# A Life Lived on the Edge

# A LIFE LIVED ON THE EDGE

**DOUG STANYON**

**Author's Note:** The names of various individuals have been changed for a variety of reasons, some, from the swinging sixties, to protect the not so innocent who now lead respectable lives, others from the past who may still be in danger of retaliation from wherever and those that were just naturally incompetent, who's families do not deserve to face the stigma of their relatives.

First edition self-published by Kindle USA in December, 2017
Second edition published in January 2018.

Cover design by the author.

# DEDICATION

This work is dedicated to

## ROGAN BOYCE STANYON

1980 – 2004

Who through an agonising twist of fate, was born with the terminal condition of Duchenne's muscular dystrophy. He spent the majority of his short life in a wheel chair. Of the multitudes of people I have met worldwide in my lifetime, I say without fear of contradiction that he was the most courageous and determined individual I have known. With accelerating muscular degeneration he acquired a Business Degree from University, qualified as a junior Rugby League Coach, was a competent self-taught artist, played the Stock Market with success and held down a full time position with a leading Australian company until the week of his death.

He was a man without peer.

Son, it was an extreme honour to have known you: you taught me so much in your short life.

I have and always will miss you so very much.

**Also to**

## SUSAN ANNE STANYON

1948 – 2011

My wife who chose to leave her comfortable life style and live and suffer with me through Rhodesia's war, where we lost almost everything and started again in Australia. She was a wonderful mother, a hard working nurse and a dedicated wife, who helped rebuild a new and successful life for us.

**And to**

My sister **Nooks** and so many of my friends and associates, – who suffered my inebriated, incoherent, inarticulate and rambling recitals, which while, admittedly the minor details were not always "totally true, however were certainly always based on facts". Always recited in an irreverent manner, with a pinch of humour, as it has been written, for the enjoyment of my listeners and readers.

# RHODESIA
## 1896 – 1980

### Some called it
### 'God's Little Green Acre'

This map depicts the country, formally known as Rhodesia, with original place names. Information on this map, covers areas referred to in this book.

In large light grey print are the names of Operational Areas in which fighting occurred during the insurgency that started in December 1972 and ended with a political solution in April 1980.

The three highlighted squares are specific areas in which the author relates his own experiences during his service with the British South Africa Police (BSAP).

The smaller area covers service from 1962-1964 & 1978-1979
The Southern area covers service from 1964 to 1968.
The Northern area covers service between 1972 and 1980.

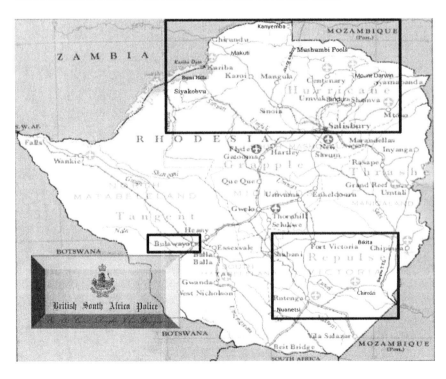

# Contents

DEDICATION...............................................................5

RHODESIA 1896 - 980.............................................6

PROLOGUE.............................................................11

IN MEMORIAM ......................................................14

**BOOK ONE**.........................................................15

THE GUN HILL SPLIT ARSE  NEW YEARS DAY 1965.............16

RHODESIAN WITCHCRAFT CURSES

AND A YOUNG POLICEMAN .................................21

The First Curse...........................................................21

The Second Curse.....................................................23

The Party and Call Out.............................................24

Third Curse and Investigation..................................27

THE WISDOM OF AN AGEING RACONTEUR ............29

SUDDEN DEATH DOCKETS:

WHAT THE HELL WOULD HE KNOW? .....................33

THE TRANSFER : BIKITA TO CHIREDZI .................38

THE BRIEFING OF STAFF AND SETTLING IN .........42

PATROLS, ATTEMPTED CONS

AND UNEXPECTED RESULTS....................................47

ESTABLISHING LAW AND ORDER LOWVELD STYLE.........53

ANTI-TERRORISTTRAINING......................................58

STOPPING THE DRUNK DRIVING.............................63

ONE THAT WALKED ALL THE WAY ..........................70

FORENSIC SCIENCE IS INTRODUCED

TO LOWVELD POLICING............................................74

DINNER WITH THE CAVEY'S.....................................79

THE LAST PATROL AND CON ...................................81

THREE YOUNG MEN GO IN SEARCH FOR

A BETTER COUNTRY ................................................86

BOOK TWO ................................................................................91

A BAPTISIM OF FIRE .............................................................92

AS MECCA IS TO MUSLIMS,

SO MUNICH IS TO BEER DRINKERS ..................................99

CLANDESTINE EXTERNAL OPERATIONS ......................106

LSD AND HARD FACTS ABOUT

BEDDING THE OPPOSITE SEX ..........................................110

AMUSEMENT ARCADES & FRUITMACHINES ........ ............114

SEX DRUGS AND ROCK AND ROLL INDEED............... ...119

MY FILM CAREER & THE ROCK OF GIBRALTA........ ........ ...124

CLARET ON THE STRAND: RHODESIA HOUSE......................129

THE ZAMBESI CLUB & CHELSEA CORPS D'ELITE ................133

THE LUCRATIVE ICE CREAM TRADE....................................139

SHOWDOWN AT THE HALYCON .........................................145

NO RESPONSIBILITIES NO WORRIES....................................153

THE LAND DOWN UNDER ...................................................158

GETTING STARTED IN THE LUCKY COUNTRY.....................162

A SHORT WORKING INITIATION

BEFORE GOING BEYOND THE BLACK STUMP .....................166

THE ORD RIVER DAM SCHEME WESTERN AUSTRALIA .....172

BEANS, AN IRISH CRANE DRIVER

AND AMERICAN LABOUR JUSTICE ......................................177

PERFUMED LOVE LETTERS IMPALEMENT AND

HOSPITALISATION.................................................................182

THE IRISH FIST FIGHT

DEAR JOHN & THE ALL BLACK BAR ....................................187

FIRST NIGHT IN PARTY CENTRAL

& ANOTHER LIFE'S LESSON .................................................192

WORKING IN THE JUNGLES OF PAPUA NEW GUINEA......197

THE LONG ROAD HOME......................................................206

WHATEVER YOU DO – DO NOT RE-ATTEST!.........................215

**BOOK THREE** ........................................................220

RE-ATTESTATION ...............................................221

UNDER INVESTIGATION FOR FRAUD ................229

CID OPERATIONAL INVESTIGATIONS ...............233

FIRE FORCE ..........................................................244

A POLICE LADY IN THE LIFE OF RENEGADES ......247

THE ART OF ANTI-TERRORIST OPERATIONS ........253

THE BEST 'GIG' IN THE RHODESIAN SECURITY FORCES.257

RECRUITMENT & TRAINING OF THE HOME GUARD.........260

DISTURBING THE UTOPIA OF THE OMAY TTL......265

THINKING ON YOUR FEET:

AN ESSENTIAL REQUIREMENT ...........................270

DEPLOYMENT OF THE NEW HOME GUARD...........276

THE BUMI HILLS AIRSTRIP ATTACK....................280

S.B. GAMES OR PLAIN & DANGEROUS INCOMPETENCE..282

JUST ON THE EDGE OF 'C' SQUADRON S.A.S...........289

CLEANING UP MY OWN BACK YARD FIRST……..............294

BUSH LESSON ONE: DON'T GET BETWEEN

MOTHER AND CALF………………....…………………300

TAME GOOKS, LANDMINES AND HAEMORRHOIDS...........304

RECALCITRANT POLICEMAN……….....................313

"WHAT'S GOOD FOR THE GOOSE

IS GOOD FOR THE GANDER" ...............................316

IF ONLY THE PEARCE COMMISSION

HAD DESTROYED THE ELEPHANTS....................320

PROMOTION IN THE FIELD & THE SMELL OF CORDITE

AGAIN....................................................................325

HOW NOT TO GET PROMOTED .............................332

JUST ANOTHER DAY IN THE OFFICE ....................338

IT'S JUST PLAIN COMMON SENSE.......................343

WHAT GOES UP  MUST COME DOWN ............................................347

WHILE THE FAT LADY WAS SINGING ........................................352

SOME FOOD FOR WHEN YOU GET HUNGRY ........................360

FAREWELL TO THE BSAP & RHODESIA....................................365

TRANSITION TO THE COMMERCIAL WORLD ........................368

THE BEER MUG NAMED GOOK ....................................................378

WELCOME TO THE LAST WATERING HOLE............................385

GLOSSARY OF TERMS........................................................................387

BSAP MEMBERS IDENTIFIED  ........................................................389

# PROLOGUE

S torytelling is slowly becoming an art form lost to the new world. Busy with "computers" fitted into just about everything we use today. Speeds and capacity constantly accelerating. News through the medium of television, radio or newsprint often inaccurate or part truth or insinuations published solely to enhance political or pecuniary interests to achieve common goals. Aimed at the gullible public to entice them to part with a few shillings/cents /drachmas/Bart or whatever currency. The world is filled with greed and corruption at all levels of society. Wars, death, suffering and momentous destruction, our daily news diet. We dare not go to the assistance of a fallen fellow traveller, least our actions be considered negligent and we face litigation. Political correctness balancing between the absurd, impractical and ridiculous.

Few now enjoy the simple things in life. A quiet amiable conversation, slowly sipping the nectar of the Gods. The gentle and re-assuring touch of a loved one. To recognise the sheer joy of a bright sunlit day, the scent of a woman or a garden of flowers in full bloom. The indulgence of poetry. The smile and chuckle of young infants, the warmth of the company of old friends, tried and trusted like old wine. To retire for a nights repose content that for the moment you have sated life's joys.

I am Rhodesian born, and some may query, and educated person. After four years of secondary education ending in 1962, I embarked on a career with the British South African Police. A misleading title, it was neither British nor South African, it was the Police Force which maintained Law and Order in Rhodesia.

Due to my parent's divorce when I was five years old, I lived with my father, but flew a number of times alone to Kenya in terms of a Court ruling that I spend each Christmas holiday with my mother. When I was nine I flew alone to England, requiring a night stop in Cairo (sleeping on a boat on the Nile). This sowed the seed of my desire to see the world.

After six years, I resigned from the Police in 1968 and embarked on a three year trip hitch hiking and working my way around the world.

On my return I re-attested in the Police in 1971 and shortly thereafter, "war" broke out, in which I was engaged until the political demise of my beloved country in April, 1980.

That it was a catastrophe is apparent today, nevertheless its disappearance would warrant no more than a single sentence in world history.

More than 50,000 lives were lost of all races, creeds and colour and countless others shattered.

I immigrated to Australia, the Lucky Country, where I thankfully enjoyed a successful career in the commercial security service industry. I reside in quiet retirement, having lived the life of "three men".

The following series of anecdotes cover personal experiences – taken from parts of my life. While I make light of each situation, I find no amusement or joy in human conflict. It is awful and will always be so.

Stories of the war are related, embodying the adage:

*'I laugh for fear of crying'.*

Covering the war period in book three, I make no pretence of being 'a warrior'. I was a trained Policeman and carried out those duties to the best of my abilities.

I acknowledge with humility, the hard yards carried out by the many highly trained and competent men of all Rhodesian Government services. Certainly, I took a wrong turn at times during the war years. Once in a while I surprisingly bumped into the opposition. I was always ready and willing to assist, I never shirked an opportunity to further the prosecution of the war. I went where angels fear to tread in the foolhardy belief, at my young age that I was invincible and would always have the capacity to return to "the local" watering hole at the end of a particular exercise.

I am no war hero, not in the slightest.

Possibly my only claim to fame was the ability to earn the accolades and admiration of the local populous while "Shangaan dancing" on the bar counter of the Twin Rivers Motel, in an inebriated state, well past my bed time.

This work is not intended to be a highly researched historical reference regarding the BSAP or its involvement in the political demise of the nation of Rhodesia, nor noteworthy academic comment on military strategies employed, world sanctions nor a synopsis of African race relations. Enough has been written regarding the politics, the Commissioners, the elite Forces and people of national interest who lived in Rhodesia.

For those with a thirst for quantifiable detail and exact commentary of why, how, who did what to whom and when and what could have been if only – may I suggest you find some other literary work.

These are true experiences, told tongue in cheek by a man who only made it half way up the promotion ladder.

He was never of any more consequence to the outcome of Rhodesia than those who merely "made up the numbers". Our names will not be recorded in any history books.

The majority of those I served with both Black and White, gave of their best. They were fine and brave men, who attempted to save Rhodesia from what it has become.

# IN MEMORIAM

*Those who have attended the last parade.*

While it is to be expected, it is with regret that many of the characters mentioned have attended *"their last parade"*. Some far too early, robbing them of the reward of their retirement. Those the author is aware of, who have passed on to greener pastures are mentioned hereunder. Others may have passed on, without my knowledge.

## MAY THEY REST IN PEACE

ROGER JOHN PEARCE 4756
JOHN WORDEN 5334
HARVEY BURR 6753
PAT CURRAN (Former DO Internal Affairs)
JOHN STANYON 3835
TOM CRAWFORD 7154
BERNARD CAVEY 4038
KEITH JARRETT 4438
NEVILLE "PADDY" GARDINER 6090
NIGEL STANYON 10203
ANTHONY "SAINTS" ST CLAIR 7146
CHARLES CASSIDY 6548
GEOFF HEDGES 5332
JOCK BREMNER 4303
PETER SHERREN 3862
PETER BEGG 5875
DAPH MORRISON (Former WDSO)
BILL HOBLEY 4234
TED PAINTING 6097
JACK DENLEY 4261
PETER ALLUM 3939
VIC OPPERMAN 6005
STRETCH FRANKLIN (SAS SGT. SB Attaché)
JOHN HICKS 5360
ERICK KRUGER 7655
TIM ALLEN 5997
MAC MCGUINESS 5197
RUFUS SYNMAN (Proprietor Twin Rivers Motel)
EDDY WEBB 4416
PADDY ANDERSON (Former DCI)
MIKE RAYNE 7368
JENNY RAYNE
BEN PRETORIUS 7552
JOE Mc BRIDE 4367.
SUE STANYON
RALPH WATSON.
BILL COETZEE 4752

# BOOK ONE

## *Policing the last untamed Frontier of Rhodesia.*

I n this, the first of three sections I relate one story from the time I spent in my initial induction training. I was one of the last European Constables and one of the first sixteen men to pass out of the BSAP Training Depot as a Patrol Officer. I am unable to explain the official reason for the rank change. My presumption is it was one of the futile and less than progressive decisions to have the world believe we were fundamentally not a racist organisation.

That said very little changed in the day-to-day relationship between the African and European members of the BSAP.

Of the fourteen 'yarns' I chronicle, the majority relate to the opening of a new police station and its operational area in the Lowveld of Rhodesia. The residents were not 'lawless' in the sense that there was organised crime. It was the history of inadequate policing to maintain the law resulting in minor infringements of Statute law rather than people committing common law crimes.

My father had emigrated from England to join the same police force in 1938, which was less than 50 years after the colony was founded. Having grown up listening to his tales of policing Rhodesia in days gone by. I really think our experiences in Chiredzi may have been comparable to working in the 'last frontier' of untamed Rhodesia.

If that statement is inaccurate, let it be my use or abuse of poetic licence.

## THE GUN HILL SPLIT ARSE
## NEW YEAR'S DAY – 1965

On the morning of New Year's Day 1965, Training Squads 6 & 7/64 were assembled on their horses, within the stable area of Depot (Police Training School). We were clad in stable kit. Recruit Constable Dan Varkevisser and I had decided to ride together. Varkevisser was an adventurous lad and had been punished for some slight misdemeanour and issued with Regimental Horse (RH) Prairie. The horse was legendary. I think it stood 16 hands and had an attitude that made the Devil himself appear angelic. The only person it respected was Farrier Staff Insp. 'Bill' Coetzee. I on the other hand was riding RH Nutmeg a very pleasantly natured horse.

We were addressed by Staff Crown Sergeant John Pearce (a true character of the BSAP, in the traditional sense, reported to be a remittance man from the Old Dart.)

*"We have been invited to join the Salisbury Equestrian Club on their annual fox hunt on the Commonage. We shall meet with them at the base of Gun Hill, where the 'Master of Hounds' shall address you further. I want you to be on your best behaviour, keep your horses under control at all times and obey commands from the Master. Make sure you do not ride too close to members of the Club."*

So assembled, the hunt was a sight for sore eyes. There were people attired in red jackets and white riding breeches, long, Black

English dress boots and black riding helmets. High ranking officers of the BSAP, in full uniform, some with dark blue hats with scrambled egg on the peaks, one or two rows of medals on their chests and obviously re-tailored breeches and long brown boots.

I surmised there would have been at least forty people, plus the same number of recruits – near on 80 in all.

A very pukka gentleman rode out in front of the assembled group. *"Good Morning Ladies and Gentlemen."*

Definitely English, most probably Eton then Oxford, one could tell from the accent. (I guessed he had not seen us, the rabble, behind his horsey mates.)

*"Welcome to the annual Salisbury fox hunt. As usual our activities shall be restricted to the area within the Commonage. Again with thanks to the police, our quarry is represented by the two Duns."*

(For those who missed out on the absolute guffaw that Stables and horse riding in the BSAP was: the Duns were two horse of a mustard hue, never ridden by Recruits, with the best stables all to themselves named Whinny and Winsome.) The Master of Hounds continued, periodically clearing his throat.

*"With riders, provided by the police, they have already been deployed into the thickets, waiting to be found."* He allowed himself a short gurgling chuckle at his own joke. There was a respectful show of gratitude by a quiet, sophisticated clapping of hands, made even quieter because many wore white gloves. We did not clap. We did not know we had to.

*"The young police recruits will represent the hounds. We again thank the police force for providing the hounds,"* again, a quiet, subdued clapping.

I was not sure what to think about being called a dog but Depot instructors had called me a lot worse so I accepted it.

*"We shall move off shortly, with the hounds riding at a slow pace in front of the rest of the 'hunt'. Once we have spotted the quarry, the trumpeter shall blow the bugle and sound.* (I just don't recall what it was, probably the last post as the fox was about to be massacred!!)

*"Then as we all know the fun begins, we shall chase the quarry at a full gallop – shouting Tally Ho! Tally Ho! There they go!"*

I thought to myself: *I am not sure the recruits will use that language.*

There being no further business, the 'Master' said, *"Good hunting and we shall re-convene at Gun Hill on completion."*

Off we went at a leisurely pace. Slowly the 'hounds' worked their way through the 'rest of the hunt' until most of them were in the vanguard of the formidable hunting party. God help the Duns I thought.

Now Varkevisser had some mischief in mind. As I started moving forward he called me back.

He gestured with his head and eyes to a rider a few yards in front of us, and a smile crept across his lips.

There was one of the blue hatted, scrambled egg officers of the regiment. I had not noticed him prior. Now I noticed he was a very short individual, he must have just scrapped home on the height requirements during the medical. With age, his body had become rotund, with more than a healthy waistline.

I had heard officers were issued with corsets or cummerbunds. This chap had obviously chosen not to wear one. Frankly he looked extremely uncomfortable on his steed. His legs were all over the place and he sat in a position indicative of a lack of recent experience. He was chatting to a lady of similar age whose face was heavily plastered with makeup, with bright red lipstick that appeared to add extra dimension to her lips. She wore the red jacket with full regalia.

Varkevisser caught my attention and looked down towards his lap. He lifted up his right hand to just above his saddle. I noticed he was holding something. I could not identify it. I was riding on his left flank. He gestured for me to ride on his right. I manoeuvred myself accordingly. Then I saw it.

I shall have to be a little pedantic so that readers will fully understand what he had.

Its botanical name, should you wish to repeat the story and try and impress your listener's is 'Leonotis Ocymfolia'. Its common names are Lion's Tail and Wild Dagga (while it has mild medicinal uses, it is not related to the Hemp plant, also known as Dagga. It does have mild psychoactive compounds).

VARKERVISSER'S
WEAPON
OF CHOICE.

These plants are common throughout Rhodesia, well wherever I have been. They grow between three and six feet in height. While in a bush form, each stem grows individually from the ground, and is square in shape. As it matures and increases in height, it sprouts a ball or whorl around the stem, from which orange petals develop. This is repeated, to its maximum height. The golf ball size whorls are in fact seedpods. Each of these pods is armed with protrusion like thorns to protect the seeds. When the plant dies it remains upstanding for months, becoming rigid and sturdy. Varkevisser had armed himself with a dried, dead Lions Tail, some six feet in length. They were widespread on the Commonage.

He was up to no good. I am not a vet and my total experience with horses is limited to my incarceration in Depot. But as a horse walks the top of his tail, his 'dock', lifts momentarily.

The dock covers the horse's rectum! This, as it turns out, was Varkevisser target; the 'dock' of the officers horse. Now his timing was nothing short of incredible. Way across the commonage, the Duns came into view – a few of the vanguard hounds shouted:

*"There the f\*\*\*ers are"*, followed by other shouts of, *"Tally Ho."* *"Get the f\*\*kers."* The recruits' language, thankfully, drowned out by the bugler calling his troops to war.

We were now very close to the officer's horse. It started getting excited, its dock lifted. Varkevisser placed the Lion's Tail so that one of the golf ball sized thorn whorls was in exactly the right spot. The horse reacted as expected and slammed his tail down hard and fast.

The whole column had broken into a canter when the senior officer's horse reared momentarily onto its hind legs, as though seeking some traction for take-off. When the front legs hit the ground it was at full gallop. Centrifugal forces, from the horse's acceleration, threw the rider's upper body backwards. His feet, still in the stirrups, rose close to the horse's ears, his cap fell onto the nape of his neck. When I last saw him, his arms and feet were wildly windmilling as he went thundering through the 'hounds'.

Having been severely startled by the antics of the horse all the other horses bolted and 'split arsed into the Commonage'. There were horses everywhere, going in all directions of the compass at full gallop.

Varkevisser and I, now on horses travelling at max speed, found ourselves heading towards a disused quarry which had a road leading down to its base. It was half filled with water from recent rains. While I was barely in control of my own horse I was thankful that it chose a course along the top and side of the quarry.

I watched as a number of recruits, the brims of their stable hats flat against the crowns, resembling cowboys from the movies. Their hands firmly clasped on the saddle, reins flapping in the air, some had their feet in the stirrups, and others were less fortunate. Most were desperately hoping to stay aboard.

As their horses realised the water blocked their progress they came to an immediate and grinding halt, trying to change direction as they did. A number of bodies clad in grey shirts took to the air then disappeared in a large splash of water.

I galloped passed the quarry and on towards the suburb of Gun Hill. My direction bore no resemblance to the location of the two Duns who were by now at full gallop, miles away.

Over the years the horses had grown accustomed, at some stage, to being 'riderless' and knew their way back to the stables. All the police horses, some riderless, some with recruits barely holding on returned to Depot. Varkevisser and I had miraculously managed to stay on our steeds and towards the end of the 'split arse' regained some resemblance of control. We cantered into the stable lines, unable to wipe the grins from our faces, well satisfied with our day's work.

We found Staff Sergeant Pearce seated on his horse adjacent to the water troughs. He was ranting and raving, abusing all and sundry, making the most ungodly threats to each and every recruit, whether they were on foot or mounted, whether injured or in fine fettle.

I for one believe, the rebel in him, had enjoyed the spectacle, he just dared not show it.

*          *          *          *          *

*It doesn't matter*
*If you come first or last.*
*All that matters is that you,*
*Finished the race!*

# RHODESIAN WITCHCRAFT CURSES
# AND A YOUNG POLICEMAN

This story is presented in four parts. It will test the resolve of even the harshest sceptics of African witchcraft. It is a true story. The first, third and fourth parts were, at the time, documented by the BSAP and may still be available in archival records for scrutiny. It involves characters that some may be familiar with. Regrettably, three are now known to be deceased, others are most probably deceased due to their age at the time and the passage of time itself. The ending will no doubt come as a surprise. The devil is in the detail – it is suggested one peruses the tale with some concentration.

A **curse** is defined as: 'The invocation of **supernatural power** to inflict harm upon someone or something'.

## The First Curse

On the 17th February 1965 I had just passed out of the Police Training School (Depot) and been posted to the Bulawayo Driving School. I had attested as a Constable but two days before the Pass Out parade we were instructed to wear the single gold bar on our epaulettes, signifying the new order of things. We were now referred to as Patrol Officers.

The Hendon School of Driving was the system and standard expected to be achieved by recruits before release to their first station. Driving school was simply a matter of instructors being satisfied an individual recruit was competent to drive both Land Rovers and ride motor cycles.

Once satisfied the instructors issued the recruit with his Drivers Licence and Route Instructions to his first posting. The more experienced and competent recruits were soon on their way. The instructors worked on getting each recruit up to the minimum standard. Over the next twenty-five days the numbers dwindled, until there was one recruit and three Driving Instructors left.

I was that recruit. For the next five days it mattered not that I kept my hands on the wheel at the ten to two position, or that I double declutched on each gear change and that my right arm was perfectly extended making perfect circles or waving up and down, or pointing directly to my right at the appropriate times, they still considered me well below the acceptable standards of a BSAP driver.

I did satisfy their needs, however, on the BSA 650 - maybe that was because they were behind me on another motorcycle and could not watch every minute detail.

Unexpectedly on the 25th March the Instructor in Charge called me in and said he was going to reluctantly issue me with my driver's licence. I still have the document with my photograph showing the Depot hairstyle and a look of total surprise and amazement on my face. I was to be transferred to Fort Victoria Province.

He informed me the OC Province had personally phoned him and claimed to be desperately short of patrol officers. I was to be issued my licence and despatched immediately. He informed me he had said to the OC that: if this man is issued with a drivers licence he will have a serious car accident within six months.

**The first curse had been placed.**

I arrived at Bikita in Fort Victoria Province on the 2 April 1965, one of three patrol officers: wide-eyed, bushy tailed and sopping wet behind the ears. Dark grey shirts and all leather shinning, like it would never shine again. I was now a fully-fledged policeman: ready, willing and able to help maintain law and order.

# The Second Curse

T he Member in Charge was a newly promoted Inspector. My summation resulted from two observations: the two shinning pips on each epaulette and the two holes in the right upper arm section of his summer tunic, where the Sergeants stripes had once hung. His name: John Worden.

As the junior troop you automatically inherited a number of duties at the station. The duty of significance to this tale was Member in Charge Prisons.

There was a small government prison on the station grounds filled with short term prisoners, whose offences ranged from contraventions of the Wild Life Act, The Witchcraft Suppression Act, thefts, assaults and other minor offences. Of course, also incarcerated were the old laggards who, with eyes on the season, committed some minor transgression so their residence at Her Majesty's pleasure over the winter months was ensured.

The Senior Patrol Officer was Harvey Burr (who left the Force in 1966) the third, John Vorster, senior to me by 30 days, and a former classmate at high school.

Sometime in late June or early July 1965, Vorster approached me with what he described as a brilliant idea. Burr, he claimed, had investigated a case under the Witchcraft Suppression Act and then with his skills as the resident Prosecutor secured a conviction of one of Bikita's most renowned Nganga's (witch doctor).

He was a man feared and held in the highest esteem from Chipinga to the east, Zaka to the south and as far away as Fort Victoria. He had been incarcerated at Bikita.

"*We should*," said Vorster, "*get him to throw his bones and predict our futures!*"

I spoke with the Chief Prison Warden, asking if he and the Nganga would co-operate with our plan. The answer was confirmatory, on condition that he be allowed to shed his prison garb and don his skins and clothing regalia, currently being held in Prisoners Property. I smelt a rat – with 'all' my service I knew something was amiss. The warder assured me all would be well.

One Saturday afternoon, when Inspector Worden was off station and Burr cared not, we took the Nganga, all dressed up, through the African police lines and out onto a flat rocky kopje overlooking the police station. Vorster pulled rank and went first.

The Nganga threw his bones, snorted, mumbled, spat and made strange faces, his hands constantly hovering over his paraphernalia, sometimes retrieving one item and throwing it independently of the rest.

Turning one piece this way and that, head nodding, now and then providing Vorster, through the interpretation of the keenly observant Prison Warder with his prophecies. He was going to get married, have children, become as big as the Member in Charge and generally experience a healthy and fulfilling life.

Then it was my turn. Vorster and I swapped places. I keenly watched as the Nganga went through the same rituals. Looking closer this time at 'his bones' I noticed a seashell and what appeared to be a Dik Dik's skull. I waited with baited breath – Commissioner Maybe? Great wealth? Overseas travel? Bevies of beautiful women? My daydreaming was interrupted when I saw the Nganga silently packing up his goods and chattels, placing them back into the grubby, dirty, hide skin bag.

My attention was diverted by the Warder's voice.

*"He sees nothing Sir!"*

*"What?"* I demanded he throw the bones again. This was met with resolute refusal.

*"He must have seen something"*, I said.

*"No nothing,"* he repeated.

*"How can he see nothing?"*

A short discussion ensued between Warden and Nganga whereupon the Warden said in a low, all most whispering voice, *"All there was, was blood and running water, very, very dark black, night, Sir. Nothing after that."*

I did not pursue the matter any further – I knew it was all poppycock anyway.

## The Party and Call Out

In early August 1965 Pat Curran, the District Officer with Internal Affairs at Bikita, invited the three Patrol Officers to a party at his house on Saturday 14th August. Nothing new there, but his wife was having three young ladies as guests.

At first I thought it a done deal, three of us, three of them. I later found out the two cadets from Internal Affairs had also been invited. The three PO's discussed this and came to the conclusion that the elder cadet, Hugh Curtis, who was very shy, stuttered, was very tall and very skinny, moved awkwardly, had a big hooked nose would be little competition (how wrong could we have been.)

Eight years later, in January or February 1973, in a very different world I met Hugh in Mount Darwin while on operational duties in Op Hurricane – he was married to a drop dead beautiful wife with a wonderful personality. I digress.

The other cadet, Mike Blake, was a raw Englishman with lily-white skin, rosy red cheeks, who was always smiling, talked all the time and knew everything: possible competition, but unlikely.

We constantly debated this huge event: What would we wear? How many beers could we afford to buy? Would these girls be stunners? Nonstop analysis and planning, in the Mess, over breakfast, supper and lunch, at beer time! We planned to get there earlier than invited, achieving the advantage of time 'in situ'.

On Friday the 13th August, the first of many surprises raised its ugly head. I was placed on First Reserve starting Friday at 1630 through to Monday 16th 0800 that meant I was first response to any request for police attendance.

Although I had only served for a period of six months I felt confident that there was little likelihood of my being 'called out'. The Member in Charge sanctioned my attendance, in mufti, at the party, but I was not allowed to drink. I had dodged one bullet.

It's hard to describe the excitement in the Mess: fear, trepidation, wonderment, hope, dreams and lots of discussion.

On the evening of the 14th August, as we were getting dressed in the best clothes we could find from our sparse wardrobes, the Mess phone rang. I answered, I was sure it would be Pat Curran. It was the orderly at the Charge Office. A Constable on patrol in the Bikita Township (some 15-20 miles away) reported an illegal beer drink in progress.

The time was about 1830 or slightly later. I sought counsel with PO Burr. He had two bars, thus must know how I could avoid attending this matter and not get myself into any trouble. As we debated and planned, the Mess phone rang a second time.

The orderly reported that the Constable at the township had rung again, he had witnessed a number of fights and the matter was getting 'out of control'. Burr's considered opinion and advice – "*attend and get back as quick as possible.*"

The time was now 1835 hours. I donned my uniform and went to the Charge Office. Our standard issue police grey, long wheelbase Land Rover was in CMED Fort Victoria, for repairs.

In exchange we had been issued with a green Land Rover, which had a yellow circle on each door with the letters TIF (Temporary Issue Fleet). It was a pickup model, long wheelbase, with canvas enclosing the area behind the driver's cabin. Not nearly as impressive as attending the scene with the real thing: spotlight, body-box roof rack and riot meshing.

The First Reserve Constable arrived. My white Alsatian, named Lady, which I had rescued from the pound, leapt into the back and we drove towards the scene. Past the party lights, down past the District Commissioner's office, Mrs Powell's African store, picking up speed all the time, past the African clinic, across the Rosva River causeway, creating great waves of turbulent water to rise into the evening sky, a sharp right at the end of the causeway and flat out, now, to the Township. Breaking every record held (PO's unofficial Bikita to the main Ft Vic/Birchenough bridge road record)

Across the sealed road into the township following the chaos to the centre of the beer drink. People were staggering, laughing, some dancing, much singing and clapping of hands, some already fast asleep, or would that be unconscious, where they had fallen.

With my time running out, I sought out the brewer, requested the permit, spoke to the Constable who had called me out. He advised the party had quietened down and the troublemakers had left. I advised the brewer she was in contravention of the law (I cannot recall her exact offence) by failing to have a permit issued by the DC. Consequently I was required to destroy the beer. So with no further ceremony I placed my boot on the top section of the 44-gallon drum and shoved. The beer spilled out and over the dry and dirty soil.

I instructed the First Reserve Constable to return to the vehicle. On opening my driver's door, the Constable was standing next to me at attention.

He asked, explaining, *"Can I stay here Sir? I am not the First Reserve Constable. Constable 'so and so' is first reserve but he was too slow so I came instead. He will be ready if called out again."*

It was around 1930 hours. My priorities and thoughts were far flung from this minor issue. I agreed.

Lady jumped into the back and we headed for home. I lit a cigarette, inhaled deeply and my thoughts went to my stratagems to be employed at the party.

I was obviously behind the eight ball but with some adept manoeuvring, success was still within my grasp.

I knew the road like the back of my hand. I drove, at speed, along the banks of the Rosva River, anticipating the sharp, 90-degree left hand turn approaching. My cigarette had run its course, so I idly threw it out of the driver's window. Unbeknown to me, the spring lock on the window had worked loose and the window had slipped shut. Suddenly a shower of sparks engulfed the cabin, which momentarily distracted my attention.

My next recollection was confusion. I was in pitch, black darkness. I could hear running water. Water was lapping parts of my body.

I felt warm liquid running across my face and into my eyes and ears. I wiped it away with my hand, realising it was blood. There were no stars. The lights of the Land Rover had been extinguished. I was cramped, confined, lying on my side, unable to move with much freedom. The knob of the gear lever was lying next to my stomach. I lifted my hand above my body as far as I could. I felt the clutch, brake and accelerator pedals above me. The water was running along my body, but not causing a threat to my breathing. I started scratching and scraping in the darkness. Suddenly to my relief I managed to squeeze my body through a small gap. I saw starlight and managed to stand. I realised I had driven over the causeway. The four wheels of the TIF were facing skywards.

I walked, along the road for about a mile, maybe less to the African clinic. The last I recall was entering the confines of the clinic and seeing the numerous cooking fires, people running towards me. I must have lost consciousness.

## Third Curse and Investigation

**B**ikita T.A.R.B. 13/65 refers. I came to in a bed in Fort Victoria Hospital. I was informed I had fractured my skull and received numerous lacerations to my face and other injuries. Nothing, thankfully, of great concern: my face was black and blue, I had difficulty with my vision, a large gash across my left eyebrow and upper cheek had closed the eye completely.

A week or so later I was transported back to Bikita, considered 'fit for duty'. John Vorster advised me he and Worden had attended the scene just after 2000 hours.

Lady was found to have suffered horrendous injuries and he had had to shoot her. The scene had been examined and photographs taken. I never did find out the outcome of the party.

Insp. Worden questioned me regarding the circumstances, which for all but the speed I was travelling I told him the truth. There remained one mystifying matter that he needed to clarify. Why was the Constable not in the vehicle at the time of the accident? He surmised that, had he been, both of us would have been killed. I explained what I knew.

Inspector Worden said he had questioned the Constable who claimed that during the destruction of the beer he had been standing next to a Nganga and the brewer. He heard the Nganga placing a curse on me. He was too scared to drive back, so he lied to me.

According to the Constable's testament, the curse the Nganga had placed was:

**"He shall not get home, tonight he will die in a crash in water."**

It had been four and a half months since I was reluctantly issued with my driver's licence, with the prediction of suffering a serious accident within six months. The prophecy of the reluctant witchdoctor had also proven amazingly accurate in regards to my demise, other thankfully, than my premature death.

The conundrum remains, how proficient is the centuries old practice of African witchcraft?

\*      \*      \*      \*      \*

*The Secret of success is to do the
Common things uncommonly well.*

*J.D. Rockerfeller*

# THE WISDOM OF
# AN AGEING RACONTEUR

I n 1965 I was a young Patrol Officer in the District Branch; my shirt was still a dark grey and the single newly acquired bar on the epaulette twinkled in the sunlight. My leather leggings still held some past shine from the Depot batman's hard work. The right legging revealed a few dents on the lower calf area, caused by pre-ignition kick back from the Matchless 500cc police motorcycle. Painful lessons learnt if wearing long blue top socks when riding. All these observations were signs of a young or new policeman with a lot yet to learn.

I was extremely excited, as I had been sent out on my first patrol. The patrol was carried out in a Land Rover fitted with an SSB radio. My accommodation: a tent. Those former members of the District branch will recall the requirements were to visit all persons of interest in the patrol area. Chiefs, important kraal heads, townships, grain mills, known political activists, missionaries, storekeepers, farmers and ranchers, as well as an assortment of Government officials from the District Commissioners Office, cattle inspectors and veterinary officers.

If we heard of any visitors within the area we were required to locate them and establish their business interests. We were expected to investigate any crimes coming to our notice.

As inexperienced as I was, I knew who Ndabaningi Sithole was. (At the time, he was the leader of the Zimbabwe African National Union (ZANU), later deposed by the Zimbabwe President, Robert

Mugabe.) One of my visitation targets was relative's he had in the area. If only I had attended some séances or tarot card readings or maybe even consulted a witch doctor with long range forecasting abilities, how different my future may have been.

One day, information reached the patrol base camp of a European camping within the Tribal Trust Land (TTL). Unless he had the appropriate authority no European was allowed, even temporary residence, in a TTL. So with the possibility of at best, making an arrest, or at worst improving a somewhat scant and unprofessional patrol report, I set off with my trusty tutor, advisor, cohort and all round good man Senior Sergeant Taringvandisho With service exceeding my age, I am certain he had endured, with humour and no doubt diplomatic patience, any number of bright eyed, bushy tailed, wet behind the ears, know-it-all members of the BSAP. What he had forgotten about police work, I was yet to learn.

Our target was not hard to locate. We came across some Africans digging, carrying, sieving and discarding soil and small rocks. A poorly dressed, grey haired European man, who shuffled rather than strode, his back hunched over forward, carefully supervised this activity. He greeted me with a smile and we passed the pleasantries of the day. With my best acting abilities I respectfully enquired what he was doing.

"Prospecting," he said, "looking for tin."

On taking me to his campsite, he produced all necessary authorities. Then with politeness and a warm smile asked if I had time for a cuppa tea.

He gestured to me to be seated. I looked around.

Under a large leafy tree, there was a central fire, still smouldering, surrounded by a few logs of wood, turned on end on top of which were dirty, torn, presumably once treasured small pillows. He sat on what looked like an old fruit box. I chose a large, quite functional rock.

He asked how long I had been in the police – while tempted to lie so he might think he was dealing with a policeman of great experience, I knew it would not work, so I told him the truth.

*"Yes, we all have to start somewhere,"* he nodded.

I looked around for the Sergeant. He was talking to a group of Africans; he knew what had to be done and how to do it – I wondered if I would pass this test?

The prospector rattled off a few European policemen's names. Did I know Sergeant *'so and so'*? Stationed at *'such and such'*, or what about Sub Inspector *'this'* or Constable *'that'*. I had never heard of any. He knew more policemen than I did!! His servant, carrying the tea interrupted us. No tray, no sugar or milk, just two old baked bean tins, with a cloth wrapped around to prevent the burning of hands. I thanked the man and looked into the tin. It was black tea. This was going to be a first. The servant was back in a flash, holding a tin, the lid of which was still attached, like a hinge. A spoon handle extended from its centre. I looked up at the man and he smiled.

*"No sugar Sir, try this one."*

Peering inside the tin I saw a dark coloured jam. This was another first. I pulled the spoon out with a lump of jam, placed it in the tea and stirred, returned the spoon from whence it came, which was then offered to my host. I looked down into my tea and realised I had learnt another lesson: unlike sugar this tea had needed a vigorous stirring to prevent what I had, a lump of jam floating on the top of my black tea.

Getting as comfortable as the rock would allow, I engaged the prospector in conversation: How long had he being doing this? What was the lifestyle like? How often did he get into town? Married? Kids? Where from originally? (Although that was obvious, he spoke with an Eton type accent. You know the one, the plum in the mouth type.) He removed his oily, dirt stained, broad brimmed hat. I noted a Guineafowl feather much the worse for wear, stuck in the outer band. His hair, grey, wavy and lifeless, dropped over his forehead.

He was clad in what was once a long sleeved white shirt, now a dark grey, obviously 'Sunlight Soap' had long lost its effectiveness.

The back of the collar and the cuffs on his sleeves were tattered, some evidence of past attempts to repair were visible.

His breast pocket held what appeared to be a notebook. The long dark blue trousers, were threadbare, the belt around the waist caused the material to gather, evidence that a long time ago he had enjoyed a larger girth. The tops of the turn-ups on both legs had been sewn, the bottoms thread bare. On the tops of his thighs the material was almost worn through where, I noticed, both of his hands were positioned. I noticed they were shaking slightly, the onset of Parkinson's or something similar perhaps.

He wore old black boots, that looked unusual, closer inspection, revealed they were not a pair; a small piece of wire held the toecap down on one boot, or maybe the whole sole?

He wore a long unkempt grey beard, his face was lined and wrinkled, the skin resembling a piece of leather that had been left to the elements for too long. His hands displayed the consequences of years of hard labour, his knuckles disproportionate to the width of his fingers, most of the nails, cracked and dirty. His palms displayed a mixture of callouses, abrasions and cuts at varying stages of healing. An old pipe was gripped between his yellowing teeth. Given the aroma of the pipe's contents, a very cheap tobacco, quite possibly floor sweepings.

My next question was to eventually produce an answer that has stayed with me for life. *"In all your years of prospecting,"* I queried, *"What was the most success you have achieved?"*

 Sipping his tea he said, *"Do not be fooled by what you see young man. You will have heard the idiom, 'never judge a book by its cover'. I am a man of considerable wealth. I was born to British aristocracy and educated in Britain's finest schools. As a consequence of my activities in my youth, I was rightfully blamed for over indulgence, careless and lavish spending, brushes' with the law and a few indiscriminate liaisons with the fairer kind, some already betrothed to others. The black sheep no doubt, whose activities caused shame, embarrassment and humiliation to the family. I agreed to emigrate to Rhodesia and am paid a fine remittance for not returning home. Over the years prospecting has got into the blood. It's not for wealth or fortune we prospect. It's the adventure of living in the unknown; of discovering what some will say is the undiscoverable. It's the solitude. I have become an introvert and recluse. Some years ago I found one of the largest gold deposits in Rhodesia. I pegged the claim, which is now held in my families' name, to secure the future of generations of our family to come."*

I interjected, *"Sir, I may be young and lack worldly experience, but somehow I find it difficult to accept you are telling the truth."*

To which he replied, *"The art son, of telling a yarn, is that it be for the interest and enjoyment to those who are listening. It is not necessary for the tale to contain the whole truth, only that it be based on fact. It is imperative however that no one's reputation or standing be sullied."*

A fine lesson indeed!

\* \* \* \* \*

## SUDDEN DEATH DOCKETS:
## WHAT THE HELL WOULD HE KNOW?

I was chatting recently, with an old friend on Skype, his grandson had set him up. I mean old in both forms, now 70 and counting backwards. I have known him since 1964, a former district trooper, so in my estimation that is from the 'the old days'. He is not into Facebook, twittering or flashing or anything like that; he prefers the old ways: Tilley lamps and paraffin fridges, wood stoves and hot ember irons. My style of man completely! I told him about my first and only contributions to the BSAP Facebook thingy.

Of course, being and still a steadfast diplomat, he enquired, *"So you tell your old stories like on an all stations radio broadcast? But now instead of a radio you use this 'Smite' system?"*

*"No it's called SKYPE, shamwari,"* I replied. *"And no, we don't use those much in the same manner as when we sent an all stations radio message."*

*"S\*\*t Stanyon, that must be hard for you?"*

*"Pray why, old friend?"* I asked.

*"Well you could never spell any word of more than four letters and the only time you told those lies were when you were pissed. Pity the poor bastards that have to try and decipher what you are saying. There were times in the Mess during the recounting of your stories that you were actually talking in Braille. We never let on we just pretended to be interested!! Have you told them the one about your sudden death investigation on the border of was it Gutu or Buhera?"*

So with thanks to my close and honest friend of 53 years, I shall try and get the story correct.

I was stationed at Bikita, fresh out of Depot. I knew just about everything there was to know about police work. How does a two bar PO know how long a one bar PO has been out of Depot?

Thinking back, that was exactly where I was. The answer lies here: The new chap walks around like a Bantam cock, full of self-importance, wide eyed, sopping wet behind the ears, barking orders at the African police, with all his leather leggings, belt and cap strap gleaming in the sun, long strides and quick movements, his lanyard still a dark blue, his grey shirt, still a dark grey.

That was me, and I was off to my first sudden death. The Member in Charge had given me some pointers to watch out for, I tried to look interested but I knew everything he was talking about.

The sudden death had been reported as "a body floating in a dam".

Now I cannot be sure whether it was on our border with Gutu or Buhera. There was an area in the north east of our police district that shared a common boundary with both.

I was sent, thankfully with Crown Sgt Taringvandisho. It was not long before all the bravado ebbed away and slowly and ever so surely I started floundering.

On arrival I knew before interfering with the body the requirement was general observations of the scene. It was a fair sized dam (I took a wild and totally unscientific stab of the surface area – who knows, ten acres – *shit how big or small is that*? *Well it does not really matter, no one will be coming out here*).

The water had receded dramatically, maybe thirty yards from its normal level, (presumption, it is just before the onset of the rainy season), sparse vegetation (not a bad observation for a TTL) evidence of rural habitation here, there and over there as well. I wrote furiously in my brand new police notebook. I was really impressed with my own progress.

Then a curved ball out of left field caught me unaware and I was stumped. A local informed us some '*majonnies*' had arrived on the other side of the dam yesterday where the body had been floating. The European *majonnie*, using a long stick, had pushed the floating body around the side of the dam and left it where I'd found it.

*"What? Sergeant what does that mean, what's that all about?"*

*"Sir, this dam is the border between Gutu (or Buhera) and Bikita"*

Let's call it Gutu for the sake of the story!

*"The body was lying in the Gutu area, it is really their case they must investigate it,"* I stated.

What the hell do I do? I'll look a fool by calling the Member in Charge. *"Well if it's Gutu's body then,"* I said to the Sgt, *"get the locals to go down on the muddy shores of the dam and push it back where it belongs."*

So it was done. Not really knowing where the boundary line was, I relied on my mentor for guidance.

I returned to Bikita. The first thing the Member in Charge asked was how I got to the mortuary and back so quickly. I just cannot recall where the mortuary was, I should do, I did so many SDD's – it was either Ft Vic or Zaka – certainly not Bikita.

*"Well, Sir,"* I said, mustering up as much of my Bantam cock image as possible, I told him how I (not mentioning the Sgt's input) had ensured that the correct police district would be investigating the matter. I also informed him about the European *majonnie* and his long stick.

Insp. Worden turned and walked back into his office. A short while later, he came out.

*"Stanyon, that matter is for you to investigate, now go back and do the job properly."*

Talk about deflated ego, from being the star to the roots within such a short space of time. Now my entire career was in jeopardy.

The Sgt and I returned. To say I was annoyed would be an understatement. Furthermore I was obviously not thinking rationally.

On approaching the dam again I drove around the other side. Technically I presumed I was now in the District of Gutu.

Seeing the body still afloat, face down, as it had been, I decided to retrieve it, and place it in the body box. I would thereafter question the locals about the person and if possible find some relative to take to the mortuary to identify the deceased to the pathologist. I was back on a roll.

I pointed the Land Rover straight at the body and drove down towards the water's edge.

The Sgt said hastily, *"No. Ishe No. Do not drive, we shall get the people to bring the body."*

Now, seriously, what would this Sgt know? Look, all we were doing was going to recover a body. What did he think I was, a blithering idiot?

The Land Rover started to labour a little and then a little more, the going was getting tough. I'll fix this!

"*Ishe, I think we should leave the car here, they can get the body,*" the Sgt said diplomatically.

What in heaven's name, does he know? (Actually he had held a drivers licence nearly as long as I had been living!!) Does he not realise that is why we have four-wheel drives! So, bang down went the magic red knob engaging four-wheel drive and foot hard down on the accelerator, or was that slowly accelerate? What did they say in driving school?

The vehicle was now really labouring, and then it just stopped. I opened the door without thinking. Of course the Bantam cock had lots of lost ground to make up. My right leg, encased in that beautifully shined and polished boot and legging hit the ground, my full weight on top of it. I literally sank, to my knee. Now holding on to the door for dear life, I tried to remove the limb. It was going nowhere. I came up with a really clever manoeuvre. I would take all my weight with my arms, and then lightly place the left leg on the edge of the doorframe, and thereafter, pushing with my left leg and arms, I would extract the errant limb. Everything worked according to plan, until, with mud now covering a fair area inside the driver's compartment, my left foot slipped. Ending up next to the right. I was now in a position to observe the vehicle was up to the floorboards in thick mud.

I was stuck, facing the inside of the vehicle. I noticed the Sgt Major, removing his shoes and then his socks, then off came his uniform pants. He called for some assistance that came in the shape of two long sticks and some 'tambo'. He was out of the mess fairly quickly.

"*Do not worry Ishe I will fix it.*"

With that he strode over and talked to the locals. While I am not certain of exactly what happened next; with the aid of a large number of kraal dwellers and a lot of very messy huffing and puffing, including the sliding of the body box across the top of the mud, achieved by tying a rope to the end handles and pulling it down to the water's edge, we retrieved the body. The body and box were then slid across the mud onto terra firma. In a most ungainly fashion I clambered back into the Land Rover.

Next came a sight that remains indelibly etched in my mind to this day. At least eight oxen had been inspanned and the lead animal was being led by a local walking with the Sgt towards me.

The police Land Rover, still facing towards the dam, had a chain placed under the rear somewhere. Then in a most undignified manner I, and the vehicle were pulled bodily out of the mud, with much cracking of whips. Locals were shouting encouragement to their favourite beasts. As progress became apparent, the women began dancing and clapping, and the ever-present piccanins ran madly around laughing and jeering. I sat facing the windscreen, hoping somehow the world would just swallow me up.

Once the very embarrassed young patrol officer saw he had arrived in reverse onto terra firma I alighted with mud covering all my legs and half my tunic shorts.

The Sgt barked a few more orders, which resulted in any number of locals using sticks to remove mud from around the wheels and mudguards. I managed to muster enough pride to interview witnesses, well actually, not, I just wrote down what the Sgt interpreted. I forgot many obvious questions as my ego was now so badly deflated I just wanted to get out of there.

Thankfully the post mortem showed no evidence of foul play and the cause of death was put down to an accidental drowning.

$*$ $*$ $*$ $*$ $*$

*Talk not of wasted affection,*
*Affection never was wasted;*
*If it enrich not the heart of another,*
*Its waters, returning*
*Back to their springs, like rain,*
*Shall fill them full of refreshment.*

*Henry Longfellow*

# THE TRANSFER:
## BIKITA TO CHIREDZI

O n Sunday 5<sup>th</sup> June 1966, whilst still stationed at Bikita in Fort Victoria Province I was instructed to attend the annual musketry course in Fort Victoria, confirmed by my route instructions in the junior PO's 'IN' basket on the Member in Charge's desk. As I picked them up I swear I saw a wry smile on the boss's face. I did my best to do a snappy about turn, which resembled, according to Insp Tacky Macintosh in Depot, a pirouette by a drunken ballet dancer. I hoped I had improved.

One time he had shouted across the hard square, yelling *Stanyon! Your marching resembles an African woman returning from a river while balancing a water calabash on her head*. I was pleased he stayed in Salisbury.

Back in 'my office', where everyone left everything, I sat down and read with interest my route instructions. The difference in my 'route instructions' from everybody else's and my previous instructions from the year before was a second paragraph. Most unusual! This read, 'Take all your kit with you. On completion of the musketry course you shall be transferred to Chiredzi'. I could, I thought, detect the sense of relief that Insp. Worden, the Member in Charge must have felt as he typed the last paragraph.

I had, in fact, not heard of a police station at Chiredzi, it was an area near Triangle and the Mkwasine. I had done no end of radio duty at Bikita: – the morning broadcasts - *ZEF 7 this is ZEF whatever*, "*Do you copy?*" "*Say again*" and "*I repeat*" etc., etc. but never a mention of Chiredzi.

With trepidation I approached the Senior P.O. Van Schalkwyk a man with a face only a mother could love, who smoked like a chimney and with hands that resembled those of a classical pianist. His grey shirts were nearly white, sun bleached. Every year he would order more shirts, but always wore the old ones – it was a status symbol. The lighter the colour the more the experience.

He told me that he had heard, on the grapevine that a new station was being built, but it was only going to be completed in a years' time.

He also politely told me, that he did not give a s\*\*t, as he was taking his discharge at the end of the month after six long years. I wondered what I was going to be doing for the next year. Waiting for the police station to be built?

I had attended my first musketry course the year before and found it to be a most festive occasion. Days were spent shooting at targets with both long and short firearms. We kneeled, stood up, laid down, left hand, right hand, picked-up doppies (strange, in a war soon to be raging in the country, I became one of those CID doppie Pickers – maybe someone thought I displayed a propensity for the task).

We showed our weapons with breach open, muzzles pointed to the ground, fingers in the breach. In the butts we patched up targets, reacted to shouts from the firing lines of; "*Where the \*\*\*\*\*\*\*\* is the number five target?*" or "*Hold target's still.*"

Some targets we twisted while they were being shot at and every now and again someone shouted, "*All clear*". It was not unusual to hear the bullets thumping into the top of the butts above your head. Mainly there was plenty of time, which we enjoyed, lazing in the sun, smoking and catching up with comrades not seen since the last such course.

Each evening saw a mass migration to 'The Phoenix', the police pub so named as it had mysteriously burnt down one night and been rebuilt, 'rising from the ashes'. I have little doubt the person responsible for naming it must have been a scholar, well read in Greek and Roman classics. Possibly the Q Rep, I thought.

Here the troops parched their well-earned thirst and no doubt discussed subjects akin to 'The Iliad', or Homer's epic 'The Odyssey' or 'The Rise and Fall of the Roman Empire', while readying themselves for the bright lights. Slowly they splintered into small groups seeking self-indulgence and debauchery in the hot spots of

Fort Victoria. Each morning the general mood was always the same, sombre, muted and dismal.

The reddened eyes of most troopers attested to the damage inflicted from the dust and sun of the previous day's gruelling workload. Five days and nights: each one following the same pattern.

On the morning of the 10th June we were given our classifications as shooters. I was never able to qualify as a 'marksman' and wear the coveted 'crossed rifles' on my winter uniform.

I actually never wore a winter uniform again. No such award was given for side arms so I spent my years as a 'first class' shootist, in both disciplines.

At midday on Friday 10th June 1966 I boarded a truck bound for a place that had no police station. *Do what you are told and don't ask questions.* We drove south and then west through the township of Triangle, through Buffalo Range, well that's what the Constable told me we did. There had been no change in landscape and I saw nothing there as I remember it. On and on into the unknown we went.

Down a dirt road I was dropped off at a brand new building, which I was told was the Mess. Next-door was another new house, beyond that some corrugated iron sheds and in the distance a cluster of small new buildings.

In between all of this was virgin bush. There were no fences. For the life of me I could not find a police station. There appeared to be some construction activity to the north of where I stood, maybe, I pondered was that the police station? Apart from the road, which was not sealed, there was nothing but African wilderness. I stood there with my black tin trunk and off white kit bag.

On entering the Mess I introduced myself to people enjoying a quiet beer. There were other newly arrived police officers at the police post with no police station: Patrol Officer Ric Williams who had been a Cadet and whose claim to fame was that his mother had been the first policewoman employed by the BSAP. I have never bothered to verify this fact.

He was from Nkai, Matabeleland, as was the other chap, Graham Hardy, whose father owned the Hardy's Inn at Gwanda. There was a single Inspector Buchanan, who wanted to be a schoolteacher or had been one – a very quiet, gentle person. Then there was a squad mate of mine, Tom Crawford, a quiet Scotsman, strong as an ox. He had been a farmer in his home country, always a smile on his face and easy going, as long as everyone toed the line. Also a chap straight out of Depot, PO Steve Botha a big strapping fellow who lifted weights for a hobby!!!

I was soon informed about two important issues:

(1) The collection of corrugated tin sheds I had seen was in fact the police station and

(2) There was no drinking or socialising facilities in Chiredzi, all that was done on the private estates know as Hippo Valley, some miles away.

This struck me immediately as an issue that would pose major logistical problems, as none of us I was informed, owned a car. Things were not looking good and I had not been on station for more than 30 minutes.

I was informed the Member in Charge lived next door and was Insp. Bernard Cavey, previously of Mashaba and Matabeleland, a man with a fearsome reputation as a hard disciplinarian.

I threw my kit into a vacant room and joined the others for a few beers, or more. After a few enjoyable hours I retired to bed wondering why this particular bunch of Patrol Officers had been chosen. None appeared to have the qualities or intentions to study for a law degree and move into a legal career. It was unlikely that any would be chosen as diplomats for the Foreign Service and less likely they might choose a career in theology and religious studies. As I drifted off to sleep it occurred to me that they were all large in stature, very fit, in your face, "*comme ci comme ça*" types.

My last thought was "*we live in interesting times.*"

As the future unfolded, similar PO's were transferred in. There was a good reason for the choice of manpower. I would be thankful, to whichever Officer Commanding (OC) had made the selection of all the new Chiredzi policeman, and little did I know it, but it was to be policing like no other, it was going to be a bumpy ride and we had no seat belts.

*     *     *     *     *

*You know by the time you've reached my age
You've made plenty of mistakes
If you've lived your life properly.*

*Ronald Reagan*

# THE BRIEFING OF STAFF
# AND SETTLING IN

O n the Monday morning, whilst consuming a leisurely breakfast, the conversation revolved around what our immediate future held in store for us. For those of us who came from small outstations we were keen to ascertain: how many of the fairer sex were resident in the town, what competition in that regard would present itself; if any sport was available, if indeed it was, would that be an avenue for introductions to the fairer sex, what was the social life like at this Hippo Valley Club? One wanted to know if game shooting would be available.

Rumour was already rife that a new, large hospital was being constructed next door to the police camp. This was met with universal approval, not for any medical considerations but for other more important considerations. I have no recollections of any discussions concerning crime patterns, clearance rates, availability of magistrates or regional courts, nor prosecutors, bordering police regions, patrol areas or targets or responsibility for the dreaded monthly returns. Nor what police transport was available. No one seemed concerned with what police equipment may be available. In fact no police issues were mentioned at all.

At five minutes to eight we ambled down to the two rows of corrugated iron sheds surrounded by a ground cover of small grey stones, cigarettes dangling from our lips, grey shirts soaking up the morning sun. The temperature? Well it was hot, maybe in the late 80's or early nineties. It did not cross my mind we were still in mid-winter and this was a mild, cloud-covered day. Waiting outside was the Member in Charge.

We were yet to learn most or all of the following: Insp. Bernard Cavey joined the BSAP on the 11/6/1946, (three months before I was even born!); along with 59 other recruits, all signed on the same day. He was from the Jersey Island, where as legend had it, he was a young man when the Islands were occupied by the Germans in the Second World War. The story goes, he and a friend, left the Islands in a boat one night, headed for England to enlist. They were shot at on departure and he was wounded. I never cared to verify the story nor did I ever have the courage to ask him. I liked the story as it was. I swear his arms were all one size. They seemed to taper, ever so slightly from each shoulder to the wrist. His shoulders seem to take up most of the area where a neck is usually situated.

Not tall, maybe 5' 9", he had spent a lot of his career in Matabeleland District, and had, until the Chiredzi transfer, been in charge at Mashaba. His discipline of troops was legendary and unconventional. I know on excellent authority, about one of his disciplinary methods. Christmas of 1965, he had given the troops the freedom to choose who was to be on 'first call' each day. His strict instructions were there would be no consumption of alcohol whilst so employed.

The long and short of the incident was all three troopers were imbibing quietly or otherwise in the Mashaba Club when the Charge Office Orderly had phoned and spoken to one of the PO's advising of the occurrence of a minor car accident requiring attendance. I have heard a number of versions as to why it was not attended, but the fact is it was not. As a consequence, Insp. Cavey attended himself. The following morning at 0530 Cavey walked into the Mess ordered the three troops (their identities are known, but not considered necessary to divulge) to get into full, blue riot gear, including wearing their gas masks, white helmets and batons.

He continued, "*report outside the Charge Office at the double.*"

Soon, with burning, mind boggling hangovers, sweating inside the gas masks the three stood in line. Cavey informed them he had attended the accident. All three, he concluded were guilty of neglect of duty and every other charge he could think of including the old favourite, 'act in a manner unbecoming'. He then marched them, at the double, backwards and forwards in front of the Charge Office for over an hour.

They sweated, vomited, shivered and collapsed from time to time, only to be told to get back up and "fall in". Some months later I sat with one of these troopers, he told me there had never been a sip of alcohol consumed by any one on 'First Call' again. Cavey's reputation for policing ability, fairness, man management and strong discipline were legendary. We were also to experience and become part of some rather unusual policing – none of which I could find in the Black Instruction Book or Green Standing Orders!!!

After my sixteen years of service in the BSAP, I say with full conviction Cavey was the finest, all round policeman I served under, a gentlemen who was able to get the best out of his troops. His reputation with the local populace was to be envied. As we were to find out, on too many occasions, he was a wry old fox; conning him was no easy matter - but we always tried.

The last time I enjoyed his company, over a few beers was many years later, after he had retired as a Chief Inspector (he was actually promoted whilst I was still at Chiredzi with him) and I was a second year DSO. We enjoyed our reminiscing – he was a first class man.

Cavey stood silently, looking at us. We staggered to a standstill. All of us were taller than he was. His hair was greying, as was his bushy moustache. In the awkwardness of the moment I found myself involuntarily shuffling into something of a 'standing to attention' position. From the noise of the boots of the others, I am sure they were reacting in a similar fashion. He never raised his voice then or at any other time.

In fact at most times, when we were in trouble, he had a slight grin on his face, most off putting while awaiting sentence, having inevitably been found guilty of whatever misdemeanour we had committed. The first time I heard him speak, he said, "*Why were you not at Stables this morning?*"

I am not sure about the others, but at Bikita one went to Stables sometimes at 0600, sometimes later, sometimes never – the trucks got washed, as did the motorcycles.

"*Whilst I am your Member in Charge your day, from Monday to Friday starts at 0600 hours at Stables. You do not have to be in uniform but you will supervise and assist in the cleaning of the police vehicles.*"

From then on, that's what we did.

He continued, with Insp Buchan at his side, "The reason you have been selected to work in Chiredzi is because the 'powers that be' (we were to later establish that he and 'the powers' had had some falling out in the past - he had no love for them) believe the current system of rotating a PO's from Triangle to live and work out of a mud hut, month about, has been ineffective."

He continued. "*I am advised the Hippo Valley Mill is filled with European employees that comprise people wanted by police in other Provinces, men who have failed to pay their wives and kids maintenance and are hiding from those responsibilities, there are former prisoners, some with extensive p.c.'s; a great deal of poaching is conducted from here, none of the residents show any respect for the rules of the road and there is a fair percentage overall that have no respect for the law or law enforcers. In fact, some of the private sugar farmers share the opinion, that there is no law here and so they do as they will."*

He continued, *"The African township, known as Chiredzi is little different – every con artist, thief, malingerer, and many wanted people are resident there – they have no respect for the law either. There has been no overt police presence at all in this area. Illegal beer drinks, dagga, prostitution and any other corruptible way of life are prevalent."*

*"Lastly, The TTL's we have been allotted to patrol have most likely not experienced a police presence for many years – I would think they are totally lawless. This being the Sangwe TTL, Matibi No.2, Ghona Re Zhou National area. There are also a number of cattle ranchers in the eastern area who will need to be visited. Cattle thefts and contraventions of the Wild Life Act are copious. It is our requirement to bring law and order to this area, the sooner the better. The police station and single quarters have yet to be built".*

We were allocated our offices. The junior troop, Botha, abiding by tradition, shared his office with the crime register and anything else nobody knew where to place. I was only too pleased to relinquish that position. While still only having one bar, there were no two bar PO's. I, by number and thus service, was the second senior PO. I was starting to move up in the organisation!!!!

Insp. Buchanan soon left us and was replaced by a single Section Officer, Eric Saul, a character of renown. He and I locked horns, until the day Rhodesia fell – he was either a Senior Assistant Commissioner or an Assistant Commissioner at the end and deservedly so. While not a popular person, he was without a doubt the most efficient policeman I ever served with. He was transferred from Chiredzi in my time.

The next time I saw him was after re-attestation, I was moving through the driving school, this time with less complication than the last. I was ordered to report to the Senior Warrant Officers office at Salisbury Central. I knew the man from previous service, Chief Inspector McBride. On arrival he greeted me cordially and asked whether there was some reasons the Officer Commanding Traffic would want to see me. I asked who that was.

"Supt. Saul," he replied.

I told him there was 'some history' there. We walked casually along the 'corridors of power' of the Mashonaland Uniform Branch. McBride stopped outside a closed door.

"*Smarten up lad*", he said. "*Place your hat on, you will have to salute him.*"

With that he knocked on the door. We were called in. There he sat, with the single crowns on his epaulets, the now Commissioned Officer Eric Saul.

McBride saluted smartly and introduced me, "*Patrol Officer Stanyon, Sir.*"

I had purposely kept my hat under my left arm and thus was not required to salute. I never had any intention of doing so. I remained silent.

Saul warned me, "*If you drive like you drove in Chiredzi, you will answer to me as the OC Traffic. That will be all thank you Mr Mac.*"

With that McBride saluted again, I turned, intentionally very casually and we left the office.

On our stroll back, McBride warned me, "*You are treading a fine line there, Stanyon.*"

"*Yes Sir,*" I replied.

We next met again in 1973 while both stationed in Mount Darwin, serving in the '*Hondo*' at the beginning of the end of Rhodesia. Fortunately at that time in our careers he had little if no influence as he had remained in uniform while I served in mufti; an extremely efficient policeman.

Other PO's moved in and out of Chiredzi in my time, including Ian Harries and Reg Graham.

In hindsight someone had done their homework well, as far as personnel selection. We were open for business. It was a bumpy ride to say the least. But as always in life ones' glass is either half full or half empty, it is a personal choice. Mine was always half full. Metaphorically and hopefully while off duty as well.

We were to experience some humorous and interesting situations.

\*      \*      \*      \*      \*

*Life was meant to be lived.*
*Curiosity must be kept alive.*
*One must never, for whatever reason,*
*Turn his back on life.*

*Eleanor Roosevelt*

## PATROLS, ATTEMPTED CONS
## AND UNEXPECTED RESULTS

G eneral patrols by the District Branch of the BSAP are
legendary. One myth circulated for years about a trooper
being sent on a six months horse patrol, with the African constable
on a bicycle, followed by a mule carrying his worldly assets and
provisions for half a year.

The story goes, the trooper was an Englishman of Great Spirit
and adventure. Soon after departure from the police station he told
the Constable to return to his kraal for a few months. He sold his
assets, left his horse and saddlery in the safekeeping of a local and
went home to England to enjoy some leave. The intention was to
return within the allotted period of time, reassemble the patrol,
falsify the patrol diary and return to the station. The myth or legend
suggests that while seated under the statue of Eros in Piccadilly
Circus in London his Member in Charge, who was on approved
leave bumped into him.

My late father, a former member of the police, Herbert John
Stanyon related many interesting yarns about extended horse patrols
he conducted from Matobo and Plumtree in 1939/40. I have a staff
photo of the Matobo Police at that time. None of the African staff
are wearing any form of footwear!!

In an earlier anecdote I described Insp. Cavey, a long serving
District Policeman, as being a wry, old fox.

I also mentioned that while the troops were well aware of his ability, we were always plotting and scheming for the day we would successfully con him and get away with it. Whether this was a localised mentality or shared by other districts I am not sure.

In the early days of Chiredzi, we still occupied the tin sheds that had no ceilings nor any form of insulation on the walls with the two lines of four offices being surrounded by small stone pebbles. After a while, it was possible to identify which person was walking outside your office, merely by the tramp noise over the pebbles of the individual. Irrespective of the colour of the grey shirts, within a few minutes after 0800 they were damp or saturated (that depended on the amounts of alcohol consumed the night before) and were dark grey almost black. Even the legendary SO Saul, who was in every way from his hair to the soles of his self well shined shoes/boots immaculate, could not escape sweating in the heat of the Lowveld, whilst sitting in a large BSAP constructed oven. I do recall we had the privilege of electricity (only paraffin lamps in Bikita and Zaka), although in my dotage I recall not if fans of any sort were a stock issue in the temporary police station – they were in the Mess. Even if they were, the 90-100 degree heat would have rendered them ineffectual.

As a young trooper my understanding of station 'general patrols' were that an explicit number of patrols, covering specific areas, had to be achieved with in a period of one year. That year, as I understood, it was from one annual inspection to the next. As to be expected some troopers loved going out on patrol, others not. I was in the former category. I loved the freedom and independence to choose my days' work. It was a welcome break from station routine. Most importantly one received patrol allowance and for the period you were out you were struck off the catering register. Meals in those days, to the horror of visiting officers when examining the mess book, came out at a very expensive two shillings and six or eight pence a meal. Officers offered their sage advice on eating healthily, which they always claimed could not be achieved at such depressed levels. With an excellent legal defence of the 'statute of limitations,' I may well explain one day how it was done.

I have mentioned my squad mate and friend Tom Crawford (senior to me by four numbers - still senior when the chips were down!!) His personality could be described as quiet, maybe shy, always smiling, inoffensive in every way, a moderate drinker, preferring, when possible whisky to beer. Never causing any alarm and despondency he was an all-round nice guy, admittedly a contrast to Williams, Hardy and I.

Out of the blue, one evening, when only the two of us were in the Mess enjoying a few quiet ones, he confided in me.

He had been planning a ruse of momentous proportion. So dastardly was the scheme that no one, including Cavey, would be capable of grasping it.

Other than 'a partner in crime', an accomplice if you will and bedding down exact dates, all the preparation work had been done but before revealing any further details he swore me to secrecy in the event that I declined his invitation. This was intriguing and coming from Tom, the quiet one - I was 'all ears'.

*"How would you like to go on a wild drunken bender for two days, at Government expense, drinking Vino, in Portuguese East Africa?"*

A most interesting proposition indeed. *"But where and how?"*

*"Exactly"*, said Crawford. *"That is where we are headed. To drink and consort with the Chef de Poste for a day or two, maybe even three."*

I unhesitatingly accepted to be part of the scheme and thanked Tom for considering me.

He explained the logistics of the operation. Tom advised he knew the patrol target was well behind schedule. He would suggest to Cavey he was willing and happy to do the southern patrol incorporating a number of European cattle ranches, Chipinda Pools and the north area of the Gona Re Zhou National Area. It was a seven-day patrol.

Independently and supposedly unknowingly, I would make a similar suggestion to Cavey but suggest I patrol the Sangwe TTL. We knew poaching was rife there. I would be heading northeast and Tom southwest - how devious the plan. I was impressed with the Scot. After he had visited a few ranchers and the Wild Life chaps at Chipinda he would head southwest for the confluence of the Lundi and Sabi rivers. I, in turn, would visit a few chiefs and townships and head directly south along the banks of the Sabi River.

In a day we could get to the crossing point, where the Sabi became the Rio Save, cross the river and into the small Portuguese settlement of Mavue, meet the Chef de Poste and thereafter indulge ourselves with the fruit of the vine for as long as we dared. We would only have to fudge three days on our patrol sheets. That would be a synch. Oh, you wonder about the African police details?

They too had been wisely selected for the task of taming the 'bad lands'. We knew the best and worst of them, our choice of partners would be wise and safe. They both loved a beer on a hot day and were unquestionably loyal to 'the cause'.

Over the next few days we pored over plans, checking every minor detail until we were primed and ready to strike.

Tom went first, I heard him walk past my office, long strides, I looked out the door as he past, only seeing his back. Within minutes I heard him walking back, I looked up from typing my non-existent docket, he did not miss a step, and with just a wink he was gone. As planned, a few days later I was in the radio room with Insp. Cavey. I seized the opportunity,

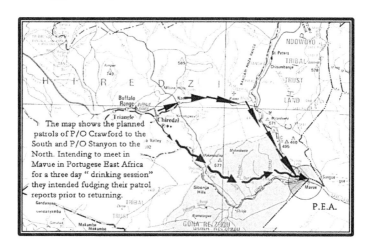

The map shows the planned patrols of P/O Crawford to the South and P/O Stanyon to the North. Intending to meet in Mavue in Portugese East Africa for a three day " drinking session" they intended fudging their patrol reports prior to returning.

*The devious plan for a three-day piss up*

*"The Sangwe Sir, I thought as we were relatively quiet I could patrol the area. I think we might be a trifle behind the patrol schedule."*

Cavey looked surprised, he smiled, I hated it when he did that, it could be interpreted in many ways, few of which were ever to my advantage.

*"That's excellent,"* he said, *"Crawford just volunteered to do the same."*

*"Well Sir,"* I said, pretending to be surprised, *"If he wants the Sangwe, I'll take the European ranches and Chipinda, it would be a shame not to use this quiet period."*

*"No Stanyon, he asked first, he gets Chipinda, you can have the Sangwe."*

To re-inforce my position but careful not to over play my hand, I said, *"I am happy to take the Mini Moke Sir".*

No one liked the bloody Moke. At the end of each day you looked as though you had been hit by an Arabian dust storm. Dust in your eyes, up your nose, your mouth, down the front of your shirt.

*"Fine, that's fine Stanyon, pick a Constable, seven days, and away you go."* He smiled and left me in the radio room.

*"ZEF this and ZEF that blah blah blah."* Who cared, I was off on a Government sponsored 'piss up" of gargantuan proportions. How bloody clever was that Scotsman.

Crawford and I quietly liaised on the dates. We chose and then informed our Constables, not of the entire plan, though they did not care as patrol allowance and getting away from the station routine was sufficient incentive. I would be billeted in the DC's rest camp on the banks of the Sabi – no tents. This was getting better all the time.

Tom and I agreed that I should leave first. I had a longer distance and more people to see. On the morning of my departure I was organising my kit in the Moke when PO Botha told me Cavey wanted to see me. I marched into his office.

*"Ah, Stanyon,"* he said. *"There you are."*

That sounded ominous. I could feel it in my bones, as a smile settled on his lips, that this was not going to end well.

*"There has been a slight change in arrangements. I have decided you will be doing the Sangwe TTL, as a foot patrol."*

*"A foot patrol Sir?"*

*"Yes."* He continued, *"It will do you good, we did plenty of them in my day. It is amazing how much you see and how few of the locals actual know you are in the area. No need for the normal routine visits to chiefs or townships."*

I was starting to feel a lack of oxygen in my system, in fact I felt very weak. I could feel the blood draining from my face - I presumed I looked like a ghost.

*"I will have you dropped off at 'x",* he said.

I started suffering from hearing impairment. I could not believe I was hearing correctly. Surely it must be time for stables, my alarm must go off any minute and relieve me of this nightmare I am going through.

He said something about walk for three days north and then return south along a different route – carry all your necessities on your back. What! That meant I would also have to carry a .303 Lee

Enfield that alone, weighed 10 pounds. How many Chinamen had I killed in a previous life?

Perusal of the BSAP archives will reveal in the year of 1967, before the rains, the last known foot patrol of the Sangwe TTL was certainly carried out by PO Stanyon. It was an alcohol free week. I was carrying enough weight! Five arrests were made, two muzzle loaders and an array of spears and bows and arrows were confiscated. PO Stanyon reported the necessity for expending three rounds of ammunition to effect arrests.

All five arrests, for contraventions of the Wild Life Conservation Act, were prosecuted in the Magistrates Court at Chiredzi, resulting in five convictions.

Patrol Officer Crawford's patrol of the European ranchers and Chipinda Pools area was cancelled. No reason was ever established.

The wry, old fox had somehow found out that we were up to no good. One more win to him. Slowly but surely the taming of Chiredzi was being achieved.

$*$ $*$ $*$ $*$ $*$

*Tis all a Chequer-board of Nights and Days*
*Where Destiny with Men for Pieces plays:*
*Hither and thither moves, and mates, and slays,*
*And one by one back in the Closet lays*

## ESTABLISHING LAW AND ORDER
## LOWVELD STYLE

T here needs to be placed on the table, for the sake of clarity and understanding, the mentality and attitudes of the times in the late 1960's, in Rhodesia.

Most of the young troopers did not mind a cold beer on a hot day. In fact, I might suggest, most of their salaries were spent in pursuits of pleasures derived in one form or another while imbibing. With very limited access to cultural and educational pursuits, off duty activities always seemed to incorporate the fruit of the vine, in whatever form it took. Generally, but by no means always, Lion Beer was favoured by the Rhodesians and Castle Beer by the English. Bar games were copied, developed, adapted and played in most bars: Darts, Bok Bok, Liar Dice, 7.14.21, Poker Dice, Dead Ants, Down Downs, Top shelf, Bottom shelf, which shelf? There were periodic 'punch ups' between the police and civilians and between the police themselves. I think it fair comment that we had a lot to learn in terms of the productive and positive use of our spare time.

Visiting Officers suggestions of building model boats and planes, gardening, research, and study for Civil Service exams or learning to speak the local dialect fell, I am afraid to say, on deaf ears.

I have no comparisons to make between District and Town Branch Police or for that matter with other Provinces.

I do know our behaviour whilst off duty, at times, was considered, to quote, 'a bit wild'. However it seldom, if ever, affected our work, which in hindsight we took extremely seriously and conscientiously.

My personal Annual Efficiency Certificate (later named, to be more politically correct, Annual Performance Report) written by Cavey, was handed to me, for my perusal and signature. Those being reported on had the right of rejection or to question, if not satisfied, that it accurately described the performance of that person. In the section that described my off duty behaviour I noted the word 'boisterous.' Not knowing the definition I consulted the Oxford Dictionary. It was defined as, amongst other things, 'unruly, rowdy, noisy, over-the-top'. Not wording I thought would benefit my upcoming promotion exam interviews that is, if I passed the exams. So within my rights I knocked on the Member in Charges door. He looked up. I had the AEC in my hand.

*"Just put it in the in tray,"* he said.

I explained my predicament.

*"What don't you agree with?"* he asked.

I explained.

*"Well"*, he said, *"I was considering something else, which I shall use if you wish."*

Relieved I said, *"Thank you Sir."*

*"I shall change it to 'a bloody drunk'."*

I immediately signed the document and left.

The Hippo Valley Club was, prior to the construction of the Chiredzi Hotel, the only premises' where one could socialise, it was run by a former BSAP Constable whose moniker was Mike Jupp who had taken his discharge on the 13th February 1965. The club had two bars, the Cocktail and Public Bars. Its position was partly concealed during the growing season by sugar cane that totally enveloped the building. Amongst other things he did, Jupp served a Rhodesian mixed grill, on a large oval platter. If you were able to consume the entire meal, at one time, you were entitled to another free one. I never saw anyone achieve the feat.

Compliance with the Liquor Licencing Rules/Regulations/Act, whatever governed licenced premises such as this club, where either unknown or just simply did not form part of the running of the establishment. I cannot recall the exact times of opening and closing, but whatever they were they bore little resemblance to the law. I think it depended on whether someone was waiting for a drink, and thus it opened irrespective of time and when the last drunk fell out the door dictated the closing time.

It was a matter, I am sure under consideration by the chief strategist and would be attended to in time as its priority reached the top of his list. In the mean time we kept an eye on proceedings.

Clientele of the two bars were fairly well defined, not by anything other than ones social standing in the community. The public bar, which had a well-used dartboard, was usually filled with artisans and their apprentices from the main sugar mill, family members and friends. While the Cocktail bar hosted private sugar farmers, Hippo Valley Estate managerial staff, a number of the growing businessmen and entrepreneurs, medical and Government officials resident in the ballooning township of Chiredzi. Oh! …and members of the BSAP, recently arrived.

The Club House was designed so both bars were at right angles to each other. There was individual public access to each bar. The bars were totally separated except for an archway on the vertex of the 90-degree angle. The archway allowed bar staff to move freely behind the two counters, facilitating service of both bars as and when necessary. This arch allowed the patrons of both bars to be able to see part way into the opposite bar.

On one particularly very busy night PO's Williams, Hardy and myself were seated in the cocktail bar after a long tiresome weeks' work quietly minding our own business while we savoured the delights of the nectar of the Gods. I cannot categorically remember the conversation. One could however accurately presume that after six or more beers the conversation would have ranged from the subjects of physics and nuclear chemistry to Greek mythology.

We were interrupted by shouts from the public bar. Looking through the arch and across to the bar counter we noted a group of young, unkempt, bedraggled and presumably inebriated patrons, all of whom we recognised as sugar mill employees. We ignored them initially. The shouting became louder, more abusive and personal.

The word, 'pigs' was repeated continuously and I, for one, did not think they were discussing some future veterinary degrees they intended studying, this was soon followed by a number of hand signs, including some idiot trying to emulate Churchill but with wrist pointing the wrong way. Soon the word Saul became audible, followed by some rather discouraging remarks about his mother and his own anatomy. I heard, something about, '*let's see, how brave you are without your uniforms on*'.

I was cogitating on this last message when I saw Williams, with the grace of an international ballet dancer, move from the seated position, with his left hand on the top of the counter, swing his legs, followed by his torso over the counter. Like greased lightning he was through the back of the cocktail bar, across to the other counter. I really do not think the chap seeking to know how brave we were, saw it coming. Williams's fist landed square on the nose of the questioner, who dropped from sight.

Then everything went into slow motion for a brief moment in time. Two people struck Williams, while I was running between the counters with Hardy we managed to squeeze through the archway at the same time. While Williams, continued his part of the melee with the counter dividing him and his opponents. Hardy and I vaulted over the Public Bar counter. There would be many ways of describing the next five minutes. One might choose ruckus or free-for-all maybe a fracas - it was on for young and old.

I am thankful to report, at the end, the three persons representing what I would describe as the 'good guys', had provided direct and indisputable evidence to the last question asked concerning our uniform.

We asked if anyone else had a similar question and wanted to continue. There were no takers. Former policeman and now innkeeper Mike Jupp, intervened with his interpretation of the Liquor Licencing Laws - he shut both bars and with words that would make a sailor blush, told everyone to go home.

Now under normal conditions this matter would have ended there. However there was the Section Officer Saul factor. As word filtered through the community of the 'brawl' or 'scuffle' it got to the ears of Section Officer Saul. He questioned the three of us, and to the best of my knowledge wanted to charge us with a contravention of the Miscellaneous Offences Act. The charge, I think was 'fighting in a public place', and knowing the efficiency of Saul, there would have been a raft of alternative charges, including a few from the Police Act, and the old favourite, to which I was personally well acquainted 'Act in a Manner Unbecoming'.

The Member in Charge got wind of proceedings. We were again interviewed. I might add, the three accused decided an outright denial of our involvement was not considered a wise defence, as the 'battle marks' remained evident. Of course there was collusion amongst the rank and file.

Individually, we explained the whole episode, it was for the honour of the BSAP and in particular we defended Section Officer Saul's honour (and his mother's I might add) We were not the aggressors, nor instigators, we were outnumbered, humiliated and abused, we defended the right to maintain law and order – blah, blah etc.

Now in this case as in many others Insp. Cavey was judge, jury and executioner. He decreed that justice was done and seen-to-be-done. The 'rabble' had been brought to a point of order, and this was to be considered a positive step to bring law and order to Chiredzi.

The matter was closed complete.

\*       \*       \*       \*       \*

### The Law of the Yukon
*This is the law of the Yukon, and ever she makes it plain:*
*"Send not your foolish and feeble; send me your strong and your sane—*
*Strong for the red rage of battle; sane, for I harry them sore;*
*Send me men girt for the combat, men who are girt to the core;*
*Swift as the panther in triumph, fierce as the bear in defeat,*
*Sired of a bulldog parent, steeled in the furnace heat.*
*Send me the best of your breeding, lend me your chosen ones;*
*Them will I take to my bosom, them will I call my sons;*
*Them will I gild with my treasure, them will I glut with my meat;*
*But the other – the misfits, the failures – I trample under my feet.*
*Dissolute, damned and despairful, crippled and palsied and slain,*
*Ye would send me the spawn of your gutters – Go! Take back your*
*spawn again.*

*Robert Service*

## ANTI-TERRORIST TRAINING

I n the mid-sixties Rhodesia experienced the first incursions of terrorists. My service (1972-1980) in assisting in the prosecution of the war effort against the terrorists, their organisation and all their atrocities and the resulting conclusion of the conflict in April 1980, has resulted in a pain that never dissipated, and a wound that never healed.

That, having been said, there will always be humour - however serious the situation. I shall now pen my very earliest involvement in anti-terrorist training in the Lowveld. In hindsight a far cry from what would actually happen, when the real situation emerged. We had heard about terrorist activity way to our north, back in 1964, which had no effect on our lifestyle in Victoria Province.

In 1965 there had been the Unilateral Declaration of Independence from Britain.

On the 11th November 1965, whilst still stationed at Bikita, we were told to go to the Mess at 1300 Hours or thereabouts and turn on the RBC. We only listened to Radio Lourenco Marques so finding the RBC took a while. We sat sipping tea. Frankly, I can't speak for the others, but I had little comprehension of what Prime Minister Smith was talking about or what, if anything, he wanted me to do, or that he might be suggesting something untoward was about to happen. Nothing changed in Victoria Province.

In 1966 there was terrorist activity in Sinoia and Kanyemba, they were both in Mashonaland and well north at that. I also established the matters were successfully resolved in our favour.

Then in 1967 we heard, along the grape vine mind you - no daily sit-reps in those days - some more activity in and around Kariba.

Well now that was as far north as one could go so if they were walking it would take aeons before they arrived anywhere near the Lowveld. Again we heard the matter was successfully resolved. So once again we returned to the policing of Chiredzi.

So there was little doubt when told by Cavey we were to undergo anti-terrorist training we were confused and greatly surprised. Night work would be required also tracking and anti-tracking training, plus important information about the enemy. Bushcraft was also on the agenda. A new unit had been formed called the Police Anti-Terrorist Unit (PATU), we were going to be trained for possible future action!!

At this time, I might add, we were resident in the new Single Quarters (The Mess). There was a brand new, brick and concrete building on the main road - the police station was, at last, operational. Williams and I had been selected to be the 'Fox and Hare'? What did they have to do with terrorists? What was happening to the BSAP!

Under instruction from Cavey and with the aid of numerous short-term prisoners we constructed a very large oblong trough, out of large rocks and filled it with, firstly, large pieces of cut, dry timber and then smaller timber on the top. Cavey explained we were preparing a large Braai, to be enjoyed after the anti-terrorist exercise.

Cavey completed his briefing by informing us Section Officer Keith Jarrett was to visit us from his base in Fort Victoria. An interesting character to say the least, he had two rows of medals on his chest, rather elderly to carry the rank he had. He seemed to be a good friend of Cavey's. While I dared not enquire, I felt he too might have had a 'brush' with the 'powers that be'. Then, as now I am not exactly sure what his role was, I think he may have been in charge of the Police Reserve. I soon established he was a person without a past life. He never spoke in the past tense. I presumed the medals were from the Second World War.

Soon after his arrival we were all told to assemble outside the Mess. The newly constructed building was built in the middle of the bush. There were a number of police Reservists, not people I was accustomed to as they had not existed in Bikita or Zaka. The Reserve was Cavey's personal domain, he and he alone dealt with all matters relating thereto. They all appeared to be men of longevity and I might add, not as physically fit as I am certain they once were. I easily relate to that as I pen this narrative.

SO Jarrett's briefing started with a synopsis of terrorist activity to date. I was less than interested, purely on the grounds he was talking about areas so far afield as to be, in my mind, inconsequential.

He talked of Russians and East German fleck, Czechoslovakian manufactured this and that, ZAPU, ZANU, Ndabaningi Sithole, Joshua Nkomo, training in Moscow, Peking, Libya and Tanzania. Was this some geography lesson disguised as a talk on terrorist activity? I was uncomfortable in my riot blues with ankle straps and boots, my floppy blue hat concealing my eyes, the hot morning sun and no shade was getting to me. I dozed off without detection.

My condition was critical as I nursed the mother of all hangovers. I considered the inapplicability and remoteness of the lecture bordered on the absurd and bizarre, I was awoken by Williams. My hangover showed little sign of subsiding.

"*Let's go,*" he said.

"*Where?*" I asked.

"*We are the terrorists and the police Reserve are going to track us, haven't you been listening?*"

The short answer was, "*No.*"

Williams explained to me we were to walk in the bush wherever we liked, as long as we remained within a designated area. If we had not been caught or killed by 1730 Hours, we were to walk to a predetermined site, where we would sleep the night, with everyone else. The exercise would be repeated the following morning. Again if not caught or killed we would walk back to the Mess. Our instructions were to get to the 'braai' early, about mid-afternoon and light the fire.

To reduce the length of the tale, we disappeared into the undergrowth, and when satisfied we were out of site, we broke into one of those Zulu-type lopping trots, by which you could literally run for miles. We were not armed, nor did we have to carry a pack. I also might add we were not issued with water bottles. Only minor issues really, how things change! The Lowveld is relatively flat, but there were a few small geographical knolls.

We positioned ourselves on one such knoll, found a shady tree and with Williams watching our tracks I returned to nursing the hangover.

We never heard or saw the 'opposition' so we headed for the rendezvous. On arrival we found ourselves to be late. Our kit had been brought by Land Rover, and as the 'juniors' we were delegated to make a number of fires.

It was a great night, with the fires blazing and then, after supper, coffee was served. Jarrett and Cavey produced bottles of rum. At first one small 'tot' was 'issued'. The rule was soon expunged. With both bottles emptied, the signal was given to turn in. Sentries? Hourly watch? If you wake up keep the fires burning. We had no sleeping bags.

In the morning, leaving our kit for collection, Williams and I headed for the hills - in a manner of speaking. Once we had done the Zulu thing for a while we rested and again watched our tracks. Nothing. At midday we headed for base – the only instruction left was the lighting of the braai. After numerous failed attempts, by both of us, I suggested to Williams to hang on while I went down to the petrol pumps, filled a jerry can and returned. I'll get it going. I then poured the four gallons along the entire length of the structure, which was about 12 feet long.

I had a Ronson lighter, silver in colour, with one of my cadet silver lion badges soldered on the side. It was my pride and joy. Positioning myself well clear of the braai area I adjusted the length of the flame. I walked up to the structure and of course (I had not thought through this exercise very well) had to bend down to ignite the fire. Such was the explosion I am sure it woke the dead. I landed on my derriere some distance away. The explosion had taken my eyebrows off and given me something resembling a Depot 'short back and sides' hairstyle. Both arms looked as though I had undergone beauty waxing.

There was a conflicting odour of burnt hair, skin and burning wood. The flames at their peak were actually higher than the Mess roof. A large black cloud of smoke rose high into the air. Williams was doubled up in laughter. The remnants of my hangover had evaporated.

There was to follow an exercise debriefing. We all agreed we were now more proficient in anti-terrorist operation capabilities. Little did Williams and I realise at that point, both of us were soon to go hunting for the real thing. A brief by Special Branch stated that one terrorist had in fact 'walked all the way' but that is another tale.

Beers, stories, yarns and lies followed well into the night with yet another *babalas* in progress.

\*        \*        \*        \*        \*

*He earns whate'er he can,*
*And looks the whole world in the face,*
*For he owes not any man.*
*Toiling, – rejoicing, – sorrowing,*
*Onward through life he goes;*
*Each morning sees some task begin,*
*Each evening sees it close;*
*Something attempted, something done,*
*Has earned a night's repose.*

*Henry Longfellow*

# STOPPING
# THE DRUNK DRIVING.

The planning and stratagem of enforcing law and order was the sole sphere of the Member in Charge, who at the time of the implementation of what was known as the 'anti-DWD operation' had recently been promoted to Chief Inspector. It was my presumption the timing of this exercise coincided with the completion of the police station and new Mess.

I might add the landscaping of the grounds had been completed under my direction, as a form of punishment for some long forgotten misdemeanour. It was done in my time after hours with periodical visits from Cavey to supervise my efforts. The Q Rep, never seen or spoken to, was of great assistance with provision of tree saplings and plants. The local prison population provided all the muscle and hard grind. Chiredzi police was for all intents and purposes a fully operational and functioning member of the BSAP organisation, complicit with its unquestionably high standards and professionalism.

One morning Inspector Cavey called PO's Williams, Hardy and myself into his office.

After entry his door was closed. With the respect we all had for Cavey, we all stood at the 'at ease position' with hands folded behind our backs, shoulders erect, immaculately presented, no twisting of the blue lanyards, all buttons done up, none missing. Belt buckles shinning and leather polished.

"*We have reached the time when it is now appropriate to deal with the drink driving in this area. My initial exercise will be to make a solid and very blatant show of policing in this regard. It will prove to be an unpopular exercise and will have a detrimental effect on police/public relations in the area. I am hoping the first exercise will be so severe that there will be no necessity to duplicate the exercise in the future."*

*"You are not to discuss this with anyone, least of all your drinking friends at the Club. Do I make myself quite clear?"*

*"Yes Sir."*

*"Here is the operational plan. Stanyon, soon after 10:00pm on (Saturday or Friday night I cannot recall which) you will position yourself, in full uniform, with a torch and your note book, on the main road to the Club on the eastern side of the railway line that demarcates the area between the privately owned land of Hippo Valley Estate and the local Government area of the township of Chiredzi.*

*Hardy you will be in close proximity to assist, also so equipped.*

*Williams, you will be in charge of the Land Rover which will be off the road, positioned facing east."*

*"Stanyon your job is to stop all traffic moving back into the Chiredzi area. You will make an assessment as to whether the drivers of such vehicles can be considered to have consumed sufficient alcohol to be deemed in contravention of the Roads and Road Traffic Act. You will carry out the usual test and if deemed to be sufficiently drunk Hardy will escort the driver to the Land Rover, and Williams you will drive that person, post haste, to the police station, where I shall carry out a further examination to determine whether they may be in a condition rendering themselves as 'drunk whilst driving'. Williams you will then return immediately for the next accused."*

*"I shall transfer the accused to the hospital, where I have arranged with the Government Medical Officer to be on duty and ready to apply the last and conclusive test of their state of inebriation. All such drivers shall face the full force of the law. I surmise we shall end up with a number of convictions. This should suffice as a warning to all."*

*"Any questions?"*

In unison the answer was, *"No Sir."*

We were dismissed with the customary wording, *"That's all."*

To say the least, we were shell shocked, our minds agog. Was he for real? There was no conversation at the station. At lunchtime we were, for some reason, the only PO's on station. SO Saul had packed his bags and gone to Chirundu I think.

The entire hour was spent discussing the upcoming operation/exercise. There was no conversation regarding our police requirements – which were straightforward but what were the long-term implications of such action. What was it going to do to our standing in the community?

We had by now fully ingratiated ourselves in the drinking community at the club, especially on Friday and Saturday nights. It would be a logistical nightmare. The possible targets were our only means of travelling to and from the club. I am not sure whether the Chiredzi Hotel was operational at that time. I think not. This was a dilemma of mammoth proportions. We were facing down the barrel and heading for a very quiet and isolated social life of that there was little doubt.

As one of the others commented and rightly so, *"It's just as well you built that bar in the Mess Stanyon. That's where we shall be drinking from now on."*

The Bar, designed and constructed by myself, was another punishment I had been given by Cavey. It took a trip to Chipinda Pools and a chat with the lads down there, resulting in the acquisition of three recently killed animal heads complete with skin and flesh. Buffalo, Kudu and Eland. We set up a number of half size 44-gallon drums on the front 'lawn' (excuse the adulating description), built the appropriate number of fires, roaming the district far and wide bringing in Land Rovers full of timber, all with the assistance of prisoners. We filled the drums with water, placed the heads there in and waited for the water to boil. This process, over a protracted time, would remove all the skin and flesh, from the skulls.

The prisoners loved it. They sat and slept next to the fires all night and day, no guards. Their only tasks were to keep the water filled to the brim, fires burning and periodically change the position of each heads. They returned individually to the prison for meals, ablutions and washing. It took a week or more.

When reduced to bone, the heads were painted ivory, placed on timber backboards, fitted with different coloured globes and secured to the back wall above the shelving in the bar. The counter and decoratively welded steel bar stools had all been manufactured for free at the Mill, by our drinking friends at the Hippo Club!!!! The conundrum was evident for all to realise.

My younger brother, PO Nigel Stanyon who I think was stationed at Chiredzi during the last years of Rhodesia informed me the bar has been dismantled. Pity really, if those walls could talk, the devil would smile.

'D-day' arrived soon enough. For most probably the first Friday or Saturday night in our careers at Chiredzi, no alcohol was consumed. We were living in interesting times.

At 2045 Hours after a final briefing from Cavey, Williams drove the three-man team to the railway line. To be honest I have racked my brain and spoken to two former members, but I just cannot recall what steps were required to be taken to determine that a driver was 'Drunk whilst Driving'. It is but a technicality, someone will remember.

The scene at the roadblock was simple. To the west of the railway line, sugar cane grew to a height of at least ten feet. The sugarcane fields spread over miles in every direction except east for almost as far as the eye could see (during the day that is). To the east of the railway line, sparse Rhodesian scrub land, a few Mopani trees here and there, varying heights of wild grass and small bushes. The police Land Rover was concealed from sight. The road on either side of the rail line was unsealed.

We waited in silence; we were about to embark on social suicide. Williams was seated, smoking, on the spare tyre on the bonnet of the Land Rover. He broke the silence with, *"Here comes the first one."*

Because of the height of the cane, Hardy and I could see nothing. I stood on the front bumper of the Land Rover and was confronted with a sight yet unseen in Rhodesia. It looked like the Aurora Borealis, the Northern or Dancing Lights. In the pitch black of the clear night sky patches of scattered clouds of light forming arcs and curtains lighting up the sky like a million fireflies chaotically flying in the night, light reflecting upwards off the thick sugarcane. It was plain to see they were approaching us.

As they came closer one could not distinguish one source of light from another. The closer they came the louder the noise of vehicles, travelling at speed. When they were maybe a mile or less away, it was actually possible to monitor the individual movement of the headlights, some swaying in longer arcs while others almost 'staggering'. The first car came into sight from my position, which was now very precarious.

I was standing in the middle of the road with an issue torch, waving. The torch was in the left hand, my right arm up and forward, palm outstretched forward in the 'Stop' position. The road was narrow, with a slight mound in the middle with limited room to manoeuvre either side.

Momentarily I thought the driver had not seen me. One wheel went up on the mound and the opposite wheel struck the cane, the vehicle rectified itself and came to a skidding halt at my feet.

A head popped out of the driver's window and a male voice shouted, *"What the f\*\*k are you doing Doug? I nearly ran you over! Where were you and the boys tonight? We had a great time."*

Conscious of the fact a second car was approaching at speed I told the driver not to turn his lights off. Hardy walked behind the first car and assumed the stop position, with torch in hand. Concentrating on the first driver I heard a similar conversation between Hardy and the second driver. I asked the driver whether he had consumed any alcohol that night.

*"Of course I have Doug, I'm pissed as a coot man. Where were you guys?"*

I asked him to get out of his car so I could determine whether he was drunk. He opened the driver's door, stepped out, and staggered slightly while he regained his balance.

*"Is this a joke?"* He asked.

I determined he was drunk and called on Williams for assistance. When Williams appeared the driver said he knew what we were up to. He said, or maybe slurred the words, *"This is going to be a continuation of the 'Hooley' in the bush – what a great idea."*

Williams took him away and placed him in the back of the Land Rover. By that time the third and fourth cars were racing towards our position' Hardy was escorting the second driver to the Land Rover. Within a very short space of time we had made eight arrests. All eight were seated in the Land Rover, occupying the back seat, front seat and one, I think, if I remember correctly, on the floor.

We radioed Chief Insp Cavey, reported the number of arrests, and as there was no further room in the Land Rover Williams drove away with the first eight accused.

The rationale of all eight men had been identical, *"What a great way to have a party", "Where have you been?" "You should have seen old so and so, he was motherless,"* and *"it was bloody funny",* etc, etc. A few queried why we were in uniform.

After William's departure there was a slight lull in the traffic. Our eyes were now accustomed to the night light and the next set of dancing lights was on their way. Hardy and I discussed a more efficient method of processing the drunks, safe keeping of their keys, and security of their cars and the transfer of any passengers where appropriate.

The next vehicle came to the usual skidding halt, the same conversation occurred, and as the truck had not yet returned, the driver was asked 'to be seated' in his car. After we had confiscated his keys I remember him singing, although I did not recognise the song.

The Land Rover returned just as I was stopping the tenth vehicle. It was travelling very slowly, far too slowly. It came to a gentle and dignified stop. I walked to the driver's door as the window was being wound down. A head lolled out, my torch shone in the eyes of none other than the doctor, our Government Medical Officer and key player in the nights' operations.

*"Hello Doug, why were you not at the club tonight?"*

*"Good evening Doc, I thought you were on duty at the hospital?"*

*"Why,"* he enquired, *"Would such a thought enter your head?"*

There was trouble brewing, I thought. This was going to be a difficult situation to extract ourselves from.

*"Did you not have an appointment and agreement with C/Insp. Cavey Doc?"*

Silence, then the penny dropped. *"Oh my God was that tonight?"* He asked.

I asked the Doc if he would accompany me to the police vehicle so he and Cavey could have a discussion. He sheepishly agreed. Hardy appeared and when he saw who my prisoner was he looked as though he had seen a ghost.

With one accused in the truck, I asked the Doc to get in the front and I gently closed the door. I suggested to Williams he park the truck away from sight at the police station and, very quietly, inform Cavey of the situation. I suggested it unwise to use the radio.

Williams drove away, returning at break neck speed. He had orders from Cavey. He told us to get in, let the drivers, most probably another two or three go on their way and we were to return to the station.

On arrival I saw a large group of men, the accused previously arrested, led by Cavey, walking towards the Mess. They were a jovial lot, chatting and laughing. Cavey instructed us to meet him in the Mess, and not to drink. The reason - we were required to drive the revellers home after their nightcap.

Cavey had told the drivers it had purely been a warning exercise of what to expect if they ever drank in excess and drove again.

A few beers on the police, a few jokes, a lie or two and we drove them all safely home. An all-round excellent police public relations exercise and the Patrol Officers still had transport to the local watering hole on weekends.

I was never involved in a duplicate operation, I am not sure there was one.

Another small step in the policing of Chiredzi had been achieved.

\*　　　\*　　　\*　　　\*　　　\*

## YOUNG & OLD

When all the world is young lad,
And all the trees are green;
And every goose a Swan, lad,
And every lass a Queen
Then hey for boot and horse, lad,
And around the world away;
Young blood must have its course, lad;
And every dog his day

When all the world is old, lad,
And all the trees are brown,
And all the sport is stale, lad,
And all the wheels run down;
Creep home, and take your place there,
The spent and maimed among.
God grant you find one face there,
You loved when all was young.

*Kingsley*

# ONE THAT WALKED ALL THE WAY
## *(With Bananas and Pineapples)*

**W**ith the aforementioned substantial anti-terrorist training under our belts and the adage 'More Sweat in Training, less Blood in Battle' being our motto we felt secure in knowing 'the boys' up north would always get their man. We were also confident no terrorist could walk undetected from Kariba to Chiredzi.

So life went on as always in Chiredzi. Now I knew of the CID Dept. As a Cadet I had worked in CID Cycles for a while, although in all my time at Bikita, Zaka and Chiredzi I had never seen one.

It was with great surprise when C/Insp Cavey called Williams and I into his office and introduced us to, DSO 'Paddy' Gardiner, Special Branch. I must be honest; I had not seen one of these super sleuths before. Legend had it that these were the "*crème de la crème*" of the Police Force. Handpicked. Not to be underestimated in any way.

"*DSO Gardiner needs some help and I have suggested you two would be most suitable,*" said Cavey introducing us.

DSO Gardiner then started talking in that geography lesson type language like S/O Jarrett had. Mentioning again ZANU and ZAPU of course, but there was a new one to add to the list SANAC. He informed us a member of a South African terrorist group (that's the SANAC bit) had escaped the net up north and was last seen, or rumoured to have been seen, travelling on foot well south of Fort Victoria. Now that was not supposed to happen in our world. Given the time the information had been received, SB calculated there was every possibility he was now past or certainly in the Chiredzi area, heading for South Africa.

We were to filter into the TTL's and make enquiries with the locals to establish his whereabouts. If located we were not to engage him, but to contact the police station immediately for assistance.

He provided a lot more information, in what's called a 'full briefing'. Sometimes I thought he was speaking in Latin or Greek.

I recognised the words 'Moscow' and 'East German Fleck' (not sure what fleck meant!!), 'highly trained, externally', 'very dangerous' and something about a 'banana magazine'.

*"Any questions?"* he asked.

*"Yes,"* I said, quite confused. *"What is a banana magazine? Surely this chap is not carrying media discussing the growing of bananas. If so why would that be important?"*

DSO Gardiner must have thought, they could have found someone a little brighter than this idiot. *"It is a description,"* he explained, *"the local tribes people understand and will be able to identify with as it is the shape of the magazine fitted on the Russian Automat Kalashnikov (AK) 47, automatic rifle, named after the Russian that invented it in 1947.* He then went on about it having a 30 round magazine and our suspect was carrying a few such magazines. He then confused the matter even more by adding that he was also carrying *'pineapple'* grenades. I decided to let that one go through to the wicket keeper!!!

Williams and I, with one Constable each, dressed in full riot blues and armed with bolt action Lee Enfield's, with eight rounds maximum, which required re-filling on total expenditure, not just exchanging, like our quarry. The Constables carried a Greener shotgun. I am not sure whether my Constable had ever fired one before.

We headed into the TTLs, driving long wheel based Land Rovers, marked POLICE in dark blue. To make a long story short we spent just over two weeks in different TTL's. I still remember the looks of astonishment when we told the locals this chap was carrying a *'sibam'* that looked like it had a banana underneath and hand grenades which looked like pineapples.

Grenades, I explained, were small, round items that looked like pineapples that made a loud noise and blew up, throwing my hands in the air, in a vain attempt to explain blowing up. I explained he was extremely dangerous, did not speak their language and if seen they should report the matter, post haste, to our base camp.

This was a serious matter of National importance, and obviously a dangerous mission, so each of our Land Rovers had been fitted with SSB radios, not the norm.

Each morning before departing on our 'seek and locate' mission we 'reported in' by radio, each morning the same message; *"nothing to report, over and out."*

Now full riot gear in the middle of summer in the Lowveld would test the resolve of many, but in the name of law and order, and regimental pride on we went seeking our quarry.

Good old basic, sound, police work: investigations and enquiries. Little did I know then what I know now; travelling with a full length NATO rifle in a Land Rover with doors fitted does not provide for ease of immediate and uncomplicated extraction from vehicles coming under fire. It never entered my mind our quarry might shoot at us whilst driving. Surely that would not be fair or within the rules?

Those who know the ways of the indigenous community will know that information spreads like a wild fire in tinder dry bush veld, fanned by cyclonic strength winds. Readers will be well aware of the confusion that reigns when messages are passed from person to person by mouth. The classic World War I example comes to mind where a message was passed along the trenches from man to man resulting in the request from the battle front to HQ to 'send reinforcements we are going to advance', resulting in HQ receiving the request, 'send two and six pence we are going to a dance'!! Not much had changed, even in Africa without a conflict, well not at this time anyway. Within the second week, the patrol areas were filled with people looking for a 'mute man, selling bananas and pineapples, heading for somewhere unknown'.

In our third week, we were no closer to our quarry, than we were when we started. The TTLs had been transformed into wide-eyed locals keen to meet this chap. One morning when we 'checked in' by radio C/Insp Cavey himself informed us to return immediately.

So the battle hardened veteran's returned from their not 'seek and kill' mission but their 'seek and report' mission. Surely we should be deserved of a medal, if not for the display of courage and beyond the call of duty performance, but that we had been alcohol free for 21 days or thereabouts and in my case had been on cigarette rations far too long.

Reporting in C/Insp Cavey informed us he had received word from DSO Gardiner, SB itself had conducted a very successful operation at Farmers Hall (located just outside Fort Victoria town, for those uninitiated) and captured our quarry alive and uninjured.

DSO Gardiner had been either so busy, or had experienced a momentary lapse in memory, or any other excuse, he had clean forgotten to inform us. I guess that's OK, except the arrest had been made three days after we initially set out on our daring mission. Thus I presume we, and the locals in the TTLs had been looking for a 'non-existent mute "banana and pineapple" salesman, headed for South Africa', wherever that was?

And the relentless taming of Chiredzi continued unabated.

\* \* \* \* \*

*Come, fill the cup, and in the Fire of Spring*
*The Winter Garment of Repentance fling:*
*The Bird of Time has but a little way*
*To fly – and Lo! The Bird is on the Wing.*

*The Rubaiyat*

# FORENSIC SCIENCE IS INTRODUCED TO LOWVELD POLICING

R emaining in compliance with the aging sage's requirements of 'it must be based on fact', I consulted with my old accomplice who now lives in the UK somewhere. He apologised for not replying sooner, but said he had his grandchildren with him for a few days and *'they took up all his time'* – how things have changed, and for the better for all of us I am certain.

The introduction of forensic science into the crime investigation armoury of the early crime fighters in Chiredzi was a very important and complex exercise. This is without a shadow of doubt the first investigation by Chiredzi Police where Forensic investigations were employed.

This story is told from the perspective of two policemen involved in this matter. Early one Sunday morning, Insp Cavey phoned the single quarters, known as the Mess (maybe for more reasons than one). Asked specifically for PO Stanyon, who, on answering the phone, thought he must be going to be accused of some diabolical behaviour.

*"Stanyon see me in the Charge Office immediately, I want you in uniform."*

The diplomatic advice from myself that *"I was not on either first or second reserve,"* was responded to with the 'click' of the other phone on hanging up. I reported immediately.

*"Now Stanyon I am going to give you a lesson in the collection, labelling and forwarding of forensic evidence/exhibits, to the FSLO in Salisbury."*

Not wishing to display my ignorance, I replied, *"Yes Sir that would be most welcome."*

Exactly who the FSLO was, and why he should get our exhibits was in that moment a bit of a mystery although I did vaguely recall one sleepy law and order lecture in Depot where forensic science and the importance it could be to police investigations was mentioned but suffering from exhaustion after riding horses in the early mornings, followed by marching backwards and forwards, with *eyes right, one step forwaaaaard, swing those ***** arms, present arms, stand at eeeeez* and being called some quite unusual and sometimes unpalatable names, I used the reprieve of law lectures to catch up on some well needed sleep.

Cavey and I got into a Land Rover. Cavey sat in the driver's seat, after having handed me a rather large, cumbersome briefcase type receptacle to look after. He drove into the Chiredzi town village and pulled up outside one of the residences.

What I viewed, was an ornate stone and concrete wall some four feet high, stretching across the front of the garden, dividing the municipal area from the owners beautifully manicured front lawn. At a position, most probably a trifle left of centre of this structure, was a hole about six feet in length. Shattered parts of the wall were strewn across the front lawn. There were some distinct tyre marks in both the municipal area and right through what would have been the wall, where the hole was and across the lawn and up to the steps leading to the front door of the residence. One other thing, that was obvious and hastily written into my police notebook, was a telephone pole. Closer examination revealed the wires that had been attached to the pole had snapped. The pole was also positioned on the front garden of this residence.

I never usually used a police notebook, but I had brought one to impress the boss.

Cavey was having a discussion with, presumably, the owner of the residence. Returning to where I was standing, a jug of water in his hand he opened the brief case and removed a packet of white powdery stuff. A rather large bowl also mysteriously came out of this case into which he poured the water and powder and gave it a vigorous stir.

*"Now Stanyon watch closely."*

I remember thinking to myself; if he pulls a rabbit out of that briefcase I am going to collapse laughing. He explained he was taking a mould of the tyre tracks. He would allow time for it to dry and then pull it up. Handing me a small square plastic bag and a pair of tweezers he instructed me to examine all the broken stones on the lawn for the minutest particles of paint.

Paint he explained would have 'transferred' from the vehicle involved onto the stone fence on impact.

He gave me a brief lecture about compound strengths and impact and how no two solids were of the same compound strength and as such there would always be a transfer of material from one to the other. He also said when the paint was examined it was the thickness not the surface that was viewed under a microscope and the numbers of layers were used in evidence. Now that was all very interesting, but I was suffering from the mother of all hangovers from Saturday night in the Mess. The brain was having great difficulty in absorbing all this very useful information.

Purely of academic interest, to show how life comes with many surprises, PO Stanyon, with promotion and a 'D' in front of the rank, was to be the BSAP Forensic Science Liaison Officer (FSLO) himself, from 31/10/73 to 3/1/75!!!

Back to the major crime scene in either 1967/68, down I went on hands and knees closely examining each rock. With deft dexterity I manipulated the tweezers in recovery of forensic evidence. Each spec of paint, one minute particle of paint after another. After a short while I looked into the bag and a hue was forming. A shade of grey, light grey maybe. I see I thought, how clever – now I knew we were looking for a grey car. I was becoming very astute at this high-end investigation work. I could not wait to tell the boys in the Mess!!

I was still on my hands and knees with renewed vigour and a depleting hangover when I heard a car pull up close to the scene, behind me. Looking under my armpit I noted the PO on first reserve had arrived. I thought how kind to come and give us a hand. That person was PO Hardy.

I now provide the story of events from the perspective of PO Hardy (BSAP Chiredzi – First Reserve) on that particular weekend.

*We had had a party at the camp that Saturday night, and as you know I was on duty. In my very inebriated state in the early hours of Sunday morning I decided to go and do a VO (Visiting Officers) check on the patrolling Constable. Somewhere in the middle of Chiredzi town, the Land Rover left the road, went through a stone garden wall, knocked over a telephone pole, and came to a halt at the front steps leading up to the house. Luckily it was a steep set of stairs otherwise I probably would have gone through the front door.*

*Well I got out of the Land Rover, looked around and figured the only way out was the way I came in, so putting the Land Rover in 4 wheel drive I reversed back over the telephone pole and through the gap in the wall. I went back to camp and went to bed. I never found the patrolling constable.*

*The next morning I got a call from the Charge Office to say there were Constables from Depot at the railway station and I had to go and pick them up. I woke up with this sick feeling I had had an accident but was kind of hoping it was just a bad dream, so after picking up the Constables I decided to drive through the town to see if I did in fact have an accident.*

*That's when I saw you and Bernard Cavey examining the scene of destruction. When I stopped Cavey asked me if I knew who was driving a grey Land Rover around town in the early hours of the morning, knowing full well it was me.*

*Anyway once we established it was me he took me to see the house owner to whom I apologised and offered to have his wall rebuilt. He said not to worry he would sort it.*

*Cavey then phoned his mate at the Post Office who said he would have the telephone pole and all that sorted that day. The amazing thing of all was that there was only a very small dent in the front bumper, right in the centre. (There lies an anomaly)*

*That was the end of that. Bernard Cavey never mentioned it again.*

I did not hear the conversation between Hardy and Cavey but I saw them talking to the owner of the residence and presumed Hardy was getting further information to investigate the matter. Cavey walked over to me as Hardy drove off, asked for the plastic bag containing all my hard earned forensic evidence, stuck his foot in the middle of the partially dried mould, which turned in to a gooey mess, climbed into the vehicle and we returned to the station. As we got out he said, *"that will be all Stanyon, I hope you have learnt something."*

The taming of Chiredzi had now encompassed the gathering of forensic evidence; we were achieving our goals in leaps and bounds.

\*     \*     \*     \*     \*

*Success is to be measured not so much*
*By the position one has reached in life,*
*As by the obstacles which one has*
*Overcome while trying to succeed.*

*Booker*
*Washington*

## DINNER WITH THE CAVEY'S

I recall sitting in the Mess one evening, while Hardy and Williams were discussing their invitation to dinner with The Member in Charge and his wife. *What are we going to wear? Have you got some aftershave? Should I get a haircut? Do you reckon we stand a chance? Will they be good looking?*

*"Excuse me if I interrupt, why do I not know about this?"*

I was informed, *"The Boss called us into the office this morning and invited us to his place for dinner on Saturday night. His wife has invited two of her young nieces, about our age, for the weekend, and we have to entertain them."*

Frankly I did not presume I had an ego any larger than the average male but in my opinion I thought, in the physical stakes, I was reasonably good looking, and would give either of the other two a fair and reasonable run in that regard.

My great strength, I humbly believed, was I had greater skills and charisma from an entertainment perspective and I was, I thought, more articulate, worldlier wise – an all-round much better bet as a dinner guest than those that had been chosen.

So at Stables the next morning, with broken pride and my nose completely out of joint, not to mention my deflated ego I approached the Boss. I would enlighten him on my many positive traits in the field of entertainment. I also intended, diplomatically, to have him realise his poor decision and right the wrong.

*"May I ask Sir, why you chose Williams and Hardy before myself to entertain your wife's two nieces?"*

"*It is quite simple,*" he said with that smile creeping across his lips, "*It is, Stanyon, because you have no panache and are an uncouth drunk.*"

"*Thank you, Sir*" I replied, returning to my duties of the washing of vehicles.

\*　　　\*　　　\*　　　\*　　　\*

## JUST THINK!

*Just think! Some night the stars will gleam*
*Upon a cold, grey stone,*
*And trace a name with silver beam,*
*And lo! 'twill be your own.*

*That night is speeding on to greet*
*Your epitaphic rhyme.*
*Your life is but a little beat*
*Within the heart of Time.*

*A little gain, a little pain,*
*A laugh, lest you may moan;*
*A little blame, a little fame,*
*A star-gleam on a stone.*

*Robert Service*

## THE LAST PATROL AND CON
*Game viewing & puncture patches*

Little did I realise in September 1967 I would undertake my last patrol at Chiredzi. It was the prime patrol of all, the European farms and the Gona Re Zhou wildlife area. Had I known then what I now know, these would have been my reflections.

I loved every minute of the patrolling experience. I cherished the solitude in the evenings, reading Kingsley, Robert Service, The Rubaiyat, James Elroy Flecker, Longfellow and others. Tying the beer bottles to the roots of trees growing on the banks of the river each morning, allowing them to wallow in the tepid waters for the day, so they were not boiling hot after a day's work. I loved watching the birds settling for the evening, having earned a nights' repose.

The log fire, flickering in the clear night sky, tended by men, whose muted speech and laughter was comforting as they pondered and discussed the matters of the day, the sheer uninhibited freedom of driving through Africa as wild as it could be, if only for a fleeting moment, being in control of my own destiny. Meeting genuine characters free from the pretentious attitudes in the new world. Roaming, almost nomadic style on roads less travelled. The only concerns to personal safety being a cantankerous aging rhino, maybe a surprised Cape buffalo or a six-ton elephant who 'just wanted to play'.

It was certainly not outside the bounds of possibility that C/Insp Cavey preferred me out on patrol as well as it was less taxing for him, so we had a win-win situation, without me even contributing to the discussion.

Daydreams or cherished memories, aging former troopers are allowed such engrossments, tis' our privilege not only of age, but that we were part of that very special period in history.

Ah, yes the last patrol, indeed, once more into the breech dear friend. I was instructed and accepted, may I say with absolutely no reluctance, to carry out what was parochially known as 'the European ranchers and Chipinda Pools patrol'.

As far back as I could remember there were 'game and birds' in my life. I had been brought up on a 96,000-acre cattle ranch, holding six thousand head of cattle, owned by the Belgium Royal Family.

The ranch had a common boundary with the Wankie Game Reserve near Robin's camp north of Wankie. My father shot lions and leopards because they attacked the cattle, elephants because they knocked down the fences, and just about anything else for 'rations'. We always travelled with Kepas, the most trusty and competent of 'gun bearers', an excellent shot when required to do so.

I recall vividly the day the three of us were hunting ration meat – we came across a herd of buffalo. The two adults discussed the wind direction, observed the herd, a couple hundred strong, and made their plans. My father instructed me to stand in a certain spot and asked Kepas to look after me – he wandered off to shoot. Being too young to fully grasp the state of things, I waited. The grass was way above my head and consequently I could see nothing. I heard a shot ring out. Kepas shouted to me to climb a nearby tree and hurriedly clambered up after me, pushing me ever higher. Standing on a reasonable sized branch, he instructed me to wrap my arms around the trunk and then I felt his arms envelope me, pulling me tight against the trunk. No sooner were we so situated when the two hundred odd buffalo stampeded around, through and under the tree – it sounded like rolling thunder.

I could feel the tree shaking, dust rose in such thick blankets that I was temporarily blinded. The sound was deafening. It felt like an eternity, but could only have been a few minutes.

As the dust partially cleared from my eyes, I saw my father running towards us. It looked like a lawn mower or grass slasher had passed under our position.

I digress - a true story, unlikely to be repeated too often.

Yes, back to the patrol. I had completed the necessary visits, obtained the appropriate signatures and dutifully written out my patrol diary. Accurately for once, I had, at that time no need to 'fudge'. I felt I was due a well-deserved reward for service to King/Queen and country, or if one wanted to be fastidious about mere detail the Rhodesian Government, now that we were an Independent Country etc. etc. So I decide to make, what in my later commercial career was called an executive decision. I took a day off and indulged in some game viewing, it was in the blood you see. Not just looking but studying the behaviour of the animals. I could and did do it for hours on end. The day soon ended and I had enjoyed it so much I followed through with a second morning of pleasure.

Cavey would not question me being a day late, surely!

We decamped and headed home. Life was good. Driving the Mini Moke with the air brushing through ones hair mixed, every time a car passed, with sheets of dust, I started to get an uneasy feeling. Would Cavey question me? What would his attitude be? I thought it prudent to conjure up an excuse and fast, just in case. I also needed time to bring the old Sergeant up to speed. Ironically in most cases they could usually present a much more convincing account of the concocted story than we could.

The best I could come up with, which was quiet lame really, was exactly what I told Cavey on my arrival in the late afternoon/evening.

"Sir," I said. "I am sorry we are late. I had a line of enquiries in the TTL to undertake at the end of the patrol."

Then putting on my Oscar winning performance of an infuriated soul, I continued, "We suffered a puncture and had no puncture kit available so I sent the Sgt on a passing bus to find one in a township. He returned, I mended the puncture then we had to await a passing motorist who carried a foot *pump to pump the bloody tyre up. All in all a bloody nuisance, but I got the job done Sir."*

Finishing with a drum roll of epic proportions to my surprise I had even convinced myself and to my utter astonishment, he replied, as is said in the Courts of Justice, 'in words of substance and effect'.

*"Well done Stanyon for using your initiative. Not calling the station and asking for a wheel to be brought down. You better go and get cleaned up. Well done. Good to see you back safely."*

So that was how you beat Cavey. You planned on the run, thinking on your feet. Simple plans, not long drawn out complex arrangements. I went to the Mess, had a shower, sat down with the rest of the Troops and told them my story. We drank long into the night. We never really needed an excuse to do so, and in fact not to have an excuse was excuse suffice to drink. I sat basking in the adulations of my peers. We had all tried and failed. I, I alone, had beaten the best of them. Oh, the taste of success was sweet indeed.

I retired to bed inebriated, exhausted and filled with pride. I remember dozing off with the thought, *"You shall do well in this career my boy"*. I awoke for Stables feeling a touch under the weather but still swelling with pride. I joined the others as we walked to the station. I had an unusual 'cocky step to my gait', chest pumped like some Bantam cock pruning itself for the mating season.

Unsurprisingly Cavey was standing, legs astride, hands on hips, supervising the cleaning. I noticed he was taking a keen interest on the concrete slab on which we parked the cars to wash. Through my bloodshot and slowly adjusting gaze I noticed the Moke was being washed, but there was something amiss. Closer examination revealed the Moke was up on blocks. Next to each wheel hub, the rim, tyre and inner tube were lined up like some military parade. Including the spare wheel off the back.

*"Ah, there you are Stanyon."*

I instinctively knew there was trouble afoot – but still it did not dawn on me.

*"Would you mind explaining which inner tube you attached the repair patch to Stanyon."*

I did not have to enter a plea. There were no mitigating circumstances. There before me lay the direct, indisputable evidence. The Crown's (or was that now the State's) case had been proven beyond any reasonable doubt.

There was no defence. I accepted, as always, my punishment.

\*        \*        \*        \*        \*

## AFRICA

*When you have acquired a taste for the dust,*
*And the scent of our first rain,*
*You're hooked for life on Africa,*
*And you'll not be right again.*
*Until you can watch the setting moon*
*And hear the jackals bark,*
*And know they are around you*
*Waiting in the dark.*

*When you long to see the Elephants*
*Or hear the coucal's song,*
*When the moonrise sets your blood on fire,*
*Then you've been away too long.*
*It is time to cut the traces loose,*
*And let your heart go free,*
*Beyond that far horizon*
*Where your spirit yearns to be.*

*Africa is waiting – come!*
*Since you have touched the open sky*
*And learned to love the rustling grass*
*And the wild Fish Eagle's cry.*
*You'll always hunger for the bush;*
*For the Lion's rasping roar,*
*To camp at last beneath the stars*
*And to be at Peace once more.*

*Author Unknown*

# THREE YOUNG MEN GO IN SEARCH FOR A BETTER COUNTRY

*Alias*

*'The Three Must Get Beers'*

On the night of Tuesday the 10th October 1967 I was partially involved in a minor incident being the passenger in a VW which rolled over, in slow motion, at an intersection within the Chiredzi township, my involvement, in comparison to others, was less than minimal. However it was to be the last straw that broke the camel's back.

Mid-morning of Wednesday the 11th October 1967 Mr Cavey approached me, informing me of the report he had received at his house the night before. He told me to return to my room in the Mess, pack my kit and then, pointing to a Land Rover with a Constable driver waiting next to it, said, *"Get in that Land Rover. You have been transferred to Nuanetsi."*

Incredulously I had been sent, without notice and as punishment, to the best District station, I believe, in the country.

On arrival at Nuanetsi, the Member in Charge, Inspector Geoff Hedges informed me he had reluctantly agreed with the OC to have me transferred under his command.

The staff on station were: SO Charles Cassidy and PO Chris Russell. (I remain in contact with Chris to this day - 50 years on)

Both were quiet, studious men, one studying for his BA in Law the other studying Churchill's six volumes of the Second World War.

Both were teetotallers, or close to. Hedges had informed the OC that even with my addition, on strength, he remained a man short. He was told he would not be receiving further staff, until an ex-Depot recruit who was a teetotaller was found. There were apparently no teetotallers of the rank of Patrol Officer in Victoria Province. He assured me he was less than happy with these arrangements, which were my fault. To begin with as further punishment, he used my presence to get his patrol targets up to date. This perceived punishment, once again caused me to land with my derriere in the butter. Life was good.

A few weeks later I happened to be holding the bar counter up in the Phoenix Bar, in the police Mess in Fort Victoria. There were two other friends there at the time, Hardy from Chiredzi and St Clair from Mashaba. We were discussing whether Rhodesia was in fact the best country in the world. What if there was some other place more suited to us. Should we not spend our lives in the best possible place?

There were few rules to this debate: however all agreed that the following deliberations were not allowed: parochialism, blinkered views, bias, one-eyed prejudice or bigotry. Contributions had to be based on either personal experience or information gleaned from exemplary sources.

One of these young men had travelled outside of their home country a few times, since seven years of age. Not far, but he had been to the 'old Dart' twice, and visited some African countries in the north. The other two relied on their impeccable sources, maybe the odd trip or two to the Republic of South Africa (RSA) or Portuguese East Africa (PEA).

That night a 'seed was sown' and over the next twelve months it blossomed. As each person served on differing police stations far from the Phoenix, face-to-face communication was seldom possible. Undaunted a plan emerged. It was unanimously agreed to conclusively prove 'the answer' whatever it maybe, that they had to travel the world to find it.

Subsequent discussions occurred, sometimes in pairs, at Common, Regional or High Court appearances. At times on the very few occasions when the three individuals could wangle 'time off' dates to coincide, the venue was always Fort Victoria town.

The inevitable consequence was a raucous piss up. They concluded they were physically capable of handling anything that came their way, they could take the good and bad times and any possible impediments to their desired goals.

With hindsight and 20/20 vision little did they know they had not the faintest idea what was about to happen, not in their wildest imagination could they perceive the characters they were soon to meet; what transgressions they would become involved in, nor how their moral compasses would find no magnetic centre in their chosen life. They would be confronted with an 'eat or be eaten' environment of unthinkable proportions.

With the arrogance, invincibility and blasé naivety that only youth can muster, they ploughed on. There were few rules to their enterprise.

They shook hands in agreement – irrespective of what should befall their adventurers, they 'would stick together'; there would only be three of them, fearing if a fourth were involved, the group might split into pairs. Surely two would not forsake one. It seemed a foolproof number for the adventure.

The objective was simple, 'all three' had to hitchhike their way from country to country, doing whatever it took, until such time as they had circumnavigated the globe. There was no time limit placed on the scheme. Thereafter they would be free to take up residence in the "best country in the world", in their personal opinion.

They believed they were beholden to no one. All necessary travel documents were obtained and the first leg planned to be a Castle Liner boat trip to 'the Old Dart'. From there into Europe and then beyond, the sky was the limit, with strong but flawed beliefs in their own invincibility.

Their debate and plans were no secret. A few others had heard of it and wanted in. Their advances were blocked in accordance with 'the rules.'

November 1967 in a pre-planned manoeuvre the three submitted their Form '46' (Application for Discharge) at 0800

Hours on the same Monday morning, at three different police stations in Victoria Province.

PO's Graham Hardy, Tony St Clair and Doug Stanyon resigned.

Unbeknown to them their plan and off shoots thereof had found traction with other men of similar rank. If my memory serves me correctly 13 Patrol Officers submitted their Form 46 in that same week, there was a total of about 30 P/O's in the Fort Victorian District Branch.

Immediately all applications for discharge were refused. DISPOL and DISPOL's number two, Supt Bremner was sent to interview those who had so applied. From my interview with Bremner I understood the Officers had a suspicion this was an orchestrated attempt of 'boycott' or 'rebellion' against authority.

The three of us had inadvertently caused this 'predicament'. There was much to-ing and fro-ing and in the end all discharges were accepted, on conditions!!! The three months' notice period was staggered. My only concern was with my two partners. Hardy was allowed to leave on his three months – 20th February 1968. – St Clair and I had to wait until 14th April, for release.

On the 14th April, Insp Hedges kindly had a Constable drive me from Nuanetsi to Fort Victoria, for which I was always thankful. I will always remember the cheetah mother and her three cubs that we passed positioned on an anthill surveying their territory for the daily meal. I met up with St Clair who had a car and as 'freemen' we drove into Mashonaland to start our adventure.

On my return, which has been documented in these chronicles, an Inspector I had known in days gone by had been commissioned and he told the tale of PROPOL Victoria visiting the Officers Mess in Salisbury, soon after the 'staffing' problem had been resolved. It was claimed it had been a pre-planned 'protest' and the three of us had been the organisers. That was just not the case. How true this bit is I have no idea, but when he announced the three of us were now long gone and 'good riddance' patrons drinking in the Police Club across the Hard Square could hear the loud clapping and cheering.

Was it that long ago all this happened? Indeed not. If measured in time and days, months or years – that is calculable. If however it was measured in human forbearance, physiological trial and anguish, of the constant mental torment, of the moral and principal dilemmas derived from ones upbringing against the present day need to survive in a world very foreign to you - in a world where the definition of honesty – clashed with your upbringing. Where 'the con' was the norm – where everyone from your Manager down was part of illicit behaviour. Where the blind eye, was turned at the right moment, where the weak failed and fell by the way side and the strong survived, just one more day. When the battle of wits and survival came with each new morning light. Where violence was the supreme tool to achieve or to resolve. There was no 'rank within society' that afforded protection.

The lifestyle cared not for the colour of your skin, the religion you practised or your former breeding wherever it was you came from. It was a tough world and one had to be wide-awake at all times. I have to say, in that regard, it was an awfully long time ago.

Some people would never live through similar experiences in two lifetimes that will own, the only one they had.

We left a former BSAP colleague, 'over there' wherever that might be. He fell victim to socialising with the wrong people, became a user of party drugs, and worse. The last time I saw him he was homeless, addicted and angry and refused any assistance – I fear he will no longer be with us. He made some bad choices in a world unforgiving of those who are tempted by 'the easy life'.

In the following contributions, I shall document some of the 'lifestyle' we experienced, by no means all bad: there was some most memorable times of lost love, wasted fortunes and missed opportunities. How we soon realised how poorly qualified, incompetent, incapable and naive we were to exist in our new world that was in fact the old world. A life style Rhodesia had sheltered us from, since birth! The uncertainty of shelter each night, no insurance of three meals a day or hot water and washing facilities, nor the comforting knowledge that was the 28th of every month – come hail or high water, the provision of a salary, in fact no longer any tenure of existence at all. Where your last meal or pay cheque may well be just that for days or weeks to come.

Where friendship and contacts were paramount to survival.

\* \* \* \* \*

# BOOK TWO

This book chronicles some anecdotes of life in a sub culture, in which I travelled with limited funds, surviving by my wits and hard labour with an overall aim to see as much of the world as possible.

In my three-year hiatus I visited six of the seven continents on earth, some more than once. I worked on most of them. I visited remote islands in the Pacific Ocean, many dens of iniquity, great cathedrals and mosques, historic buildings and sites, viewed original paintings by great masters, witnessed pageantry and met hundreds of interesting characters, worked for a pittance and made bag loads of cash, fell in love a hundred times. I met a few less than desirable people, witnessed lost wretched souls abusing drugs, spent a few nights in police cells, participated in fighting the protesters outside Rhodesia House on the Strand in London, worked in the jungles of New Guinea and the desert in Australia. I hiked over the Andes Mountains between Chile and Argentina, visited the Aztec pyramids in Mexico and Lima, Peru, suffered a part winter in Canada and drove by car from Kenya to the Chirundu Bridge between Rhodesia and Zambia.

In April 1971, as I crossed back into Rhodesia, my total worldly assets and wealth comprised of; a dirty torn rucksack, with the names of the 37 countries inscribed on the shoulder straps, two shirts, three pairs of underpants, one pair of jeans, the shoes (no socks) I stood up in, a copy of Robert Service's Poems and a copy of the Rubaiyat. My mother kindly gave me $200 US at the bridge in Zambia. I had lost 35 pounds in weight since my departure.

Then as now:
*I don't regret the things I have done,*
*I regret the things I did not do,*
*When I had the chance.*

## A BAPTISIM OF FIRE
*Questioning Values, Friendly Ladies and White Lightning*

The reader is requested to reflect on their own journey into adolescence and beyond. There is no instruction book, no guidelines, advice from parents usually ignored as too conservative, plenty of advice from peers, although usually the loudest knew and had experienced the least. The quiet achievers chose not to divulge their experiences.

So three young men from the ultraconservative Victorian upbringing in Rhodesia dived headlong into Europe in the swinging sixties of sex, drugs and rock and roll. Think back when Playboy was banned in Rhodesia, irrespective of content and the Bob Dylan song *Lay Lady Lay* banished from the airwaves.

**Sex** – Generalisation is never a fair barometer to make any judgement with, however my experience (which was extremely limited) was Rhodesian girls who were well brought up, dignified, conservative and educated, always well dressed, on dates anyway, and had, I might add, a touch of class and panache. It sometimes took forever to get to 'first base', the rituals of parent meetings, and big brother dropping by, a type of covert threat against any intended or even planed unscrupulous behaviour. Those were the girls I knew before. I am sure they were other characters.

Many of the girls in the subculture bore little to no resemblance to my experiences. They were independent, confident in their abilities and determinations and went for what they wanted.

**Drugs** – irrespective of our law enforcement background none of us had any inclination in this regard. We drank enough to get silly and irresponsible, there was no need to bend the mind any more. In comparison to today, drugs on the streets that were readily available and used was limited to cannabis/marijuana/hash/grass and LSD – I never actually came across any other drugs.

**Rock and Roll:** This depended on ones interpretation of the age-old cliché. Many thought it 'dancing', some believed it encompassed 'all forms of a social lifestyle while others chose to define it as each situation presenting its self, including 'illegal activity'. Also of course it was broadly defined as being 'all three'.

For the entrée/appetiser on our trip, to find a better country and lifestyle, we spent 14 days on the Edinburgh Castle, traveling from Cape Town to Southampton. It had a reputation of being a 'Love Boat', an anything and everything goes cruise, the big 'party time'. We soon became associated with a group of South African youngsters, and spent the majority of each day on the rear deck drinking and telling lies. The ladies in the crowd varied in age from 20 to 35.

The three Rhodesians held their own in the drinking stakes, but fared less well in consorting with the opposite sex. Now I dare not speak for the other two but in my case, having be brought up in an all-male household since I was six, attended an all-male boarding schools, then two years later resident of the "backwoods" of Victoria Province, I was inexperienced, shy and if the truth be known had no bloody idea how to get off the starting blocks when it came to the fairer sex. I had lost my virginity, after being set up by a European Constable at Donnington, at the age of 16 with a 37-year-old divorcee. It remains one of the funniest stories I tell. Not that I found it funny at the time.

Now where was I? Drinking was my forte, it shielded my lack of confidence to approach the fairer sex. Two things remain memorable. I had my eyes set on a very pretty, young nurse from

Groote Schuur Hospital. She was quiet and not as vivacious as the others. Consultation with my two accomplices, who were enjoying far better results than myself, provided this advice, "*ask her to walk with you to the stern of the ship one night and show her the florescent lights in the wake.*"

This was seven days into the voyage, so after I had plied myself with enough 'grog' to build up the necessary courage, I approached her. To my absolute delight she agreed.

We left the madding crowd and under a bright, starlit night we walked close together every now and then our shoulders brushing together (no hand holding, that will come, I thought). On arrival at the stern, I mentioned the wake and the bouncing and dancing lights. It was a truly touching and romantic moment. Her eyes seemed to sparkle. She moved forward, towards me, closer and then held both my hands in hers.

Jackpot!! I was on a roll.

She looked into my eyes and with a beautiful smile said, "*Doug I think you are a lovely person. I want to tell you something.*"

Was I on the move or what?

"*You are very special.*"

Now we are on our way!!!

"*I have had an affair with a doctor at the hospital and he has paid for me to go away for a few months so he can try and get back with his wife.*"

My mind racing, "*Well that's OK.*"

She continued, "*I have been hurt so much* (I can fix that!) *I am so much in love with him – I am sorry it is going to take me a long time to get over him. Can we just be friends?*"

My first thought, 'There goes first base, that's a disguised full frontal rejection.' I answered, "*Sure it must be painful – I hope everything goes well for you.*" I lost that one and never even got off the starting blocks.

My only other dalliance with the fairer sex during the trip was as I was standing at the railing watching Southampton appear through the smog. I was actually on crutches, on loan from the ship. I had to hand them in on disembarkation. It had been a silly game played at height and I fell off a roof. I had been warned that any further similar activity would result in my incarceration in the brig. My ankle had been sprained.

I was pondering my future and where it would take me when I became aware of someone very close to me. I felt an arm go around my waist. I found it was one of the 30-year-old girls, with a most attractive face and body. She had been in the crowd since day one.

*"Doug do you mind if I tell you something?"*

*"Sure go for it."*

*"I would have gone to bed with you any time you wanted. In fact on a few occasions I actually propositioned you, it fell on drunken, deaf ears. You are very young and inexperienced, don't be so shy in future."*

Now that was surely a proposition and indication of future intent?

*"Well, when we get off we can meet up,"* said I.

*"No, I am going to Scotland and you and the boys to Earls Court."*

Then with a big squeeze of my waist and a tiptoes lingering kiss on my lips, she said, *"Good luck Doug,"* and walked away.

I never saw her again.

This 'make love not war' thing was going to need some intense training and very quickly.

The 'main meal' of the adventure started in the renowned 'backpackers, hitchhikers, bums' suburb of Earls Court, London, known colloquially as 'Kangaroo Valley'. It had three bars other than the Grotto, located in the Overseas Visitors Club (OVC), a number of restaurants and take away food joints, an employment agency catering for 'us types' and any number of residential flats, that varied in price, quality and position. We learned on the first day it was cheaper to live one or more tube stops away from Earls Court. Consequently we leased a flat in West Kensington. One tube stop, a 3-penny ride from 'where it all happened'.

The flat was one of those 'underground units' (basements) accessed off the street by walking down an eight to ten foot staircase. We had arrived in London using British passports. Apart from long unknown relatives somewhere, we knew nobody in Europe. Our first residential lesson was the 'stairwell' providing access to our flat was also used by passers-by as a disposal area of half eaten fruit, banana skins, cigarette butts, fast food wrappers, a urinal and even rejected 'fast food'. Occasionally we would step over a sleeping homeless man taking refuge from the wind outside our front door.

Given our background and unquestionable talent in frequenting 'ale houses' we boarded the tube and found a suitable ale house and drank our first British pint – it was not warm, it was hot!!! Lesson one of most probably thousands if not tens of thousands of lessons we were to be educated in. We had not been there long when I was offered LSD! I had never heard of it – this Pommy bloke opened the palm of his hand, revealing a square piece of blotting paper with an absorbed drop of light blue ink in the middle. It was cheap – something like eight bob. (80 cents) I declined. It turned out to be more common than a misty day in England. In the first week, we gathered knowledge of the "sub culture" that was to be our way of life within that community.

I was a Vodka drinker, as was Hardy. Saints did not mind a bit either.

We were introduced to the ' brew of choice' for those who were constantly broke, needed a fast reliable method of reaching 'take off' in the shortest possible time which would then consign one to a state of 'comatose' for the following 24 hours. They called it 'White Lightning', imported Russian Vodka - 85% proof. When you drank it, it felt like a piece of sandpaper being rubbed against your inner throat.

One day, within the first week, at around about 3.00 pm, we decided to grace the 'Grotto Bar' with our presence. Having been educated not to consume British beers, we now joined a large section of the Valley's population in drinking Fosters. It was an Australian beer, served in blue aluminium cans, not much to my liking but at least it was served cold and had some similarity to Lion Lager.

The Grotto Bar was in the basement of the Overseas Visitors Club, furnished with parallel bench seating that seated four or five to each side bench, others joined us. The party was soon in full swing, or would that be a number of parties. The atmosphere in any drinking establishment in England is a combination of electric and sheer unadulterated pleasure. Someone suggested rather than having to return the empty cans we would place them neatly in the middle of our bench top. Slowly bench space became a premium as the wall of cans widened, then a second and third tier were erected. The beer cans became a visual hindrance when trying to converse with the person on the opposite side of the bench. Realising this it was decided to continue erecting the wall, constructing apertures within the wall providing at least some sight of the person opposite.

I became increasingly niggled by this now large, blue wall of cans in front of me. I was also fairly inebriated. I took the law into my own hands and picking up what I thought was an empty can I threw it with some force at the wall directly opposite me. Most unfortunately, although given the ending, thankfully, the can was either half or still full. The projectile shattered the wall and sped past my fellow conversationalist and hit the back of the head of a person on the next bench. It was a bench full of Aussies, male and female.

It was as though someone had lit an instantaneous fuse – the place erupted. There was general confusion as to where the projectile had been launched from.

Not only had the projectile I had launched hit a male on the head.

A good number of the cans in the three feet high wall had sprayed across the bar like a blue aluminium hand grenade causing people to duck and knock over beers and fall off perches.

A full on punch-up ensued, not initially, involving us. It must have been our angelic looks that caused the brawlers to fail to identify us as instigators. Not for long – somehow one of the three *'must-get-beers'* was punched as the melee widened, which of course invoked a retaliation and presto, before you could say Jack Robinson the three of us were in the middle of the action.

As always things settled down, guilty parties and known troublemakers were evicted from the premises (we were not in either of those categories). We resumed our seats and I ended up sitting, as it transpired, next to this Aussie girl who had been with the chap initially hit on the back of the head. They had had an argument and he left. We chatted and got along famously. She obviously had a keen eye for detail, as she observed I was 'horribly drunk'.

She asked, *"Where are we sleeping tonight, my place or yours?"*
*"You said what?"*
*"If you are going to argue about it I shall leave you to it."*
*"No! No! No! I'm with you. Either place is good."*

So it was. The relationship was enjoyed for a few months. She returned home to Australia, as most did. A year later I got to Australia and met her again, therein lies another yarn.

＊　　　＊　　　＊　　　＊　　　＊

## A Time to Rise

*It's six, my son, and time to rise;*
*The sun has shot through the darkness*
*And the long day spreads before you like a kaross;*
*Start now, dear son; the journey is long.*
*There will be thunder and hailstorms*
*Although the weather appears calm for the moment;*
*Beware of shelters offered you;*
*Rather brave it and be a Man.*
*Should you fall, rise with grace, and without*
*Turning to see who sees, continue on your road*
*Precisely as if nothing had ever happened;*
*For those who did not, the ditches became graves.*
*If ever you fall in love with some woman,*
*Ask if she can walk at your pace to the end*
*Of the Road....*

    *From*
    *"On my Son's sixth Birthday" by Eddison Zvobgo*

# AS MECCA IS TO MUSLIMS,
# SO MUNICH IS TO BEER DRINKERS
### *From Sir Walter to Arrest*

W hile continuing our education in this 'new world', that was really the 'old world', the *'Three Must-get-beers'* settled into their new life, with great gusto I might add.

We heard whispers on the streets that said that however much of a 'big' beer drinker you claimed to be you can never claim to be a true beer drinker until you had partaken of the nectar at the Oktoberfest in Munich, Bavaria, Germany.

I recall in the BSAP there were a few men or should that be a few too many men who professed to be 'big' drinkers. At Chiredzi in 1966 three PO's were engaged in a discussion and with the bravado of youth all three professed to be able to drink the other under the table. This was settled by a contest to see who could drink the most beer in one sitting. The resulting competition started at 12:00 noon one Saturday afternoon in the Mess and came to a very undignified closure in the public bar of the Chiredzi Hotel in the early hours of Sunday morning.

The competition supervised by the manageress of the Chiredzi Hotel who, at the time, was a Petite Amie or Amoureux, of one of the competitors and in hindsight I cannot be certain who had the better deal the 39-year-old mentor or the 20-year-old student.

The first chap dropped out - literally from a bar stool - at a count of 52 beers. The second passed out at a count of 55 and I cannot recall if the winner just stopped and claimed victory or drank one more.

Many years later the Australian wicket keeper Rodney Marsh claimed a beer drinking record by consuming 50 beers on the flight from London to Sydney. The flight takes 22 hours. But high altitude drinking is in the Super League, as the author was to establish in his commercial career after the Police.

Sorry where was I, oh yes the Mecca for beer drinkers. One thing led to another and Graham Hardy (Hardy's Inn, Gwanda) and I decided that Germany was the next port of call. Once we had the cash together, the logistics mapped out and down to a 'tee', all we had to do was get there. We understood we would be attending the 'biggest piss up' in the world and in so doing, rightfully claim to be 'qualified beer drinkers' having paid homage in the beer drinkers' Mecca.

My current research for this project shows the 'festival', as the Germans call it, has grown exponentially since our visit. It started as a festival to honour some German aristocracies wedding in October 1810. It lasts between 16 and 18 days starting late September and closing in the first week of October. In our day there were 12 beer tents (there are now 25 plus), six tents on each side of a road.

Each tent was run by an individual beer brewer and only sold their wares. A tent had a capacity of about 2,000 plus people (now 4, 000). In the centre of each establishment was a brass band playing Bavarian music, (an oompah band). The seating was made up of long bench seats, 6 to 8 per side (remember this for what's coming) In our time, one could only order a Stein of beer, presented in a grey pottery stein mug or glass jug, of one litre capacity; the alcohol content was 6%. Each full stein weighed about 3 kgs.

We understood from our discussions in London, one had to get to the tented area early and the challenge was to consume one 'beer' in each tent. At day's end, well night's end, the winner was the person who exited the twelfth tent, on foot (rather than on a hospital stretcher!!).

We teamed up with some other hikers who had purchased a cargo/passenger vehicle, similar in shape and size to a VW Combi, from a shonky second hand car dealer for 100 pounds. It was equipped with two benches in the back and two well-worn seats in the front. We aimed to take up residence in a camping area, in close proximity to the Oktoberfest grounds.

In mid-September 1968 with backpacks filled, sleeping bags checked and some very questionable quality two-man tents, we clambered aboard and headed for Dover.

With nothing-untoward happening we travelled through France and arrived safely at our intended destination. We pitched camp and I experienced my first shower with a member of the opposite sex. It was purely to conserve money as the hot water was metered. Yeah - that's right!!

Our first visit to the road of beer tents was considered a 'recce', as we all agreed we needed to get the lay of the land before we started in pursuit of the 'one beer per tent' mission before closing time.

On the second day we got there early and found a bench with Graham, my girlfriend and I all sitting on the same side. The 'recce' had proven useful, providing the wisdom to occupy a seat next to the exit door thus facilitating access to toilets and food.

Soon all the benches were full, the beers were flowing, the band was playing and 2,000 odd people, including us, were having the time of our lives. In fact we were having such a good time we forgot about having 'one beer per tent'. On realising our mistake we postponed the 'contest' to the following morning, and continued drinking in the first tent.

I was on the end of the bench that all the people wishing to exit, eat or relieve themselves, travelled. There were four young men on the opposite side of our bench. One came from Aussie and the others were European tourists.

Now I have to admit the Lowenbrau beer was tasty indeed and was going down singing hymns. The proximity of the exit/entry door also provided access to an unusual variety of delightfully tasting hot German sausages with mustard. Life just could not be better – so we drank a now common toast:

*"**To all those poor bastards still serving**."*

In my peripheral vision I saw a young lady walk pass the chap opposite me, who gave her a friendly pat on the 'backside'. She turned and gave him a nasty look.

I asked him if she was a friend.

"*No*," he said, "*but she had a nice derriere*." Well he actually said arse.

Now well-oiled with the nectar of the Gods and forgetting momentarily 'that when in Rome' and for reasons I shall never know, I thought the movement improper. So I voiced my concern to this chap and suggested he desist from any future similar action. He thought I was joking and laughed.

A few minutes later the same girl was on her return trip and as she arrived at a point close to my new drinking 'mate' he gave her another affectionate rub on her tail. Again she looked around in disgust and shouted at him.

I had no idea what she said. I did not even know what language she was speaking. She walked away annoyed.

Now that was when everything turned 'turtle'. I stood up and took a swing at this chap landing my blow right in the middle of his face. He did not expect it, nor did he see it coming. He landed flat on the floor on his back, at which point, believing I had played the part of Sir Walter Raleigh, I sat down well satisfied with having defended her honour.

Without a 'beg your pardon' or 'how do you do' I received a fist on the end of my jaw that sent me plummeting to the floor. I dragged myself up, now positioned at the end of the table and saw a most amazing sight. The punching across the table had progressed down our table and spilled over onto other tables. It was as though someone had set off a bomb. My girlfriend ran out of the tent. I must have been hit by a least two more people, which put me back on the floor.

The 'Greens' intervened – they were either local police or local security dressed in very smart green uniforms and armed with sizeable batons. My girlfriend headed for the internal balcony above the main 'beer hall' floor. She told me later that on her arrival she looked down and saw at least one hundred or more people fighting.

I decided the best course of action was to head for the exit and get as far away as I could. That was just not possible as I was being assaulted from every direction. I decided on Plan 'B' – I would fight my way out, only striking those who were barring my egress from the tent. I was doing OK, until a rather large 'Greeny' hove into sight. He was swinging his baton with wild delirium, the blows landing wherever. I thought if that baton hits me it's going to split my head clean open. Just as the thought crossed my mind, everything went into slow motion. I saw the 'Greens' arm drawn back sidewards and the baton coming towards me. It hit me square in the chest so hard, it broke two ribs and bent a steel cigarette case that was in my shirt pocket. I dropped like a sack of potatoes. He stepped over me, still carving his way through the crowd.

It was at that point I made my second mistake. I stood up, walked after the 'Greeny', who now had his back to me and with everything Insp Winchcombe had taught us in 'unarmed defence' in Depot I struck the man with the base of my right palm, at the base of his skull.

Just like Winchcombe had said he would, he 'dropped cold'. Turning back to Plan B I started trying to exit by fighting my way out.

My little trial of BSAP 'unarmed defence' had unfortunately not gone unnoticed, even in the confusion of the melee.

Two 'Greenys' grabbed me and dragged me out, and then to my surprise, placed me into an ambulance. They handcuffed me, and then handcuffed the handcuffs to the bodywork of the vehicle. I received a few reminders as to just who was running the show.

As I lay there the Aussie, who had been at our bench, jumped into the ambulance and started punching me in the face. Two 'Greenys' subdued him with a couple of well-aimed strikes to the head and body, rendering him unconscious on the ambulance floor. He was soon in handcuffs as well.

The ambulance drove off with two guards in the back with us. They were very angry and I think had I understood German, they would have been threatening us with the most dastardly fate conceivable.

One thing life has taught me, is you never know your future – from one minute to the next and what was to occur in the next hour, Hollywood would have been thankful to have thought up.

We were transported to a local hospital. On the trip I asked the now conscious Aussie why he had jumped into the vehicle and beaten me. He retorted, I had actually hit him several times during the melee and when he saw me in the ambulance thought he would balance the ledger.

We ended up in a corridor full of 'wounded'. It was not unlike some scene from a movie; they were on beds, on chairs, on the floor, lying sitting - it was like a bloody war zone.

The Aussie and I were still handcuffed.

He said to me in the unmistakable Aussie Strine, *"Hey Mate, I reckon we are in the shit! They gonna patch us up' mate, and lock us up. Then we's gonna get the flogging of our lives."*

It was an unpleasant thought indeed.

When our turn came we were marched into this 'operating room'. It was equipped with two 'slabs'. We were placed on a slab each. The doctor or I presumed he was one, spoke to the 'Greens' after which they removed the handcuffs and left the room. I was lying so the back of my head was facing the door. I noticed we were in a hexagonal shaped room. There were sash windows on three walls. I could see trees outside. I guessed we were on the ground floor.

There was a doctor and two nurses with us. One nurse came up to me and placed a mirror in front of my face. She said something in German.

My face was in a sorry state; I had three maybe four lips, both my eyebrows had deep wounds across them and one cheek had a nasty gash on it. My hands were painful. On examination I found both thumbs were dislocated. I had obviously attempted the Jerry Winchcombe manoeuvre a few times, missed the palm of my hand, connected with the thumb and bingo – 'hanging thumbs'. My chest was also very painful.

To cut the story short, both of us were stitched, bandaged and in my case thumbs relocated to where they should have been.

The two nurses left the room. The doctor then said, in immaculate English, I think you Aussies always bring a bit of flair and excitement to Munich. (In 1968 all young men carrying Australian passports had been banned from Munich. They had apparently hi-jacked the trams, trussed up the drivers and offered everyone a free ride.)

The doctor continued: "*If I release you back into the custody of those two men waiting outside you will be back here within a few hours with twice the injuries. I shall open a window, your best bet is to run for it, and get out of Munich – come back next year.*"

Now that presented a quandary, if I went with this madman he may start assaulting me again. On the other hand I was going to get beaten up anyway.

I said to the Aussie, "*Are you up for it?*"

He sat up, the doctor turned opened a window and we climbed out: the coast was clear and we ran for our lives. Within an hour we were at his campsite. I stayed in his tent that night and bid him farewell the next morning. He gave me his address in South Australia – saying I was welcome to stay if I ever got 'Down Under'.

"*Thanks,*" I said, "*What do you do for a crust?*"

"*Merchant Navy mate. I am the current Merchant Navy heavy weight boxing champion of Australia.*"

I did get Down Under – but had lost his name and address.

I have been to the beer drinkers Mecca, just once and can claim now to be questionably qualified, depending on how I tell the tale.

As a reformed and part time consumer of 'light' beer only, I think I might seek a new Mecca!!!

A quieter one, like the Muslims, I might find somewhere to walk in circles a few times and head home.


＊　　　＊　　　＊　　　＊　　　＊


*Hath man no second life?*
*Pitch this one high!*

**Mathew Arnold**

# CLANDESTINE EXTERNAL OPERATIONS
*Before War was declared*

S ometimes in life one has to do what one has to do. Opportunities to work for good money, whether classified as honest, opportunistic or just plain criminal, is a matter for sages, bed wetters, do-gooders and left wing minority groups to argue and debate. Sometimes, to put food on the table, one has to take whatever measures are available and if required to work for honest and normal pay, so be it.

'*Hickory, Dickory* and *Dock*' were broke, homeless, beer less and most critically were down to '*roll your owns*': smoking poor quality Turkish tobacco floor sweepings. Not exactly the way a refined gentleman should be seen in public. Other considerations occur when the '*moola*' becomes scarce. An already poor diet, now limited to one meal a day, causes hunger pains, which forces unfortunate and never lightly taken considerations of 'doing a runner'.

Another survival tactic learned in the 'new world', not as high risk as one imagines, it involved a number of players, in a convoluted and intricate set of devious manoeuvres, some 'ham' acting and an ability for all but one player to make an inconspicuous exit, and the final player to be in a state of utmost fitness with an ability to run the 100 yards in less than 12 seconds. The reward: a free meal of their choice, for all participants.

We, along with some South African friends, were thankful to find employment in the East End of London. We were issued with overalls. It was labouring work in the outdoors – in England that is not necessarily a pleasant place to be making a crust.

Our job was to pack second hand military canvas equipment. This meant we had to fold a variety of different sized tents, with the guide ropes and poles, in a specific manner. Thereafter we packed them in containers. In due course an Englishman arrived on a forklift, picked up our work and disappeared into a warehouse. We also packed small canvas items like hand basins, outdoor shower containers, small roofless cubicles and water containers, in fact any manner of 'canvass equipment for military use'.

The pay was regular, and average for labourers. All of us kept our ear to the ground, looking for better paid work. In the 'new world' the type of work was actually an irrelevance, it was how much it paid, and whether there was a tax deduction before receipt that counted. Where the work was, geographically, in relation to Earls Court was also an irrelevance. We were now all highly experienced 'tube travellers', which in essence meant irrespective of the cost of a tube fare we travelled 'free'.

Given our longevity in Earls Court we were well known and enjoyed a good reputation among the local populous, so, in dire times, the cost of a bed was also an irrelevance. At times one might be fortunate enough to be enjoying a dalliance, which provided a bed, shower and often a meal or two. Other times and more usually, it was never difficult to get 'carpet space' in one of the main 'digs'. Which also usually provided an opportunity to shower, but no food.

After a few days at work in the East End, whilst having our morning tea of 'buns and coke' (memories of workers back home!!!) someone in our group, who had been paying attention to what we had been doing, asked a reasonable question, *"Has anyone been involved in the labelling or shipping of our tents and equipment? Where would it be going?"*

It was second hand stuff. The general consensus was reached that we would all make an effort to establish 'to whom the equipment was being shipped'.

'Recces' were deployed and soon enough we established a truck transferred the 'kit' across the street to a covered warehouse.

It was obvious that it was there that our answer lay. One of the group volunteered to take a walk and see what he could find out.

He returned with the news that they were packed into very large steel shipping containers. He also reported the full containers, now locked, were placed out in a yard where there was no security, well no overt security and no cameras had been identified.

A new 'recces' team was sent and returned with the information that all the containers examined had been bound for Tanzania. Now that was interesting - it was common knowledge Rhodesian Africans were undergoing terrorist training in Russia and China and were funnelled through Libya and down into Tanzania.

A call to arms echoed through the dismal setting.

Someone halted the conversation, *"What if we are jumping the gun and it is for Tanzania's military establishment?"*

That was a reasonable thought. So a third 'recces' was deployed a few days later into the warehouse across the road with a briefing to locate and meet the 'locals' who worked there. The briefing was to suggest, on auspicious grounds, our wish to enjoy the pleasure of their company, imbibing in a few 'after work' tipples. The 'recces' returned with the necessary information.

So on payday we duly presented ourselves at their 'local'. After the normal men's chat about sex, drugs and rock and roll, and then more sex, most of it fantasised and highly exaggerated, a few casual almost boring questions were floated to keep the conversation alight. It was established the equipment was to house and equip 'freedom fighters' living in Tanzania before they departed for southern Africa.

The following day an 'O' group was held amongst the leaderless legion and plans made to assist 'the poor bastards still serving'. The first observation was we were aiding terrorists and a suggestion we immediately resign en masse. This was considered a short-term solution and ineffective as our labour would be easily replaced. The next suggestion, 'sabotage' was unanimously adopted. It was agreed wholesale destruction would be less effective than surreptitious destruction.

While each operative was left to their own devices the aim was to cause sufficient damage to make life irritable, and demoralise the 'freedom fighters' but allow the distribution of equipment to continue for as long as possible. Sharp instruments were acquired then the gang set to work by partially severing the guide ropes to a point where, when tightened, they would snap. The poles all had removable caps on one end, these were detached, and anything from three inches to nine inches were sawn off and caps replaced. Large sections of roof canvas had small, almost undetectable apertures inserted. Hopefully undetectable while the sun shone, but providing annoying leaks in the rains. Water containers, including many canvass water bottles, were punctured along seams.

We hoped this would require machine repairs to rectify, something that would take time. In all, we aimed to cause as much discomfort and frustration as possible, and hopefully reduce moral.

We remained there for weeks, increasing the tempo of our work production, drawing praise from our 'Masters' as good and solid workers.

Did we achieve anything worthwhile? Most probably not! Were our clandestine operations worthy of recognition for awards for bravery? So highly classified were these operations, they were categorised with a 50-year censure. So now when released, it turns out we lost the war. No one cares.

Did we ever hear the results of our treachery? No.

It is however reasonable to presume our op's pissed off a lot of terrorists, Tanzanian officials and English sympathisers and cohorts who hopefully lost their supply contract.

Was it worthwhile? I guess it made us feel we had made some contribution, on top of which we certainly got a few free beers from interested parties in Kangaroo Valley, which resulted in a few laughs at the bad guy's expense.

As usual we drank a toast to:-

**"The poor bastards still serving."**

*         *         *         *         *

*Times change and we change with them.*

*Harrison*

## LSD AND HARD FACTS ABOUT
## BEDDING THE OPPOSITE SEX

O ften the *'Three Must-get-beers'* discussed their current situation. Never once was there any mention of remorse for the decision to leave Gods Little Green Acre. Whether 'flush with cash' or 'down on their luck', their discussions were always fortified by the 'nectar of the Gods'. It must be said, during these debates, many pearls of wisdom sprouted forth, the more nectar the higher the quality of the pearl.

Illegal drugs, the availability of, the effects on those who partook and the long term effects of possible addiction was a common topic, most probably not as common as the 'bragging' of realistic or fantasised conquests of the fairer sex, nor of the prospects of making it 'rich' and the aftermath dreams.

One debate focused on how we, the 'three-wise-men', could make any honest appraisal of illegal drug use when we had never taken a drug of any sort in our life. Over most probably a dozen 'nectar's' it was agreed we should try it - just once - so we had the 'experience' and therefore the credibility to make comment.

Being cautious, we decided only one of the three would take the drug, and the other two would remain in personal contact until the effects wore off. A sound workable situation in that the 'consumer' would be able to factually report the effects on the mind and body.

The two assistants and protectors would also have firsthand experience, from an outsider's point of view, as to what had occurred.

All three made a solemn promise that when the drug was taken they would be sober (yeah!, that would be interesting) and no alcohol would be consumed until the 'taker' had fully recovered.

All that was left was to choose the 'consumer'. *"Do we have a volunteer?"*

There was a deafening silence, no takers.

*"Let's make it fair, we shall put the names in a hat and have one of the other flat dwellers draw it out,"* I said.

The type of drug to use was now discussed. Dagga or 'Merry Jew Anna' was considered 'not a real drug' for the purposes of this experiment. That left one option. All agreed LSD was the appropriate choice. It was agreed it was the most popular. The whisper on the streets had it that it took the mind on a magical mystery tour with bright and vivid colours allowing the mind to remain in a perpetual state of bliss. That would do us!

For reasons unknown I was allotted the task of the acquisition of the drug. It was most probably because I was the more innocent and angelic looking of the three and posed less risk of arrest by 'Constable Plod'.

So it was one wintery morning, in the basement flat, the 'three stooges' sat in a circle and penned their names on identical pieces of paper, and scrunched them up. A kitchen bowl was placed on the coffee table and the three pieces of paper dropped in. They looked forlorn on the bottom of the glass receptacle.

The first 'flat dweller' to come in sight was a very pleasant young lady, a Cape Town University Student, studying psychiatry. All three would have wished they had an intimate relationship, but she was far too wise to be more than casually associated with any of them. Unfortunately I do not recall her Christian name, however I know she had the old Scottish surname of van der Westerhuizen.

On being asked to draw out one of the pieces of paper, she enquired what we were doing. She listened intently as the whole plan was exposed. There were four of us seated around the table as she had kindly served everyone a cup of coffee.

She agreed to do her bit on condition she be permitted to advise us on research conducted into 'acid' (LSD). We agreed. It took her some time, with many questions in regards to some of the 'wording' she was using.

In the end her summary sounded something like this.

The risks you are running by taking LSD are these:

In some people there is an immediate and uncontrollable addiction.

You will have a 50/50 chance of experiencing a good or bad trip.

In some people the trip, good or bad can last many hours – bad trips are described as varying between scary and petrifying.

Lastly, and you should heed this warning well, some users may experience 'flash backs' many years after the initial experience, even if they only used once, with no warning and this may place you in a position of potential harm by lacking the ability to be in control.

I looked into the bowl like some clairvoyant. This was no good. How was I going to extract myself from this situation and keep my pride and reputation in tact with the other two, I wanted out! Sometimes fortune favours the weak.

St Clair stood up and said, "*F\*\*k this, I'll have a beer instead.*"

Followed by Hardy who was already walking to the 'liquor shelf' where he seized a bottle of 85% proof 'White Lightning' and returned to the table with an empty glass.

Being the opportunist and carpetbagger, I slowly rose from my seat, shook my head slowly side to side, and said, "*Well that's me done, I was happy to have a go, but not on my own.*" I wandered into the kitchen.

Christ if I had been called out I could have died I thought. I returned fondling an empty glass, poured a stiff measure of 'White Lightning' and we drank a toast, "*To those poor bastards still serving.*"

It was whilst we were drinking Miss van der Westerhuizen came out with an absolute pearler. She said she had often heard our discussions about 'bedding the opposite sex' and had listened, with silent amusement and mirth, to our bragging of how charming and charismatic we had been in our achievements. She also noted with scepticism and cynicism the many manoeuvres, ploys, gambits and ruses we had cleverly engineered to get damsels into the 'cot'. How often we applauded and commended each other on our efforts.

There was an awkward silence in the lounge, 'Faith, Hope and Charity' were looking very sheepish, shuffling, tinkering with their drinks and blowing cigarette smoke up to the ceiling, embarrassment was universal. Now the young lady picked on me!

"*Doug, how many of your so called 'conquests' have you taken to bed and raped?*"

"*Heavens forbid! What kind of question is that? That's a terrible and shameful slur on my reputation!*"

"*All we need is a number Doug.*"

"*Well obviously none.*"

"*That's exactly what I thought*"

"*Saints?*"

"*Never! not me!*"

"*Graham?*"

"*Never, that's stupid talk.*"

"*Well now all three of you Don Juans, do we agree that these conquests were willing partners?*"

"*Yes of course.*"

"*They entered into the relationship freely and voluntarily.*"

"*Yes.*"

"*I suggest then gentleman, initially the girl may have been drawn to your personalities but the ultimate decision to 'go to bed' with you was actually hers, not yours. She had in fact charmed you, she was the one who lead you to the boudoir, and* **she** *was the one who allowed the 'blossoming of the flower'.*

*Interestingly you will find, if you watch the process closer next time, she allowed you to think you were in control, but actually at no step of the process were you.*"

"*Pass the Vodka, please Graham. My throats dry. My ego lies in tatters on the floor, any chances of recovery are remote. I wonder if I shall ever pass this way again.*"

∗          ∗          ∗          ∗          ∗

*For my part, I travel not to go anywhere, but to go.*
*I travel for travel's sake.*
*The great affair is to move.*

*Robert Louis Stevenson*

# AMUSEMENT ARCADES
# & FRUIT MACHINES
### *Just Help Yourself*

B eing unemployed my friends in the employment agency sent me to an interview, this time with a 'gaming' company.

*"What does a gaming company do?"*

*"They own Amusement Arcades. It's good money,"* I was told.

The interview was not too arduous.

*"Have you worked with these machines before?"*

*"No Sir, No."*

*"Have you been in trouble with Old Bill?"*

*"Never."*

*"Any previous?"*

*"No Sir."*

*"Have you handled large sums of money before?"*

*"No Sir."*

*"We will give you a jacket and long trousers, you have to wear a collared shirt and tie, black shoes. Your Governor is at our Strand shop. Your pay is five quid a shift. You start on …."* (whatever the date).

I reported to the Strand on the given time and day. The décor was exemplary. It was spotlessly clean with soft piped orchestral music. It had large chandeliers hanging from the ceiling. No internal walls. It was an oblong structure, with large doors opening onto the Strand. The name of the premises was flickering in lights.

Plush, deep red carpet, it had all the hallmarks of a luxurious, wealthy man's playground. I was to learn that is exactly what it was, but identifying the owner was a task even the local police force would fail to do.

'Fruit Machines', as they were called in the UK (known elsewhere in the world as Slot Machines or One Armed Bandits) were positioned side-by-side, inches apart along the entire length of both external sidewalls. On the back wall a closed door, next to it more 'Fruit Machines'. The centre of the room was filled with much larger machines allowing multiple players to engage at once, including miniature racing car circuits and football games.

Although it was early evening the premises was jam packed with people, known in the game as 'punters'.

I introduced myself to an employee who directed me to the door on the rear wall. I noticed a small glass peephole at eye level in the door. On knocking I heard some movement within, then the door opened, slightly. What stopped the door opening any further was a substantial chain, not unlike hotel room doors are fitted with – but far more robust.

The chap inside questioned, *"Doug?"*

*"Yes, that's me."*

The door closed and then re-opened. The room was furnished with a desk supporting a phone, devoid of any paper work or writing equipment, three dining room chairs, a moveable full-length cupboard and a large, very large safe. On the floor were some oblong containers made of metal of sorts. Each fitted with a good quality hasp and staple and padlock.

He reached into the cupboard and produced a pair of long black trousers and a bright red jacket.

He said, *"The 'Gov.' said you were a tall lad, these should fit."* Continuing, he remarked, *"The 'Gov.' said you were green."*

I was not sure what he meant but agreed. I needed the money.

*"Follow me."*

He opened the door and walked out, locking it behind us. He took me to a vacant 'one armed bandit' and showed me the ropes. This was training al-express, no frills, all the possible machine malfunctions and on the spot remedies.

He pointed to a locked steel container, *"that's the most important part of the machine, it's the 'drop box'."* With the door still open he inserted a coin in the external slot, then pointing with his index finger, followed its path through the machine, it flicked a wire, which rang a bell.

It slowly moved further down a chute, eventually entering an aperture on the top of a 'drop box', so positioned and sized to accept only that denomination of currency. Closer examination showed the distance from the base of the chute and the top of the 'drop box' would have been three quarters of an inch. He extracted the drop box and gave it to me.

*"That's just over half full."*

Taking a key from his pocket, he opened the lock. So it was.

*"You will get used to two ways of knowing when it is full, by the number of punters playing the machine or the time between exchanges."*

He revealed a hidden cupboard, containing a 'Hoover', broom and dustpan. There were also a number of leather and material cloths and a large spray bottle. He explained the cleaning regime, how often to carry out regular cleaning and *"cleaning the bloody mess the punters make."*

One last and very important thing, he pointed towards a sidewall, *"On each shift, you work that wall and your mate works the other. The senior man gets the back wall. You do not touch each other's machines."*

A few days passed and I came to the conclusion the chap I worked with was either fairly incompetent at his job or maybe the senior guy got the older machines because they seemed to break down much more often than mine. He certainly did his fair share of cleaning, regular or when the 'bloody punters' left a mess. I was thankful he did regular maintenance on the central machines. They were large and complex.

We got paid late at night on my first payday - I was thankful for the cash. If that was good pay I needed to change jobs. My newfound work colleague suggested we stop off for a beer. I declined, informing him I was short of a bob.

As we strolled down the Strand, headed for the Tube station, he casually enquired, *"Did you not 'top up' enough?"*

*"I am sorry I do not understand."*

*"You know 'graft', did you not get a 'sling'?"*

*"I have no idea what the hell you are talking about."*

*"Hop into this 'boozer' mate."*

He ordered two pints, and placing his hand in his jacket pocket took out a tiny oblong piece of rigid cardboard placing it on the bar counter.

*"You need some of these."*

There was nothing special about it, it looked as though he had made it himself, and it had little finesse.

*"What's that?"*

*"That's a dosh stick, mate."*

I was becoming adept at smelling out a good investment when it passed. I just needed to play this one quietly.

*"May I buy you a beer my friend?"*

He then 'spilt the beans' in similar words as follows:

*"You see mate they give you poor wages because they know you are going to nick the 'dosh'. They tried cameras, but they didn't work. The system is like this, you 'help yourself' to some 'dosh' each shift. When you take the drop boxes to the Governor, he opens them and counts what's inside.*

*His Governor knows he is going to take some as well, so they don't pay him too well. He takes all the coin to the bank, exchanges it for notes and hands those to his Governor. The Gov. helps himself to some 'dosh' then it goes you know where!"*

*"No I have no idea." "No one knows the big fellow, the Big Kahuna. They get it from all over the country. How many machines have they got? Few people know and nobody asks. You just do your bit, don't ask any questions."*

*"Well how much can I 'help' myself to?"*

*"As much as you like, you take too much you don't have a job. You take too little and our Gov. gets a bigger slice of the cake!"*

*"That does not answer my question, I don't want to get fired. As I see it, it's like a 'commission'. Well how much is too much?"*

*"Look, use your smarts, take a bit more each shift. Count it at home. When you 'go over' slightly, the Gov. will say, 'not many punters in last night' that's the time you take the foot off the pedal a bit."*

*"OK so how do I do it?"*

*"You make 30 of these dosh sticks – must be stiff cardboard mind, do not write anything on it. Soon after you start your shift open each of your machines and place the dosh stick over the hole in the drop box. When the punter puts a*

*coin in the machine it rolls down the chute, triggers a game and then rolls down to the drop box. The coin hits the dosh stick and rolls onto the top of the box."*

*"So how do you know when to go back to the machine?"*

*"The punter tells you, boyo! The punter tells you, it's that good. He squeals he dropped a coin and never got a game. You open the machine, he can't see. The coins are stacked up on the top of the box, up the shoot and now jamming the trigger wire so it can't give him a game. You scrape all the coins into your hand, put them in your pocket, clear the jammed chute, and hand him his coin back.*

*You want a tip, give him a couple of coins, he will be stoked and put the whole lot back in plus some. Just a regular money making machine. Oh, just before you close the machine, don't forget to replace your dosh stick."*

I made a very tidy living out of 'Fruit Machines' for a while. The organisation offered to promote me to shop manager, advising there was plenty of scope within 'the organisation' for good quality men like myself.

I was not really interested in a career in crime, I was just a bum, 'living the good life' and learning the ropes of the 'new world', which was really the old. These things had been going on before Methuselah and well beyond his time.

Politicians vote themselves salary increases, pension schemes and benefits during and after office and white-collar executives have it down to a fine art. They have different names for it, share bonuses, effort reward, annual premium, even 'guerdon'. Salesmen call it 'commissions' and Profit Centre Managers call it simply the 'annual bonus'. Trade Union members call it 'perks of the job'.

The education of a Rhodesian cattle rancher's son continued in his first semester at the 'University of Hard Knocks'. It would not be his last either. Unbeknown to him his first 'Degree' would take three years before he got home.

The truth was he would never leave that 'University', there was too much to learn.

*   *   *   *   *

*If you're already walking on*
*Then ice, why not dance?*

*Gil Atkinson*

## SEX DRUGS AND ROCK AND ROLL
## INDEED

I t was the European summer of 1969. We were still in London, England, attending our daily meeting in the board room, when someone, mentioned an opportunity to make some money and have a barrel of fun while doing so. Where the other two "must get beers were" is shrouded in the mists of time, I feel they may have returned to the mother-land.

I thought the venture was worth investing my time in and signed up, with some South Africans, two chaps from Swaziland and an assortment of others. We ended up in the village of Maidstone in Kent – on a hop farm. The job I was allotted was simple enough, stand on the back of a trailer, being pulled by a tractor and cut down the "hop vines", place them on the floor of the trailer and when full transfer them to a building, on the farm. I am not sure what happened thereafter, the "old-timers" has kicked in, but I do remember (thanks to Photographs, I recorded) they ended up "baled, not unlike the tobacco, back home" Bales were stamped with the Farm name and address (thanks again to the photos)

Our accommodation was a most liveable house on the farm. The owner, who lived in a very large mansion on the estate. He was an elderly pucker English Gentleman, with the RAF moustache, a real McCoy Eton/Cambridge accent and tweed jacket, plus of course the large Jaguar. What was of interest to the "labourers" was our observation of the farmer's wife, about 25 years his junior, dripping with fine gold jewellery, driving past, and frequently stopping and talking to the labourers. She showed more than an agricultural interest in one or two of the young men. To my dismay, I was not included.

Resident in the "farm house" we found were a fair number of young female globe trotters, who worked on the farm and elsewhere – they were billeted in two bedrooms separated from the male quarters. That situation lasted one night, and within a week, it was hard to distinguish which bedrooms had been allotted to which sex. As in most of England, there was a fine English pub not far from the farm, and most nights we all gathered there for nightly prayers and other activities. In this pub was one of the old style jute boxes, with a domed plastic covering through which if you were drunk enough you could watch your chosen record turning.

We had been living the good life for about three or four weeks and true to the intelligence provided to the boardroom back in London, "fun" was certainly a large part of the agenda.

In fact I got to know three or four of the young ladies well and enjoyed their company immensely.

One memorable Friday night, we had been advised the "hop picking season" was drawing to a close. Many were making plans to move on – we were all sitting in the "old pub" discussing meaningless subjects like Homers Odysseys. A friend of mine a South African Accountant and I got into a serious conversation about politics in Southern Africa. It started getting a little personal, with the South African representative saying Rhodesia or Rhodesians could not handle the terrorist incursions, and what's more he knew why I was in Europe.

*"Why"?* I enquired, "would that be".

He replied with conviction, *"Because you are too scared to go home and fight the terrorists"*

There after he provided intimate information about parts of my anatomy or the lack there of. Also a few other derogatory remarks, suggesting in a less than diplomatic turn of phrase that I was illegitimate.

What happened next was inevitable. Punches were thrown, haymakers launched, more often than not missing their targets, followed by the normal wrestling match where both parties fall to the ground. The last I recall was we were back on our feet and I was trying assiduously to put his head through the plastic bubble on top of the Jute box. There was a fair amount of claret smeared and splattered over the bar and jute box, originating from both pugilist's. I recall people intervening to stop the "punch up". The South African was very groggy, and had to sit down and listen to my abusing him and everyone and anyone associated with him.

Needless to say the owner banned us for life, and all parties reverted to the "farm house" except my opponent, who was unfortunately transported from the public house by ambulance. I later ascertained he had suffered a broken jaw and returned to his homeland.

Now one would surmise that would be the end of the tale. On the return journey to the farm house, I was talking to a young lady, who had all but "put me on a promise for that night" and the immediate future looked rosy indeed. The reader would realise I had consumed far too much of the amber fluid with intermittent top ups of any other poison which had been on offer.

When we arrived at the house, I became separated from my "mon amour", and in my inebriated state, I got her identity mixed up with another more than friendly young lady. So I peeled off my clothes, actually I staggered around disrobing, and got into a bed with, the person who, I thought had made the promise. The occupant rejected me outright, saying I had had my chance and blown it, and referred me to the other young lady. I apologised profusely and staggered across to the correct bed, as I sat thereon, I got a swift kick in the derriere, and an angry voice said, "Go and sleep with her, who you think you are?"

I was actually so confused I ended up sleeping on the carpet in the lounge, after having tripped over one or two other bodies in the process.

The following morning, as we were packing, one of the girls invited me to a party in London that night. I accompanied her, by train and tube to the suburb of Bayswater. She offered me a piece of carpet for the night and we awaited the arrival of her guests. I noted were on the third floor. Overlooking a street. She informed me she was going out to get some "stuff" for the party. Inviting me to join her. I needed a bottle of white lightning, lemonade and some Lime juice so I sized the opportunity.

I made my purchases, nursing the mother of all hangovers. I could feel the effects of the previous nights "fracas" increasing. A passing glance in a mirror revealed my eyes had gained what looked like poorly administered mascara. I realised my friend was not getting the same "stuff" as myself. Hers came in plastic/paper wrapped parcels. I knew what kind of party to expect, it would not be the first nor the last.

As the party progressed into the night, some loud speakers were placed in the middle of the lounge floor. Many participants lay on the carpet, heads as close to the speakers as possible, and formed what from my position on the couch looked like a star.

A "reefer" was lit and passed between users, who all inhaled deeply each time it rotated past their position. The music being played very loudly was not much to my liking, the band was well known in those days, calling themselves, "The Cream"

I was about half way through my bottle of white lightning, and feeling pleasantly joyous. When a young lady stood up and started peeling off her garments. It was no strip tease. The top, then the jeans, then the bra and last the panties. She had no bikini lines and obviously had been in a country without sunlight for a long time, she had that English "pure white", pale skin.

She did a bit of a dance, announcing to all she was, "free and could fly". I had never seen a naked lady dance before nor one that could fly. I therefor watched with as much interest as my inebriated state allowed. Suddenly she headed for my position. She lifted one foot, and slammed it on the opposite arm rest, with her next step, her foot landed on the backrest of the couch, and ran towards my position. *"Watch me fly"* she screamed with joy. At that moment I realised the sash window was open, and remembered we were three stories above the streets of Bayswater, London. I made the correct presumption she intended "flying" out the window. I was about to witness a suicide or terrible accident.

I turned to my left, seeing her ankle, just as she jumped. I desperately grabbed onto the foot and ankle, and pulled her towards me, as hard as I could. She fell over my head, hit my lap and then bounced onto the floor.

*"See I can fly"* she proclaimed, apparently oblivious to her close brush with death or serious injury. With that, she crawled back to help finish off the ever rotating reefer. I would like to report that I did not spill a drop, actually I lost the entire contents of my glass. Thankfully she missed the bottle, which had its cap off. Otherwise we would have had a catastrophe.

I have often told this story, and wonder whether as a member of the Police I would have received a Commissioners Commendation of crossed white lightning bottles or been arrested for possession of "dagga"( marijuana).

Sex Drugs and Rock and Roll indeed.

\*　　　\*　　　\*　　　\*　　　\*

*It isn't the moment you are*
*Stuck that you need courage,*
*But for the long uphill climb back*
*To sanity and faith and security.*

*Anne Morrow Lindebergh*

# MY FILM CAREER &
# THE ROCK OF GIBRALTAR

I am reminded of a time when General Franco (in charge of Spain, in 1968/69) removed all Spaniards off the Rock of Gibraltar during a political dispute with Britain over who was the rightful owner of the rock. I had been resident of a garden park in Alicante, south of the Costa del Sol in Spain. I was doing it tougher than usual. Whisper on the streets had it the Americans were making films in Malaga. There was a desperate need for extras, the pay US$75 a day. That's like hitting pay dirt in the El Dorado.

I and a South African accountant hitchhiked south to Malaga. We went to the hotel, soon finding those responsible for hiring extras. We were told to report to the hotel each morning at 0500 hours. We located a park close by and the next morning after a sleepless night (because we did not have an alarm clock) we presented ourselves. A bus took us out onto the film set. We had made it! All the riches of the world were ours, who knows, we dreamed, we could even become famous film stars with flocks of beauties to choose from.

On that first morning an old hand warned us, *"Don't volunteer for a speaking part, you will never get any work after that."* Hundreds of hopefuls mingled in front of a caravan. A Yank appeared.

*"Who can ride a horse?"*

*"Me I can, – Depot trained!"* My arm shot up, along with 100 others.
The Yank chose his extras. Those chosen went to the side for makeup. I was excluded.

*"I need cowboys."*

*"That's me,"* my hand shot up – he chose his men. I was excluded.

*"I want barmen, and idiots, a sheriff, brothel keepers and priests, laymen and angels, candle stick makers, butchers and farriers"* and each night I was back on the park bench again.

Although the statute of limitations does apply, I shall not advise how we were gaining sufficient nourishment to survive, safe to say, if we were caught we would be spending some valuable time in the local 'big house'. Things were desperate. The truth was starvation was more certain than stardom.

It was at this delicate time in my life politics played a helping hand. As I have mentioned General Franco pulled all Spanish citizens off the Rock of Gibraltar. Smelling a work opportunity we hiked further south. My friend and I were one of the last people to walk out of Spain across the famous air strip, where Sir Winston Churchill is alleged to have arranged for the RAF plane carrying the Polish general to crash into the Med, killing all aboard. Franco closed the border at 12 midday - behind us.My friend and I got positions as scaffolders. Our job was to continue erecting scaffolding on the external walls of the new hospital.

*The Author attends to scaffolding on the New Hospital on Gibraltar.*

To suggest the scaffolding was 'unsafe' would be an understatement. Scaffolding was attached to the building by bits of rope, string and wire. Needless to say, with the high winds coming off North Africa and the Mediterranean, they snapped so it was not unusual for one to sway, four or five stories up, three or four feet from the wall. The road less travelled was always interesting. We slept in the hospital, moving our kit up a floor as each level was poured. The pay was awful. We were paid the equivalent of Spanish wages.

We met two young ladies, a Rhodesian and a South African, both bar maids in a local hotel. A friendship ensued from which we derived a lifesaving bowl of soup with large chunks of meat and fresh vegetables in it each evening at the back door.

My friend and I did not have sufficient funds to get back to England so we worked and saved. We did not drink alcohol, which I am sure did us the world of good.

From the top floor of the hospital scaffolding I saw the mountains in Morocco! That was Africa, my home continent. After a few weeks I took a few days off and travelled back to Africa, by ferry to Ceuta and on to Tangier in Morocco. My friend was travelling on a South African passport and was refused entry to the country.

I stayed in a doss house, called the Pension Chaouen, Mohamed Torres no.24, Tangier. There were a few drug abusers in the premises. One evening I had left my room door partly ajar when it was flung open and a naked woman came tumbling through and staggered onto my bed. I am not certain which planet she was on, but it certainly was not the same one as I.

Each day, with my entire worth on my back, I walked through the city markets. It was a fascinating part of the world. Back at the doss house I entered in conversation with an aging hippy. He had been on the road for ten years. He wanted to know if I wanted to make 'easy money'. I was all ears.

He explained, *"With my contacts, both in Morocco and France, it is a 'cakewalk'. You take a bus up into the Atlas Mountains* (they had snow on them, I could see that much) *there you will be handed five bags of compacted hashish* (cannabis resin). *With an unidentified and unknown escort you will travel a pre-determined route to Paris. You will be followed. You* *will then hand it over at an address, which will only be provided to you the night before the exchange. You will be paid in French francs the equivalent of US$1,000 dollars. Each successful trip allows you the next trip. You can quit whenever you wish."*

It seemed ok; I thought it might be a way out of my current financial dilemma. Just the once, I mean it was really serious criminal activity, but I knew I was not a criminal at heart.

The following day I boarded a southbound bus for the Atlas Mountains. As always luck comes in a variety of packages, this time in the form of an American man. He sat down next to me. He informed me he had seen me talking to the aging hippy and suggested he knew where I was going and why. While I emphatically denied it, he offered some advice.

*"My brother and I did it once and then he tried it alone the second time. He is doing eight years in a Spanish prison."*

At the next bus stop I got off, went back to Ceuta, boarded a ferry and returned to Gibraltar.

A few weeks later while having 'dinner with the girls', sitting on some garbage cans in a back street alley, the girls asked if we were prepared to 'escort' them back to England. They had a small Morris car – they would pay for petrol, all we had to do was feed ourselves. Lady luck was working overtime for me.

*An Evening meal south of Lisbon, Portugal.*

With the names of the two countries of origin painted on the boot, we hit the road. I found a novel way of making some money on the move. I sold my blood. I sold it more times than recommended, but stayed in reasonably good health, only passing out once in a hospital when I sold a pint on two consecutive days. We bathed in dams and rivers and slept on the side of the roads. I would plead guilty to the occasional theft of fruit and veg from fields and orchards - only sufficient to keep the four of us afloat, so to speak.

Through Huelva, up to Lisbon, across the border to Madrid and then into Toulouse, France, and back across the channel to Blighty.

\* \* \* \* \*

*Ah, my Beloved, fill the cup that clears*
*To-day of past Regrets and future Fears*
*To-morrow?- Why, To-morrow I may be*
*Myself with Yesterday's Sev'n Thousand Years.*

*The Rubaiyat*

## CLARET ON THE STRAND:
## RHODESIA HOUSE
### *The Rhodesian Embassy 1969*

T he Strand is one of the world's most exclusive addresses. In the late sixties Rhodesia was very much in the forefront of world news. At Number 429 Strand stood a symbol of Rhodesian pride – it's British Embassy. It has been occupied by Rhodesians since 1923. On the roof of the fifth floor, was a flagpole on which the Rhodesian flag was raised every morning and lowered each evening. The Embassy was closed to the general public as politically Rhodesia was an 'illegal state' with world sanctions applied. So as far as the bed wetters, extreme lefts, and rent a crowd people were concerned, Rhodesia just did not exist.

In reality there were people working and resident in the building. In November 1968, I and many others attended a UDI function there. We had entered and left through a side door, as inconspicuously as possible. The ever-present British sense of humour had a 'Bobbie' stationed at the address, a 'Black Constable'. There were no incidents, and to the best of my knowledge all Rhodesians entering and leaving the premises, treated him with the civility and respect that policemen were due.

He was front-page news worldwide.

***The British papers reported in 1968:***
***"London's only coloured Policeman guards Rhodesia***
***House.***

In early 1969, a Zimbabwe group of Rhodesian dissidents, calling themselves The Zimbabwe Solidarity Action Committee partnered with the Black People's Alliance to organise 'The March of Dignity', a protest against the British Government for failing to remove racialism in its existing colonies.

In 1963 I had been a Cadet stationed in CID Cycles Bulawayo, my first Member in Charge was Detective Constable 6021 Terence 'Terry' John Tooher. Tooher resigned from the police as a PO on 30[TH] April 1966.

Back in Earls Court, word had filtered through about the intended protest march by black dissidents and white sympathisers, focusing on Rhodesia House. Rumours swirled of anticipated violence and property destruction. One rumour had it that it was the aim of protestors to occupy the premises.

Like all pubs, the local clientele knew each other, at least by sight. So it was one evening I sat with my cronies experiencing the fine taste of the nectar of the Gods when I saw, what I thought was a familiar face in the Prince of Teck. Why would I know him? He was not one of us. He was older than the usual 'bums'. I was puzzled but not fazed, I maintained a wary eye on who he talked to and what he did. He was not dressed like the normal crowd. He had a suit and tie on! He was drinking a British beer – few from where I came from did this after the first taste. Was he new or was he a Pommie? I left the pub without resolving the issue.

The following night we were positioned in the same place holding up the same bar counter. In came the same man. I walked over and stood next to him. I did not speak. After a few minutes he engaged me in 'chit chat'. From his accent, immediately I knew he was English. He said he knew my accent and asked whether I was Rhodesian. I told him I came from Kenya, where whites spoke with a similar accent.

*"Oh,"* he said, and told me he had lived in Rhodesia and been in the police there.

*"And what do you do here?"*

*"I am in the Metropolitan Police- plain clothes division."*

*"Is this your local? "*

*"No I am looking for people to help me in some work I am undertaking".*

*"What would that be?"*

*"The Police are concerned there are a number of Rhodesians in London, many of them in Earls Court. Information to hand was that the Rhodesians planned on going to Rhodesia House to 'combat' the well-publicised protest march."*

He confirmed it was the protesters aim to break into the Rhodesian Embassy and occupy it.

*"I need to speak to as many Rhodesians as I can, to be able to report back to police who will be on duty at the time. It is feared the Rhodesians will re-act*

*violently and we would prefer it be a peaceful demonstration,"* he told me. *"Oh by the way sorry, I am Terry Tooher, Detective Constable."*

I told him I knew no Rhodesians and was awfully sorry I could not help. Now the puzzle had fallen into place.

I spread the word as fast and as far as I could. Those receiving the information had to do what they would with the intelligence. We, in my opinion needed to have as many people there as we could to retaliate any attempt at occupation.

On the given day in March 1969 as many Rhodesians as possible attended outside Rhodesia house. Two demonstrators managed to climb onto the roof of the Embassy, lower the Rhodesian flag and raise the Union Jack. Rhodesians later climbed onto the roof, lowered the 'Jack' and raised the rightful flag. While they were so doing, violence broke out on the Strand - it was the Rhodesians verses the protestors and the good old Bobbies against both parties.

This is an excerpt from a Pathé news report given on the day while filming the clash; *"Despite the menacing mood of the mob, the police stood firm and repelled them."*

As I was a participant I considered that an accurate if not somewhat biased report. The police were shoving and 'crowd controlling' the Rhodesian 'bums'. I guess there may well have been some 'more sophisticated types' present but we were actually 'delivering the goods' so to speak. There was a fair amount of 'Claret' spilt on the Strand that day, and if I may suggest the larger portion was not Rhodesian. The Pathé News finished its broadcast with; *"Having been repelled, the demonstrators went on to South Africa House where etc., etc., etc."*

As we left the Embassy the Rhodesian Flag was fluttering in the breeze five stories up. There were piles of burning cardboard placards and placard poles. Some other rubbish was also burning. Smoked waft into the still cool evening. The Strand would be back to its immaculate condition by open of business the next day.

Satisfied we had stopped any occupation, we entered the nearest public houses and drank our fill – again!

\*        \*        \*        \*        \*

# THE ZAMBESI CLUB &
# CHELSEA CORPS D'ELITE

*A Walk on the Wild Side*

I f you think the heading has a 'typo,' research may prove otherwise. The original owner, a Rhodesian I believe, admitted to spelling Zambezi incorrectly on his official paper work.

Whether it remained at the same address for its lifetime I do not know. There is evidence in my research suggesting a drunken Irishman, who was thrown out of the club, put paid to the establishment in 1970 by throwing a petrol bomb through the window.

I believe the premises in Barkston Gardens, Earls Court, which I frequented, is now one of London's 'posh' bridge clubs. Strangely enough founded by another Rhodesian.

My readings reveal the 'Zambesi Club' was a 'notorious' establishment where 'dubious characters' could be hired for 'mercenary work' in Africa!!! We socialised with a number of Biafra mercenaries; some would-bes, could-bes, may-have-beens and certainly some who were the real 'McCoy'. Yes some of us were approached for recruitment.

In the main the Zambesi Club was a great spot for the 'hoi polloi' of the global travelling sect. Its biggest attraction was the extended hours available in the pursuit of 'the daughter of the vine'. The Zambesi was different to our normal watering holes in Lower Earls Court.

Yes while the 'rabble' like us were well represented there were always a sprinkling of the Corps d' Elite, 'A-listers and upper crust Brits from the neighbouring Chelsea and Knightsbridge areas. Well dressed and refined. As I was to find out on this occasion there were some free spirits amongst them, when they chose to be.

It's gone now and not unlike our fading lives we, that partook there over the years are left with beautiful memories made when we were young, innocent, naive, dewy eyed and unworldly.

The Zambesi was three blocks from the Prince of Teck. The time it took to walk there varied by the amount of alcohol previously consumed. The whisper on the streets had it that one of the Great Train Robbers had a 'patch' en route as a flower seller. There was a flower seller, barrow and all, on Earls Court Road but needless to say he was not one of the Robbers as they were all in the 'Big House' in our time.

On the weekend in question where Hardy and St Clair were remains shrouded in the mists of time. I was accompanied by a Mtoko tobacco farmer, Ralph Watson who, myth or legend had it, had twice been a contender for the Rhodesian heavy weight boxing title and lost.

I can vouch for the man's fighting ability when, one wild night in San Sebastian, Spain, he turned to me and said, *"You remind me of my elder brother."* (Who had been decapitated in a motorcycle accident). With that he let go an upper cut that landed square under my lower jaw. It lifted me off my feet, my body passed over a table occupied by two old Spaniards and I hit the top of a set of banisters, bounced once and tumbled down the steps, leading to the wine cellar.

Ralph and I returned to Earls Court late one day to find the normal pubs were just closing so in an unusual state of sobriety we walked down to the Zambesi Club. Walking into the Zambesi Club sober was a first with many people, like the well-known patron 'the English belle,' Julie, looking different. Situated between the street and the actual bar counter was a short corridor. The bar area was always very dark, the seats were attached to the back wall and as always there was standing room only.

Ralph and I decided to be seated. We took turns in walking to the counter to get another beer, drinking Carling Black Label – chilled. Late in the afternoon, maybe early evening, it was my turn to get the round.

I struggled and pushed my way to the counter, armed with two empty glasses, it was so 'infra dig' to drink out of bottles!!!!

As I was politely awaiting my turn to be served a heated argument was ensuing close to my chest between a short, hot tempered Aussie, known to me and a much taller Englishman, unknown to me. Nothing unusual there really, it happened all the time. I was served and had to retrieve my full glasses by passing between these two characters. Holding one glass in each hand I took one step backwards and shouted "coming through". At that very moment in time the Aussie smashed a glass on the counter and shoved it in the face of the English man!! Claret sprayed all over the place.

Thankfully, being relatively sober, I kept backing away as the fight spread like a wind assisted bush fire. Women were screaming and punches were being thrown left, right and centre. Beer was raining down from  splattered glasses. I made it back to the wall where Watson remained seated. I handed him his beer. We watched the 'punch up' with interest. It was apparent it was spreading and that we may unwittingly become involved. I suggested we get out of the bar, Watson agreed. We downed our beer, stood up and immediately received a few glancing blows from poorly aimed punches. It was going to be futile to attempt to walk out of the bar. Someone shouted, *"The Cops have been called."*

Watson came out with an absolute pearler, "Get down on our hands and knees and crawl out."

Ingenious. So that's how we set off for the front door, hopefully, we would be in the Kings Head having only lost 30 minutes drinking time.

I was in the vanguard of the retreating duo. Every now and again, stopping to navigate around sets of legs, Watson would periodically bump into me. It was comforting to know I had his 'backup' if the need arose.

As I cleared the bar area, fairly well drenched with just about every assortment of alcohol served in the club, I caught my first glimpse of the front door. The planned exit was not without its risks, more than often the boots of one of the pugilists, practising the 'Ali Shuffle' or just so pissed they were trying to maintain their balance, found their mark on our bodies.

Then it happened, I saw the distinct trousers legs and boots of the 'Bobbies'. They were pushing their way in. Also at this time I saw someone else on their hands and knees approaching me from behind the bar area. One of the employees, I knew him well. He was pushing a cardboard carton ahead of him.

*"Do us a favour, can you take this out to the Combi outside, I'll get the next one."*

I acquiesced. Inside the box were unopened bottles of 'hard' liquor. I managed to get the cargo outside, saw the Combi, its doors open.

I walked to the doors with the cargo and jokingly said, *"Where's the party?"*

Ralph was right behind me, with a second box, *"Here's your box of booze."*

Soon after our 'crawling' friend from the bar reappeared as cool as a cucumber with yet a third box. There was no rush or panic. Police cars were stopping and more Police entered the premises. A chap in the driver's seat yelled, *"All aboard for the party."*

I was in like a flash. I could not entice Ralph to join me.

*"Where is it going?"*

*"Who cares?!"*

In the end the barman slammed the side doors and we were away. I took stock of my situation. There were a few young, A-listed ladies in the van. We ended up in Chelsea somewhere.

I helped carry the booze through the front door and up the stairs. On entering the flat I thought I had arrived in a time capsule, the place looked like a scene from a Roman orgy during the era of Nero or Caligula. I was requested to undertake a second and third trip, there were cases of beer as well to be transferred.

There were an unmistakeable disproportionate number of women to men, now that was another first. The young, now not so sophisticated ladies christened us 'the bootleggers'. An extremely good looking lady pronounced the reward for 'the bootleggers' efforts to be free grog for as long as they remained in situ. Well, well, well, that was right up my alley. I don't mind if I do. I found a bottle of good quality Vodka, a clean glass, a bottle of lemonade and some lime juice. I was on a roll.

I asked a passing lady, *"Any ice?"*

*"I'll get you some darling!!"*

Leaning on the back of the sofa. I watched the party. Shortly my ice arrived and was delivered with a rather long and lingering 'peck' on the lips. I could swear something passed gentle cross my crotch area.

I was indeed 'living the dream'!!

The debauchery continued unabated, the Vodka warmed the spirit. More ice, more kisses, more 'Darlings' and now no question that with each contact I felt a hand, what else, brush my groin. After some time, things were getting a littler blurred for this bootlegger, time had passed me by, I had consumed more than my fill.

I was most probably in full stride discussing classic Greek literature, the works of Hippocrates and Plato, Aesop's and Homer, all of this in a classic braille language, never heard in Chelsea before.

My last recollection, of that very entertaining evening, was being approached by my newfound friend the wonderful young 'ice' lady who, holding my hand said, *"Darling you are so drunk, let me take you to bed."*

Right! On both counts! I woke the following morning in a double bed in which I lay alone - buck-naked. Light poured through the window causing me to shield my eyes, my head felt as though it was in a washing machine with a mallet sporadically pounding my skull.

I found a bathroom. I stole some toothpaste; my mouth resembled the driest parts of the Sahara. I dressed and found my way back to the lounge. The party had either not stopped or started again without me. There was my friend,

*"Did you sleep well darling?"*

I had just recovered from a coma. What could I say? I had no idea! *"Here's a little pick-me-up to get you started."*

Whatever it was, down it went. That day was a carbon copy of the previous afternoon and evening.

I woke up the following morning, fully clothed, lying in an empty bath with an empty bottle of Vodka. I presumed the night had not ended romantically. I walked into a much quieter living room, thanked my hosts and bid them adieu. I wandered back to Earls Court. Nobody had missed me. No one even asked, and if they had and I had told them the truth, they would only have said, *"You are bull shitting again Stanyon."*

 I was reminded, by friends I was unemployed. I needed to find work.

Life just does not get any better than this!!!

'I was living the Dream!!!'

*     *     *     *     *

*'Tisn't beauty, so to speak, nor good talk necessarily.*
*It's just IT. Some women' will stay in a man's memory*
*If they once walked down a street.*

**Kipling**

# THE LUCRATIVE
# ICE CREAM TRADE

We had ingratiated ourselves into the Earls Court scene, coming to know many Rhodesians. In 1968 the average labourer's weekly wage in Britain was 12 pound 10 shillings. The average wage: 22 pounds.

We became friends with staff in the employment agency at Earls Court.

In fact, one young lady, 'Jenny', married a good friend of mine from my Bikita days, Michael John Wilson Rayne (7368/8448) who retired as a Superintendent and joined CIO.

Over dinner many years later in England, when I was visiting on business, he was head of security for a large chain of supermarkets; he confided that it was his biggest mistake. He left CIO disgusted by former BSAP members buttering up to the new government to the detriment of their own. I am saddened to advise both Jenny and Mike have now passed on.

Our relationship with the staff allowed us to get the pick of available work. When our friends thought an appropriate vacancy came in they would contact us by phone, we would get there as fast as possible, knowing that the job would not be offered to anyone else in the meantime.

So it was early one morning, in mid-1968 as I lay in bed, unemployed and desperately short of money, the rent was in arrears, and a few friends were calling in loans. As usual, I was nursing the mother of all White Lightning hangovers when one of the staff members phoned.

*"I have a job for you and Graham."*

In Earls Court we attended the 'make believe' interview, she told us the job was selling ice creams at the Earls Court Tournament. It was annual work, for close on two weeks. Each year there was the biggest Military Tattoo in the world staged right in our backyard. She was not certain how, but the ice cream sellers made a lot of money. I was flabbergasted. I had dragged my sorry body out of bed and risked being caught evading 'transport fares' to become a Walls Ice Cream salesman.

*"You are not serious, please tell me this is a sick joke. I suppose the next thing you are going to tell us is that we get a pretty uniform and an ice cream tray to hang around our necks"*

*"Yes Doug, that is in the job description".*

Desperate people do desperate things. Hardy and I presented ourselves, as required, at the Earls Court Exhibition premises. We found the Walls Ice Cream manager and he hired us without question, we came well recommended. There would be two shows a day and the 'gig' lasted for, I just don't remember, about two weeks.

We presented ourselves prior to the Matinee on the first day. There were two levels of seating, one above the other, with access from the rear. The seats were divided into 'blocks' demarcated by aisles. I cannot recall exact numbers, but there would have been 20 rows, bottom to top. Each row containing about 40 seats.

This might seem obvious, but what it meant for us was that we were required to spend the duration of each show, twice a day constantly climbing and descending stairs.

The Manager allocated two or three 'blocks of seats' per salesman. A quick, well as quick as the state of the White Lightening comatose I suffered from allowed, calculation revealed about 800 seats per block – two blocks, 1600 – if only half of these people wanted an ice cream, we were going to be run off our feet.

We were issued with an ill-fitting uniform jacket each, a little hat and a tray with numerous compartments fitted with an adjustable strap, which hung around the neck. The last item issued was a small torch.

Apparently for most of the show, the audience was 'in the dark' as all lights shone onto the arena. That meant we would be working with the torch to locate product and issue change.

We noticed we were the only foreigner workers – all the rest were English. Clearly some were regulars, as their relationship with the Manager revealed prior contact.

Before the commencement of the Tattoo, that's what the regulars called it, we lined up with our empty trays, and by double count with a member of staff, we took possession of a number of ice creams, they came with different values, different flavours and just to make life really interesting, differing sizes and shapes. Once 'loaded' we had to sign for the monetary value of the stock we had been provided. The rules, we were told, were simple. When your tray was nearly empty you returned to base, restocked, with the value of each 'load' added to your initial total, and so on. At the end of the show we were to report to the office, return any unsold stock, the value of which would be deducted from the amount issued and the net amount was payable by ourselves. If for some reason you were short, the amount was deducted from your pay. You were paid at the end of the second shift daily.

This exercise was not as easy as it sounded.

The tournament was first performed in 1880 and had been performed every year since, historical drivel? Well maybe, but for an ice cream salesman this presented yet another hoop he had to jump through. There were 'mass' or 'block' bookings from European countries. Who cares? Well the ice cream salesman for one. Why? In essence this contributed to the chaos that is the ice cream salesman's lot.

All European countries operated on a decimal currency system, the 'Old Dart' was still using pounds, shillings and pence and no foreign currency were permitted to be exchanged for ice creams. These 'purchasers' were in fact 'day trippers'. Many of them were not fluent in English in fact, at best, they only had a smattering of the Kings English. Neither Hardy nor I were bilingual or multilingual and our linguistic flexibility was limited to Swahili, Shona, Ndebele and Fanakalo, which proved to be worthless for this exercise.

So from a service point of view, there were fiscal and linguistic issues. Customer service proved excessively challenging as well, given that the salesman spent two hours being shouted at in French, Spanish, Greek and any other number of languages, from people ordering ice creams.

Now while this difficult, no insane, activity is occurring, there are some highly charged events on show, guns going off and extremely loud military music, played by hundreds of people at a time. Horses running amok. Soldiers and seamen competing in races requiring the dismantling of cannons, carrying the pieces over an obstacle course and then reassembling them. One would think, from a salesman's perspective what was happening 'way down on the arena' was of no real consequence, the more exciting the event the more excited the patron, the more excited the patron the higher the demand for sales. This becomes a compounding factor on the first two dilemmas of finance and language so it was not uncommon for representatives of multi block bookings attempting to gain your attention at the same time, so you were over whelmed with excitable Greeks, Portuguese, Italians or Russians.

A patron may order five ice creams, prior to payment. You send the ice-creams down the line, with a request for three shillings and six pence in payment. Two shillings and nine pence comes back down the line, accompanied by a return of two sixpenny ice creams, viewed but not wanted, and a re-order of *"two da sam as fore"* accompanying the product and inappropriate payment. The problem being; initially you sent three different ones down in the first place, so which one did he want to duplicate! Then suddenly, the excitement heats up in the arena, the people assisting in the sale, those passing the ice-creams and money backwards and forwards, shout loudly, start clapping and urging on their favourite. You are forgotten, but still awaiting full and final settlement of 'the deal'.

Of course you have no idea of the identity of your customer, because he is halfway down the row, in almost pitch-blackness and your torch is designed only to light up your tray!

There is also a 'children issue' one had to learn about. It was not at all uncommon for little kids to desert their parents and use the front of your tray as a swing, trying to get your attention, only to find when you give the little 'so and so' his ice cream he does a runner on you and disappears like a black shadow on a dark night.

You would not believe the multifarious behaviours of mankind witnessed by an ice cream salesman; old ladies adamant that they have been short-changed, waddling up to you and clearly abusing you, had you been proficient in their native tongue of Polish, Swedish or whatever.

It is almost indescribable how a salesman has to converse by sign language or broken English with a prospective customer seated in the middle of a row and so many people, with good intent, trying to interpret the discussion, of course in their native tongue, which only amplifies the problem.

Another trap for the inexperienced salesman, is the, *"I am so sorry, I have to go to the loo in a hurry"* con. That's when you are standing close to the chair on a row whilst serving customers and the chap in the aisle seat suddenly and without please or thankyou stands up and his head 'accidentally' hits the base of your tray. The end result is numerous ice creams are 'lost'.

There are a million inter related stories, to the main theme. The big question remained. How the bloody hell is this a money making 'gig'? The pay equals 12 pound a week, payable at 2 pounds at the end of the second shift. Minus of course any 'owings' you might have.

After the first matinee I duly did the hand-back, total-up and the result was that I had over changed some people, lost some ice creams, had some kid swipe one while my attention was diverted so I owed Walls Ice Creams four shillings and some pence. A quick calculation revealed that at that rate, if continued, I would be paid less than 18 shillings a shift or a total of 10 pounds for the week.

Dismayed and pissed off I waited at the top of the escalators for Hardy. He arrived with a newfound 'English' friend, a long time Tattoo ice cream salesman. As we were descending I told

Hardy my dismal fiscal predicament. I also complained about these bloody Europeans and their block booking and the fact they had no understanding of the British currency system. Hardy retorted he too had suffered a 'Net Loss' on the day.

The Englishman was incredulous, *"How come you lost money? I made twenty-five quid!! Excluding my pay."*

*"Excuse me Sir, are you in a hurry to go anywhere, right now?"*

*"No."*

*"Could Graham and I buy you a few beers in the pub and you provide us with the wisdom of your experience as an ice cream salesman?"*

*"Sure, only a pleasure."*

We sat and enjoyed his company for the best part of two hours as he went over every 'con', 'cozen', 'fleece', 'scam' and 'bluff' he knew in minute detail. He immaculately described the setup, the sting and the '*munson*' - the exit strategy.

Hardy and I never lost another penny in the last 11 shows. We made on average 24 pounds a show, clearing a total of 264 pounds. We happily contributed to our tutor's pension fund.

The 'set up' had been going since 1880.

As I said, we were living in the new world that really was the old.

∗     ∗     ∗     ∗     ∗

*Lost, yesterday, somewhere between Sunrise and Sunset,*
*Two golden hours, each set with sixty diamond minutes.*
*No reward is offered, for they are gone forever.*

**Horace Mann**

# SHOWDOWN AT
# THE HALYCON

*The contribution of this story is from my friend* **Colin Lowe**, *who formed part of our world travels. This is his account and well written I may add, of an incident involving Rhodesians in 1968, some of whom are mentioned in other escapades in this book.*

The fact is, like the rest of the world, there's not much money to be made working on farms; so most of us ended up being employed on the oil rigs, steel erection and even in labouring jobs on construction sites. The wages for this type of work, on an hourly basis, paid much better than most farm work but the other side of the coin was that it was often dangerous and dirty in very cold and wet conditions. This dangerous downside, to us twenty-something year olds, was of little concern; we were, after all, indestructible.

Rob Beaton and I both happened to be in London and out of work at the same time and we were debating whether we should look for another job or go off on holiday to Europe. While giving this dilemma some serious thought in the pub at the Overseas Visitors' Club (OVC) in Earl's Court, we were approached by an Australian character who introduced himself as Rick Freemantle. He asked us to confirm that we were both Rhodesians and then offered us a contract over four weeks to do some steel erecting which paid really well, but it was on the condition that we find at least another three Rhodesians to work with us. I was suspicious of this Australian as he was way too smooth for me and I wondered if he'd been part of one of several Australian shoplifting gangs that operated in London that had hit the headlines recently when most of them had been arrested by the British Police.

You will be asking yourself why an Australian would want to employ a bunch of Rhodesians. I cannot answer that with any certainty but it was a known fact that Rhodesians rarely had any difficulty finding a job in this line of work. I saw it time and time again and especially when applying for a job on the oil rigs where Rhodesians would leap-frog right to the front of the long waiting list of hopeful Kiwis, Aussies, Canadians and even South Africans. Reading and Bates, one of the oil companies drilling in the North Sea, even went so far, on one occasion, to employ Marty and me when they didn't really have a vacancy on the rig. Management kept us in reserve, busy at the dockside in Lowestoft loading and unloading the oil rig supply boats which caused the local dockers who saw us working, to go on strike as we weren't members of their union, but that as they say, is another story.

All of these manual labouring jobs were physically demanding and it was usually twelve hours of pulling, pushing, supporting, lifting and carrying heavy metal machinery and equipment so it was like going to the gym every day for twelve hours. It was probably the fittest and strongest any of us had ever been. Rob and I scoured through the Gwebi guys in Earl's Court but all of them were either away working in the north of the country, on holiday or gainfully employed in London. Nevertheless we managed to get together with another three Rhodesians who we knew, who fitted the bill perfectly.

Ralph Watson's family farmed at Mtoko and he reminded me of an amiable and cuddly teddy bear but he was built like a brick long-drop and proved to be immensely strong, carrying lengths of steel by himself that usually required two of us to lift. As I recall he was a half-brother to Bob Courtney, a well-known wrestler in Salisbury who called himself the Masked Tornado back in the sixties. The other two were Tony St. Clair and Doug Stanyon, two policemen who knew each other from their time in the BSAP. I had briefly known Tony at primary school before his parents took him off somewhere else but in that short time he'd earned a reputation as a bit of a boxer in the playground. Then there was Doug, a tall rangy guy who worked, drank and played hard, enjoying life in large bites.

Rick met with the five of us at the OVC to clarify the contract, the financial return expected and where the work was located. This turned out to be the new Freeman's mail order warehouse in a small city called Peterborough, about a hundred and twenty kilometres north of London. What we had to do was to assemble and bolt together all the metal shelving which reached up to more than six metres high, almost to the roof. The warehouse was enormous and the work would be hard but the great advantage was that it was all indoors so the weather wouldn't bother us as it had done in previous jobs. The Poms would describe it as being a doddle!

Rick decided he would drive us to Peterborough in his car and he picked us up early one Monday morning outside the OVC, apologising that he had one stop to make before getting on the motorway. Rick parked at an office block in the northern part of London saying,

*'I'll be back in ten minutes.'*

Doug, who was sitting in the front, wasted no time in opening Rick's briefcase which he'd left on the seat and looked through all his documents explaining as he rifled through the papers,

*'We need to know something about this guy in case he does a runner with our money. Keep a lookout for him coming back.'*

It gave me some satisfaction to know that I wasn't the only one wary of our Australian friend but in fairness to Rick, he did, at the end of the contract, pay us out in full, but I had to smile to myself – once a policeman, always a policeman!

Peterborough turned out to be a rather flat featureless place, dull in appearance and dull in nature. Rob and I quickly found digs with Mrs. Wilson whose house was within walking distance of the Freeman's warehouse and the other three found similar accommodation around the corner. We wasted no time in getting to work straight away and soon got into the rhythm of working a twelve hour day – the sooner we finished the job the sooner we got paid – and we were getting through the work at a rapid rate.

***The Rhodesians hard at work steel erecting. Photo Doug
Stanyon***

We'd trudge back to our digs after six, jump into a bath, then
wolf down our supper, or tea as the Poms called it, maybe watch a
bit of the news and straight to bed. After two or three weeks of this
rather repetitive existence and with the end of the contract in sight,
we all decided to go out on Saturday night and have Sunday off.
Great idea! Tony said he'd heard of a pub which was a well-known
watering hole for the local yokels, not far from us and within
walking distance of our accommodation.

We met up and soon found the pub which was called *The Halcyon*.
This name had two meanings; it can mean calm, peaceful and
tranquil, which later on turned out to be a bit of a joke. It is also the
poetic name of the kingfisher in England and because of this the
pub had a large fluorescent image of this bird flicking on and off
over the entrance. I seem to remember that the wings moved

position and the beak opened and closed on every second flick. *Cheez, how naff can you get?!*

The pub itself was in the shape of a 'T' with the bar at the top end and about twelve rectangular tables each seating ten people, down each wall of the longer room. Presiding over the bar was the landlord, a big bluff man with a bald head who was sweating profusely by the time we arrived. I named him Mutton Chops as he sported this familiar facial hair so fashionable in the swinging sixties. He was assisted behind the bar by a couple of young men who were kept busy serving the traditional mild and bitter beer out of kegs. The pub had several double doors, obviously only opened in summer, which led onto a large parking area which was quite unusual for England where land was usually at a premium. You can gather from this description that Mutton Chops had very little imagination when it came to décor and ambience – as far as he was concerned he provided a place where the locals could drink, and this they did, in copious quantities, caring little about the atmosphere and character of the pub.

We grabbed ourselves the last remaining table and settled in with our beers to discuss the news from home. Doug's father held a senior position in the Department of Immigration in Rhodesia and of course both Doug and Tony still had their contacts with their friends back in the BSAP; Ralph's family kept him up to date with the latest news on the farming front, so there was much to talk about.

Every now and then one of us would wander up to the bar and order the five beers required for each round. When it was my shout I glanced around and noticed there was only a sprinkling of girls in the establishment and I detected a feeling of animosity towards us – a little bit of shoulder shoving at the crowded bar and a refusal to move out the way as I clutched five glasses full of beer on my way back to the table. It didn't help our standing in the community when our table won two of the five raffles announced by Mutton Chops. The rest of our group had also picked up on this antipathy towards us but the consensus was to just to ignore it, after all, they were Poms and didn't know any better.

In those days pubs closed at eleven and when Mutton Chops shouted his *'Last Orders Please!'* everyone scrambled to get their final drink. With that Tony got up and started to make his way to the bar where I thought he was about to put in his final order. But he didn't, he stopped half way down and I watched with astonishment as he jumped up onto one of the tables. There was a lull in the general hubbub of conversation as many of the customers stopped in their move towards the bar, wondering what Tony was up to, when in his loudest parade ground voice he shouted:

**'All Pommies are bastards!'**

*February 1969: Ralph, Tony, Doug and Rob standing in the snow outside the warehouse. Photo Colin Lowe.*

He accentuated the last word into two syllables to give it added emphasis and from that moment everything froze for about five seconds while a deathly hush descended over the whole pub as this piece of information about their ancestry was absorbed by their addled brains. Then there was a huge eruption of noise as the mob turned towards him with the intention of dragging him underfoot to deliver their version of English foot justice. For me the whole scene was moving in slow motion and I watched in fascination as

Tony jumped, seemingly suspended in space for a few seconds, before descending feet first into the mob, taking down about three assailants with his steel capped builder's boots without falling down to the ground himself, then that he started to use his fists. Of course a second mob had quickly formed and was advancing with intent towards us and that was when the brawl really started. The four of us shot out of our table and advanced at a run at the second group which must have been disconcerting for them, causing some of them to break away before contact was made.

Besides dealing with the imminent threat of what was in front of me I could hear Mutton Chops screaming hysterically for us to break it up as he was calling the police and if we didn't stop fighting he would lose his licence. Of course no one took the slightest bit of notice of his request as we were having too much fun but he must have instructed his staff to open the double doors and the whole brawl spilled out onto the car park area. Interestingly we didn't stand together as a band of brothers; we each had our own area of conflict to manage. In between opponents, I threw a quick glance at Rob to make sure he was OK. I needn't have bothered, I could see his arms flailing like windmills and there was a pile of Poms on the ground in his proximity and the other three, although a bit further away, were obviously having a whale of a time.

I don't remember being hit at all, not once, but then neither do I remember hitting anyone either – there were people in front of me showing a lot of unfriendliness, and even aggression on occasion, and then they just seemed to disappear. Only recently have I witnessed this same sensation when one of my grandsons was showing me his latest video war game and you press a button on the hand held control and the bad guy on the screen in front of you just disappears – well, that's what it was like for me that night.

All of a sudden the action came to a stop and there were just the five of us left standing in the car park but there were quite a few bodies lying on the tarmac, some groaning, some attempting to crawl away and some not moving at all. I looked around and couldn't believe the devastation we had caused.

*'Well, I guess that's it,'* said Doug with a note of disappointment in his voice, *'it didn't last very long, did it.'*

Tony didn't say much but I could tell from the satisfied look on his face that the whole evening had come together just as he'd planned. Mutton Chops, however, hadn't finished with us and his language had deteriorated, along with his customers, but his conversation was done from a good fifty metres away – he was not interested in engaging with us on a personal level.

*'You f....... Australians,'* he shouted, *'I don't know why we let you into England. Why don't you piss off back to your own country.'*

It occurred to me he must be annoyed with those Australian shoplifting gangs as well, and was venting his anger on us, and to be honest, I couldn't blame him. We could hear the sirens of the approaching police cars and Doug cocked a professional ear in their direction and said,

*'Those Police are less than two minutes away, we'd better leg it.'*

I couldn't help myself but I shouted at Mutton Chops as we were about to take off,

*'No worries Bruce, we'll be back next weekend.'*

His reply was unintelligible which is probably just as well but he took off like a scalded cat when I suddenly remembered that I'd left something at our table and sprinted back to the pub.

*'Colin, where the hell are you going?'*

*'We left the boxes of chocolates that we won in the raffle at our table,'* I shouted over my shoulder.

I retrieved the chocolates and soon caught up with the others and we were long gone by the time the Police arrived.

Of course, we never did go back there.

So what is the moral of this story? The moral or the lesson to be learnt from this incident, is that if you want to have a quiet drink with a couple of friends then don't, under any circumstances, include a member of the BSAP in your group.

\*      \*      \*      \*      \*

*Our deeds still travel with us from afar,*
*And what we have been, makes us what we are.*

# NO RESPONSIBILITIES, NO WORRIES

O f course there are multitudes of stories, depending on the attitude of the reader, some, the purists, may be 'tut-tutting' while others may see the humorous side. A few short incidents come to mind of life on the roads less travelled. I shall relate them for good measure.

## The Football Match
## England vs the Rest

T he British are well known for their love of 'football', and while most of the Rhodesians and South Africans, plus the Aussies and New Zealanders were avid Rugby Union followers, we did find the 'Pommie' game skilful.

One night we were kicked out of the local pub in Earls Court after last drinks. A larger than usual crowd were milling around the front door, in small groups. Suddenly some 'African' shouted, "*We challenge the Pommies to a game of 'football'.*"

Faster than a cat moving out of a room full of rocking chairs a pitch was set up on a road intersection with Earls Court Road with goal posts marked by empty beer cans brought out of the pub and a 'ball' was presented – a Fosters Blue beer can.

I was part of the 'Rest of the World' team. There was a referee. I have no idea where he came from. Nor whether he was familiar with the rules of the game.

The residences on this road were three stories high on both sides.

As the game progressed more and more lights, in residential premises were turned on. Occupants were yelling and screaming. Now it may have been and most probably was time for us to "go to bed" but the players and spectators on the ground had different intentions.

With each goal scored there was thunderous applause.

The players would return to their positions with the 'ball' placed in the centre, awaiting the ref to blow his whistle.

For a minute moment there was silence. A loud clapping could be heard, the slow, mocking style of clapping but only two people were clapping. All players turned to see who it was, clearly looking for trouble.

There they were - two Bobbies in full uniform, slow hand clapping. Once they had the players and the crowd's full attention, one addressed us.

*"Be good fellas now, and go to bed, people are trying to sleep."*

With that I estimate 30 or 40 people walked very quietly away.

*     *     *     *     *

# Auditing
# The Financials

With my two friends having returned to Rhodesia, I was at a bit of a loose end.

I just drifted from job to job, taking short trips in to Europe. My next trip I planned was to go to Australia. Trying to hitchhike across Europe, part of the Middle East, across India and Asia was just a 'bridge too far', even for this idiot.

One morning, after having outlived my welcome in a person's digs, I gathered all my belongings and headed for Earls Court tube station. As I walked amidst the busy commuters and transient hikers I wondered what my future really held. I did some serious soul searching. Was I troubled physiologically? In reality had this lifestyle, of no responsibilities, no care, easy-come-easy-go, just replaced a fear of living in the real world?

I got to the tube station, found a spare section of floor with a wall behind it and sat down. I have always been fascinated by human behaviour; if you just take the time to study it, it is immensely interesting. People rushing to get on tubes and rushing to get away from tubes, lovers holding hands, mothers fighting with kids, people in distress and those, right next to them filled with joy and laughter. All living the same day and same conditions, but struggling with the lives they had made for themselves.

I turned my thoughts inwards. I opened my wallet – there were no monetary notes. I searched my rucksack – and all its contents. My worldly assets amounted to this:

Two pairs of jeans,
Three very badly worn shirts,
Two tee shirts.
Three pairs of underpants,
A copy of the Rubaiyat,
A copy of Robert Service poems,
A 35 mm camera - no film,
One pair of shoes,
A Parker jacket/wind cheater and
The rucksack.
Total cash available - six pence.
I had also smoked my last cigarette.

I was homeless, unemployed, a vagrant with no one I could really trust.

I needed to get my act together. I thought I must be fairly close to the 'bottom', so there is only one way left and that is 'up'. I could use the sixpence to make a phone call, apply for work, after seven days I could be back on the way up. But I needed a cigarette badly. In those days one could purchase a single cigarette. If I did so, I could not make the phone call. If I made the phone call, I could not have a cigarette. What a dilemma!!

I walked towards the cigarette sales counter, bought a cigarette, bummed a light and walked to the Prince of Teck. Most of the crowd had moved home, Australia, New Zealand, Africa, the States and Canada. Surely if I hung around outside long enough I could bum a drink, borrow some money, have a few laughs, might even get some floor space to sleep on!

That is exactly what happened, it is and remains the poorest I have ever been in life.

*　　　*　　　*　　　*　　　*

# Sorry Officer I Can't Help
# I've just come off Night Shift.

I recall attending a party in a basement flat in the west of Earls Court one evening. I was clad in a pair of jeans and wore a World War I flying jacket, which was common attire for the likes of myself. They were cheap and readily available from Army Navy second hand stores.

With lamb's wool lining and good quality leather exteriors, they provided quality warmth on cold nights. Lamb's wool decorated the collars and could be pulled over the nape of the neck, to stop the wind.

A fight broke out on the street and soon word spread through the party. As usual many of those attending the party were curious so rushed upstairs to watch. Including yours truly. My initial thoughts were; it was a drunken melee, which would not be unusual.

A closer more attentive observation revealed it was actually three men against one. While I considered that unfair, such was life.

Suddenly I realised the lone pugilist was a Canadian I had spent many hours drinking with, on and off. This changed the status quo. I moved closer, they were on the street, next to the pavement. A blow delivered on the Canadian's head, dropped him, he landed with his head on the street jammed up against the curb. The assailants put 'the boot' in.

I weighed into the fight from behind the three assailants and with the advantage of not being seen or expected, two dropped to the street -thanks again to Insp. Gerry Winchcombe's unarmed combat training. The use of the base of the palm, in an upward motion, landing at the base of the skull, if executed well, worked wonders.

With two now neutralised the third spun around and realising he was at a disadvantage took flight.

I went to the aid of the Canadian and was alarmed at the damage that had been made to his face in what I considered a very short spell of time. I suppose with three boots pumping away, I should have expected the result.

I asked the gathered crowd if there was a medical facility in close proximity. I was directed along the road we were in, maybe six or seven blocks. My patient was very groggy, conscious, and in some pain. I placed my arm around his waist and helped him walk to the medical facility.

On arrival I handed him to the staff, declining to provide my details, saying I found him on the street.

As I had been in a position of doing rather well with a particular young lady, I hurried back to the party. On approaching the scene of the fight, I noticed the police were in attendance.

A plan formulated in my mind. I walked casually past the first policeman, with a cherry, *"Good evening Guv."*

He was an Inspector. He enquired where I was going and where I had come from.

*"I have just come off night shift, and I heard there was a party here, so I am going to join the party"*

*"Do you know anything about a fight here on the street?"*

*"Sorry I can't help you Sir, I have just woken up. I have not been in this place for weeks."*

*"Constable Jones. Take this man downstairs and let him have a good look in the mirror will you."*

*"Yes Sir."*

*"Come with me Sir,"*

I was escorted down the stairs, and there in the full-length mirror of my party host's flat, I saw my image. My face was covered in blood. The white wool collar was entirely red, and there was enough blood on the left jacket shoulder and surrounds for a reasonable blood transfusion.

I looked at the Constable and smiled.

I spent the remainder of the night in the Kensington Police station at her Majesties pleasure.

I never saw the young lady or the Canadian again.

$*$     $*$     $*$     $*$     $*$

*"Failure is not falling down.*
*It is not getting up again."*

*Mary Pickford.*

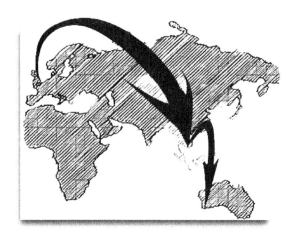

# THE LAND DOWN UNDER
## *Europe Adieu*

B y October 1969 my two friends had returned to Rhodesia for personal reasons. I decided it was time to move on. Destination Australia. I had tried to contact a few of the Aussies I had met, only one replied, an old flame from Earls Court. As they say on the road, a 'bird in the hand is worth two in the bush'. I flew on a very 'iffy' chartered airline.

My notes verify that I travelled to Southend by coach, caught a flight to Frankfurt - here my notes say simply 'no fuel', this is followed by 'Athens cancelled off flight schedule. Then 'first stop Bombay' then my notes read 'Bombay – Bangkok- Singapore' the next line reads 'Lions City Hotel, Queers, Whores, Change Alley and Aussies.'

It must have been an interesting flight to Singapore although I have no recollection of running out of fuel or missing Athens. The beer served was cold at least.

The Aussies, co-passengers on the flight, were young professional men; two lawyers, an engineer and I forget, all single, and desperate to find the wild life. I wondered what they did in England in their spare time, while getting their degrees.

Allow me to plagiarise some notes from Wikipedia, and then allow me to de-sanitise their report.

I quote: *"Infrastructure-wise, Change Alley was made up of small shops and makeshift tables, roving salesmen with their wooden boxes containing wares such as pens and watches. Improvised awning for the alley was created using zinc, plastic or canvas sheets that sometimes failed to prevent leaks on rainy days. Change Alley grew even narrower, congested and stuffy. Shopkeepers could speak phrases in various languages such as French, German, Italian and even Russian to conduct business. Money changes, most of whom were Indians, ran their businesses within their own shops. Bargaining and touting were key features of the alley. This created an atmospheric and unique place in modern Singapore that continued to be fondly remembered by locals."* Unquote.

Change Alley was all those things, plus hundreds of touters selling live sex shows in any configuration that took your fancy; girls of the night (and for those so inclined boys of the night) from a zillion different countries, all who offered the full spectrum of the Kama Sutra and more. The price of services rendered was 'bargained for', the later in the night the cheaper the same service. Drugs in many forms from chewing gum to biscuits, loose to compacted grass, LSD tablets, liquid, and blotting paper, free mystery rides, which in a worst case scenario could get you a one way ticket to the big man in the sky with a white beard, and best case scenario a visit to the police station reporting, certainly, the loss of every asset you had at the beginning of the evening and other possible hurts and injuries. Plus delicious, cheap street food, cold beer and a great lot of fun, as long as you kept your wits about you and were quick on your feet.

I spent some time, on and off, in Singapore in the mid 1990's on business and once asked a taxi driver to take me down 'memory lane'. Change Alley was a modern shopping plaza surrounded by two enormous skyscrapers - it was sterile, characterless, humdrum and monotonous - even the busker cleaning shoes resembled a resident of the local mortuary. The same went for the very famous 'Long Bar' located in the famous hotel, 'Raffles'- in times gone by a rough and tumble bar where you could get motherless on Singapore Sling's, while discarding nut shells on the floor. My revisit saw a politically correct, money hungry establishment with as much appeal as a pair of pork chops on a synagogue step.

My plane landed in Perth, Australia. I approached the Immigration booth and handed over my passport. He gave me one of those looks of total despair.

*"Morning,"* he said, I noted the absence of the 'good' bit, *"How long do you intend to stay?"*

*"I have no idea, depends on what I find."*

*"What assets do you have?"*

*"Nothing, not much, just what you can see."*

*"How much money do you have, mate?"*

I did not know then 'mate' could be used in a variety of connotations. I thought he was being friendly. I took my wallet out of my back pocket opened it and luckily I had had the forethought to change currency on the plane.

*"I have $12.50!!"*

*"Well, in your bank account?"*

*"I do not have a bank account."*

*"Is that all you have?"*

*"Well no I have a copy of the Rubaiyat and Poems by Robert Service. Plus a change of clothes."*

*"Do you have a TB Certificate?"*

*"No Sir. No I don't have that."*

*"I shall give you an entry permit for seven days, you are required to present such a certificate to an Immigration Officer within that period or you will be deported."* (I still have the restricted entry in one of my passports).

*"Thank you,"* I said. I accepted my passport and walked into a brand new adventure.

There, waiting at the arrivals, was my old friend, she looked more beautiful than ever. A big hug and kiss!

*"Have you got some carpet space where I can sleep?"*

*"Sure I have a room for you at my parent's house!!"*

*"That could be tricky. What do they know about me? You know, I mean you and me, in England."*

*"I told them we were lovers."*

*"How did that go down?'*

*"Like a lead balloon. Mum was not impressed and Dad just said I hope he is a clean cut, cultured type of bloke, not one of those bums."*

She drove us towards one of the exclusive inner suburbs of the city.

Oh dear, oh dear!! What in heaven's name was going to happen next?

*     *     *     *     *

### The Elephants Final Walk

*There is a far place unknown to man*
*Beneath shaded canopies of tall acacia trees,*
*Standing silent sentinel on mud greased banks*
*Congealed in fetid weed and reed,*
*Where these great beasts walk their last mile*
*While above the vultures ominously fly,*
*Hovering, patiently in the sky,*
*Casting their wheeling shadows over the backs*
*Of the slowly parting great grey beats,*
*Awaiting the Elephants Final Walk*

**Susan Cook-Jahme**

# GETTING STARTED
# IN THE LUCKY COUNTRY
## *Australia*

For those who may not be familiar with Australian '*strine*', the Black Stump is a fictional 'marker', so 'beyond the black stump' is beyond civilisation, deep in the outback, whereas something that is 'this side of the black stump' belongs to the known world. A 'sheila' that 'doesn't scrub up too bad', is a 'good looking woman'.

It was with some trepidation I travelled towards my former belle's parents' house. Her father was hoping for a clean cut, cultured man – not a bum. I was hardly likely to fill that bill. I had just spent three days on the turps in Change Alley. My anorak had not been cleaned 'ever' and smelt as though it had been awash in the cheap perfumes of a million ladies of the night. My tattered jeans were much the same. I had not shaved in a while.

If I were to describe my appearance I doubt that dapper, suave, debonair or well-groomed would be applicable. My hairline had been receding for some years and the fact that I had not had a haircut in over a year also tended to fly in the face of 'father's expectations. The fact that mother was 'not amused' was a quandary. I mean I was not taking out their daughter, nor asking for her hand in marriage.

We travelled through tree-lined streets with well-tended gardens. The vehicles parked outside suggested well-heeled residents. My guess was, they would be ultra conservative, middle to upper class, professional, university educated men with wives who played bridge and had very discreet affairs.

She opened the front door, *"Come in, Mum, Dad, this is Doug."*

There was an awkward moment, just fleeting, but obvious, when their eyes looked me up and down. Their faces revealed receipt of conflicting messages from their brains. There was a pregnant pause – father proffered his hand.

I said, *"How do you do, Sir,"* in my best take off of an Eton accent, *"I am so pleased to make your acquaintance."*

With a look of alarm and despondency he replied, *"Struth, Gloria he's a bloody Pom."*

Mother extend her hand, a smile crossed her face. I made sure I did not    grip her hand too hard and looking her bang in the eye I said, *"How exciting to be here."*

*"Yes"* she answered, *"You are not exactly what we expected!"*

That was a bit of a conversation dampener.

*"Come in,"* father invited, *"We have a room for you, you may stay until you get your own digs, follow me. Not hard to find board and lodging in the city. What you do for a crust mate?"*

*"Anything that pays, Sir."*

We walked to the end of a corridor and into an enclosed veranda area. He pushed open a door that revealed a very comfortable room with a bed and a wardrobe, a side table, and a window overlooking manicured lawns.  I dropped my rucksack on the floor.

*"Now, mate, we are going to have to educate you a bit. We don't like this 'Sir' stuff in Australia. My name is Norm. Now if you want to get work you are going to have to work on that 'poofta' accent of yours. Aussies don't like people who are up themselves, there is no class distinction here mate."*

Referring to his daughter, he said, *"She is pretty sweet on a young lad now. She said you were very good to her in London so we were only too pleased to return the good will. I'll show you the rest of the house. Once you have had a shower we will knock the top off a tinny and see what we can do for you."*

*"Thank you. Sir Norm."*

Back in the bedroom I sat on the bed and thought, well it could have been a lot worse. Forgetting the door was ajar I stripped off my clothes and tied a towel round my waist. I became aware of the presence of someone else. I looked at the door and leaning in the frame, was my former 'belle'.

*"Still in fairly good nick I see Stanyon. We might have to see if the performance standards are still the same!!"*

*Oh Dear, Oh Dear.* The following morning after a good nights' sleep I was grateful to find that all my clothes had been washed and ironed. My poetry books neatly stacked on the bedside table. I walked into the dining area, and joined the family for breakfast. There was a younger sister.

I thanked 'mother' for doing my washing and ironing.

Shirley, my former belle, interrupted saying, *"I did that for you Doug,"* and then with a knowing wink and a smile, she said, *"You will be receiving the invoice shortly."*

I ascertained the bus timetable and the address in the city to alight. I also established where I could get a TB x-ray and the location of the Immigration Offices and most important of all, the address of an employment agency catering for 'labourers'. I managed to satisfy the Immigration Department and as I was travelling on a British Passport I received permanent residency. Strangely, in those days, that allowed me automatic access to the 'Dole'. My principles never allowed me to use the social security service, then or in the last 38 years of my time in Australia. In Rhodesia those facilities did not exist, I never utilised them in my travels or since.

On my first morning I also managed to secure a job as a builders labourer on the first high rise, commercial block in Perth (there are now numerous – I see the one I worked on is still standing, which as you will read is surprising.)

I did have one problem, minor as it may have been, and that was a fiscal issue. I had arrived in Australia with a total asset value of $12.50. The x-ray had cost me $7.80, various bus rides dwindled my financial stocks by 80 cents and a packet of the most cheap and nasty cigarettes on the market (while I did not think it achievable, Australia had been able to manufacture a cigarette that made STAR from back home, feel like a luxury item) and a box of matches had caused a major financial bleed.

All this high finance dealings had left me with a worldly asset valuation of less than $3.00. Although I cannot recall the day of the week, I remember it was at the start of the week, which meant payday, always on a Thursday, was a financial eternity away. I would only get a few days' pay, but at least I was on the starter's blocks.

When one moves by roads less travelled, tumult and trouble are a companion that never leave your side.

On payday I offered to pay what I could towards my board and lodge. Thankfully this had been kindly declined, so with limited assets, I sat 'at home' on Friday night and watched the local television.

I established that 'father' visited the 'boozer' on the way home on Friday nights and habitually got home late and, most times, in a state of disrepair. I thanked 'mother' and retired for the night. I dozed off well pleased with my efforts. I had not informed anyone, but I had a tentative offer of board and lodge with a fellow worker, which I intended to accept.

I was awoken by someone getting into my bed. It was my 'belle' of old. She said she had brought the invoice and expected immediate settlement. Now I ask you, what should a man do? I hated being in debt for any longer than absolutely necessary. I wanted to maintain my credit rating as high as possible.

Well, well, well, clothes washed and ironed, employed, roof over the head, food in the tummy and debt free. It just does not get much better than this!!!

\*      \*      \*      \*      \*

*It doesn't matter*
*If you come first or last.*
*All that matters is that you,*
*Finished the race!*

# A SHORT WORKING INITIATION
# BEFORE GOING
# BEYOND THE BLACK STUMP

*Urban Work and Into the Australian Desert*

I told Shirley I would move out on payday. She was not enamoured with my plan and requested I stay a few more weeks. We approached her parents, who were not really warmed by the idea. They reluctantly agreed, and thankfully still refused to accept payment for board and lodge.

Labouring on a building construction site, as some will know, is just hard, physical 'yakka'. Like most labouring jobs, I found it more challenging from a mental perspective than physical, the monotony of the repetitious cycle of activity, the total absence of the need to use any initiative.

I do recall one task on the high rise I was given – it was the reading of the 'plumb bob'. To ensure the building went up totally perpendicular there were a variety of measurements taken, the plumb bob was one. The 'bob' would be lowered from a position many meters above. A pre-inscribed blue cross was painted on the concrete floor. I was always issued with, what they termed, the 'silly' or 'dumb' end that was at the bottom. The instrument was a heavy brass semi-cylindrical moulding with a fine point at one end and a ring on the other, to which the string was attached. The chap on the 'clever end' would adjust the string along a fixed piece of timber. When the fine point matched the exact point where the crossed lines intersected I would shout something and the string would be secured at that point. Theoretically we now had a perfectly perpendicular line from which all manner of building measurements were recorded.

There would be any number of these same procedures occurring all over the site. I found the wind played a significant factor in hampering total accuracy. It was the prime impediment to my achieving total accuracy. I was aware the chap on the 'clever end' was becoming frustrated with my efforts. I told him on numerous occasions I was not in control of the wind and unless he could communicate with the foreman in the sky he was just going to have to hang on a bit.

Lesson one – building a high rise Australian style.

I was down on my bended knees, eyes as close to the ground as possible, intricately touching the string to counter the wind movement steadying the 'bob'. *"Nearly there … left … left just a touch…. no right a little …. hold it … just wait … no left … a little more … just a tad … no, no … too far."*

Then this voice, in that slow laconic Australian drawl said, *"What the f\*\*k do you think you are doing mate?"*

I gazed up, and there was the dreaded foreman. He was as close to God in this industry as was possible. The right to hire, fire, strike and corrupt.

*"Making sure the plumb bob sits right on the intersection, like I was told."*

*"For f\*\*k's sake mate, this f\*\*king building is going up forty-five stories. Close enough is good enough, if she's a couple feet off centre when she gets to the top who the f\*\*k is going to care. Pull your finger out or get the 'pinkie'."* To translate - hurry up or leave the job.

As I said, she is still standing, and no she is not exactly perpendicular and yes that's right nobody did or will ever care. I understood the rules.

Once I was flush with cash I joined my new found mates at the boozer after work. I had a fair bit of experience in beer drinking back home and in England so I felt comfortable there would be little they could teach me. On entry to the 'boozer' the conversation went something like this:

*"I'll shout ya mate, whatalyaav?"*

*"Just a beer thanks."*

Turning to his mates he said, *"We've got a right f\*\*king clown 'ere. This is the boozer mate that's what they sell – what kinda beer?"*

*"I am not sure!"*

*"Do you want a Swan, VB, Tooheys Old, Tooheys New, Pilsner, Fosters, Four X, Coopers, etc. etc.,"*

*"Thanks just a lager."*

*"Just a regular comic, hey mate, we ain't got all f\*\*king night. What size?"*

*"I am not sure."*

*"Get a load of this p\*\*\*k. Now mate, will she be a pint, schooner, pot, middy, seven, pony or Shetland?"*

*"Are you pulling my leg?"*

*"What a f\*\*king d\*\*k head just given him a POT."*

Turning to his mate he said, *"She's a bloody bottler mate, I have been flat out like a lizard drinking."*

They were good lads I just needed to learn their language. And I thought they spoke English in Australia.

As for Shirley after a few weeks our dalliances had become more frequent and more intense, my belle was no longer sweet on anyone but me. I too found her company, in the new country, comforting and her circle of friends entertaining, generous and fun to be around. The wild ways of London/Europe in the swinging sixties were now a thing of the past. At times our discussions encompassed settling down, getting a place of our own - a love nest overlooking the beach with long walks on the beach at sunset, sipping cold Vodka lime and lemonade and picking up sea shells. I was doing fine with 'the oldies' but my movements were restricted, through my respect for their generosity.

I had only been eighteen months on the road but it had been hard, sleeping under bridges, in parks and derelict houses, eating once a day if you were financial and the food sometimes just palatable and working mindless jobs. The love nest was more than appealing. Maybe this was the end of the road. Maybe this was the country better than Rhodesia.

I took on a second job as a barman at the University of Western Australia to increase my income. It was night work.

I had once held a job as a food waiter in a seaside Butlins Holiday Camp in Bognor Regis, in England. Promised by the employment agency there would be an overabundance of available 'skirt' I had reluctantly taken the position. My mate Graham Hardy also worked there as a barman. It was apparently an annual, English holiday getaway for the less affluent. From the moment a holidaymaker arrived everything and I mean everything, other than your personal visit to the 'toilet' was pre-ordained, organised, controlled and announced verbally and in writing on a variety of signboards.

There were people running around convincing you that you were having a great time.

There were loudspeakers announcing and encouraging 'exciting activities you may wish to participate in,' the place was very popular.

One phenomenon was that they employed people to mingle with the holidaymakers encouraging them to enjoy themselves. *This is fantastic! Aren't we having a wonderful time, oh well-done on winning the boat race/ bingo or egg and spoon race!* I called it the 'no think holiday'. From a food waiter's point of view my work was simple and un-taxing. The  culinary choice was a set menu, restricted to three course meals; entrees - usually a soup, mains - a stew and veg, or roast and veg and always their beloved fish and chips, finally sweets – jelly and ice cream or strawberries and cream. Followed by tea/coffee. Next sitting please. One had no choice, if you did not like something on your plate, it was served, and you just did not eat it.

Hence my getting the job, without experience was easy. Here's a tray full of food plates, drop them on any tables where they have not been served, now go around and hassle them to finish, as the next sitting is due, pick up as many empty plates at once as you can, and roll out the sweets. None of that; *"did you enjoy that madam?"* It was just hurry please, next sitting coming in.

I met one of those people who thought the world owed them a living. A man who always complained, nothing was ever right. *I know my rights; I do not have to, I shall be speaking to, go and get, my soups cold, her soups cold, the ice cream has melted.*

One evening, I had had as much of him as I could take and when he started again I lost the plot. I told him his fortune, and threatened to do no end of injury to him.

That was the final night of my 'food waitering' career – I was fired and marched off the premises. The overabundance of skirt had failed to materialise. I took the train back to London.

Sorry, where was I - In the bar at the University in Perth. I did eight hours on the construction site, terminating at 1500 Hours, bussed it back to have a shower and change into some decent clothes, which had been chosen for me. Now that was a worry, I should have seen something developing from that move. Then I worked from 1800 to 'close and clean' at about 2300.

I managed to get Sundays off on both jobs – I think the new age people call that 'us' or 'me' time.

Christmas came and went and talk turned to marriage – I am not too sure what happened, how that came about as I never actually approached Sir Norm and officially ask for her hand in marriage, it appeared, through general family conversations, the plans were laid bare.

I was having a 'jug' with Sir Norm at his boozer one Friday evening when he ambushed me from left field. *"You and Shirley are going to marry?"*

I was not sure whether that was a question, command or a vague drifting statement of supposed fact. I concurred but said nothing had been set in concrete. He asked how we would manage with obviously limited funds. Sir Norm was on the staff at Head Office of a very large American construction company with the contract to build one of the largest dams in Western Australia. The site was 3214 kms by road or 2223 kms by air from Perth. Norm suggested he could get me a job there, and I could save a lot of money in a short amount of time.

Working 'beyond the Black Stump' had started in South Australia in the early 1950's. Literally thousands of men were hired to live in 'camps', 'beyond the black stump', 12 hour days, 14 days straight, one day off and repeat. Wages, far in excess of 'the norm' were paid with lucrative tax concessions available to those who chose so to work, plus free board and lodge. Rumour had it that people set themselves up for life when so employed.

Although strong objections from my 'belle' were aired, it struck me as a positive step in the right direction. I had a car, on hire purchase, which was a financial burden, which would be paid off a lot sooner.

There were farewell tears and promises to write every day.

*"I will wait for you for ever my darling, Stay safe. I love you. I am going to miss you so much."*

I was soon on my way on a company paid internal flight.

Once again on my own, oblivious to the fact I was heading for the 'Bad Lands', still in pursuit of that elusive 'degree'. I was about to attend some far-reaching lectures and lessons.

\*      \*      \*      \*      \*

*And, as the Cock crew, those who stood before*
*The Tavern shouted –'' Open then the Door!*
*You know how little while we have to stay,*
*And, once departed, may return no more."*

**The Rubaiyat**

# THE ORD RIVER DAM SCHEME
# WESTERN AUSTRALIA

*The Camp Environment*

I t is not the middle of the desert, with mile high sand dunes, but more what the Aussies describe as 'the scrub outback'. In those days it was certainly 'beyond the black stump'.

With hindsight, I am surprised there was not more violence than there was. In my time no really serious crimes were committed, lots of fights - which was to be expected when the majority of the workers were young testosterone fuelled men with few outlets in that regard. There was any number of people evading 'the law' from all States for violations ranging from failure to pay maintenance to who knows, most probably the full gambit of human crime. An ever-present 'instant fuse' was the newly arrived immigrants (one a Rhodesian) from countries like Yugoslavia and the Balkans, Poland and Ireland amongst others.

Their upbringing standards and codes of conduct in 'personnel compatibility' differed enormously from 'western civilization' standards. Their means of dispute resolution did not involve any form of 'arbitration'. Immediate violence was customary, fists, knives, bottles, iron rods, whatever may have been handy at the time and place of dispute. People generally only mixed, socially, with their own communities.

Social life encompassed a weekly film, the bar, which closed around 9.00pm and private games of cards and other gambling activities. There were of course the 'mobile brothels', some arrived with vehicles well-appointed for their trade, while others hired out worker's rooms for the duration. *"Tut-tut"* go the bed wetters and hand wringers.

The world's oldest profession will always thrive as long as men are men and willing to pay for *'femme de la nuit'*. While I have never personally availed myself, I have heard convincing argument to do so.

The quality of food was nothing less than extraordinary. One could literally eat as much, of whatever was on offer, as they liked. There were always multiple choices of meals, hot and cold, three times a day. It was well presented and cooked by quality chefs.

Ablution facilities and general cleanliness was of a high standard, they were not short on any home comforts. I felt they were on a par with any District Station facility, so I was right at home.

A mobile bank was available on payday for you to 'do your banking', no EFT or ATM's of course. Most of us had 'bank books' that recorded deposits and withdrawals, better than having it under the pillow and susceptible to possible theft while you toiled on 'the dam'.

Two men shared a room, eight feet wide by ten foot long. A small cupboard was situated at the bed end. Your clothes were washed and ironed.

Over time 'roomies' fell out and had to be separated. I was fortunate I bunked with an old Russian chap, not too many Russians or Rhodesians in the camp! He could speak a little English, but could not read or write the language. I used to read his daughters letters to him every week, I am not sure if he had a wife. He was clean and quiet, more than I could say for many others. I spent the evenings mostly writing to my 'belle' and reading poetry and autobiographies. I also enrolled in a correspondence course on Art trying, vainly, to find the talent that came naturally to my father. I failed.

I thought it might be interesting to understand the basis on which about 1,700 men and less than 40 women existed 'in the camp – beyond the black stump'. I am guessing there were a few raised eyebrows about the disproportionate numbers. Some married couples arranged to get work together, few survived, either they separated or returned to the big smoke, with broken dreams. Some ladies brought their own partners of a 'similar sex'', the consequence, disappointment suffered by the men who made an early advance (referred quaintly in Aussie as 'putting the hard word on her') when informed of the state of play. They survived but suffered limited social life. Other ladies were 'desperate' to find a man.

Presumably unsuccessful in 'the big smoke' for whatever reason, they believed there would be a huge variety of choice and eventually would end up with a charming prince or the man of their dreams – my observations were they usually ended up in tears, having been promised the earth and all that was in it but ending up having to pick up the pieces after being lied to and used by 'ne'er-do-wells' with which the camp was littered.

The most successful ladies were those whose personalities earned the respect of the men - they were there to do their job, make good money and get out as soon as possible, just like the intentions of 99% of the men and nothing else, they made it. Good luck to them.

The dam would eventually be 200 miles in length covering 741 square kilometres. It would provide hydroelectricity for the local region and irrigations for vast tracks of land for agriculture.

As I have mentioned, as a fatalist, globetrotters have 'tumult' and 'strife' as constant companions. Norm, bless him, got me a job requiring 'no skills' as a steel fixer. For those unfamiliar, your only tool, a pair of "steel nippers" rather like pliers, but with bladed ends. Your only requirement, the tying of two pieces of reinforced steel rods together. There was only one way this was done; it was called the 'saddle knot', simply threading a single piece of wire in a certain pattern, twisting the ends together and 'snipping off'. Job description and requirement completed. Brain surgeons and rocket scientists need not apply.

I spent a week in the Perth warehouse before departure. I laboured, and came across my first obstacle. It would remain with me, for the duration in the Ord Camp. Unknown to me the steel fixer ganger (rather like an SO without any brains at all) was also there. My fate was sealed when he saw the boss's daughter picking me up and dropping me off to and from work with a 'tender kiss' each day. He smelt a rat, which was fine, except for one thing - he was a poorly educated Irishman, taller than I, about six feet six inches, he had this strange posture and gait, not dissimilar to an ape walking on its hind legs and his hands were the size of hams.

When we shook initially on introduction I thought I had placed my hand in a vice, I swear my index and small finger knuckles briefly touched, there was a sound like crushed dried grass. He had this wild look in his eyes, pale blue, penetrating and dismembering, of hate and contempt. He had this large ripe pimple/boil behind his left ear, which remained so for weeks. I also noticed the dirt behind that ear, increased daily, a clear sign of a lack of hygiene.

His body reeked, the hotter the more pronounced. His fingers were akin to miniature salami rolls. His knuckles just about dragged along the floor, with this odd gait and he kind of grunted when he spoke. His accent was very pronounced and difficult to comprehend, he was my direct boss. I just had this feeling 'in my water' the future was not going to be a walk in the park.

I became very adept at tying 'saddles', recognising deformed from normal steel, and identifying the different circumferences of reinforced steel bar, I actually picked up a bit of the 'lingo'. I feared, though, my fate was sealed, for 'Paddy' was going to spread the word of this Head Office stooge and unqualified worker who had snuck in through the back door taking work from paid up union members, most probably best described as a 'scab'. I was living in interesting times. I conjured up a fall back plan if Paddy got too heavy. I am pleased to report I never had to use it. It consisted of a lighting quick strike and a fast exit, I knew if it did not work the consequences would be a painful and ugly confinement in an outback hospital somewhere.

On landing at Kununurra I was transported by bus to the camp, allocated a room with my Russian 'roomie' and told where the 'tucker' could be found, where the boozer was and where and when to catch the bus each morning to work. Few people came up and proffered a friendly hand of introduction. They walked past, a slight nod of the head with a mumbled "*g'day*". I noticed some very mean and ugly looking people, most of them in exceptional physical condition. Unlikely to find many 'pen pushers' and 'desk jockeys' amongst this lot I thought.

I lay on my 'pit' and found solace with Robert Service – I flipped through the well-worn pages, *"The Land of Beyond," "The Ballad of Blasphemous Bill", "Athabasca Dick,"*

Ah! And one of my favourites:

## THE QUITTER

*It's easy to cry that you're beaten — and die;*
*It's easy to crawfish and crawl;*
*But to fight and to fight when hope's out of sight —*
*Why that's the best game of them all!*
*And though you come out of each gruelling bout,*
*All broken and battered and scarred,*
*Just have one more try — it's dead easy to die,*
*It's the keeping-on-living that's hard.*

\*　　　\*　　　\*　　　\*　　　\*

*Life is a onetime offer,*
*Use it well!*

## BEANS, AN IRISH CRANE DRIVER
## AND AMERICAN LABOUR JUSTICE

During my first supper (Tea to the Aussies) I heard much talk suggesting we were in the 'vanguard' of the project. That was proven false, the following morning. I was initially confused by the lack of any water whatsoever. Surely a river had to be present to be 'dammed'! It transpires the Ord River had been diverted some years previous. My second observation were two very large tunnels had been drilled through the middle of a large hill, the tunnels would have been 20 feet in diameter and it turned out they were 1200 feet in length. In between the front and rear of the tunnels was a 45-degree drop, the height of that drop, about 15 feet. I was to have a very painful, life threatening experience involving the 'elbow' as it was quaintly referred to.

I observed bulldozers moving earth, nothing significant in that, but here they advanced on the dirt, in line abreast, blade to blade, 12 machines across. Very large trucks were being loaded with dirt by very large excavators. The wheels of the trucks were double the height of a normal human being.

What was not known to me on that first morning was that I, along with my 'steel fixer mates', would be bending the steel ribs and then fitting them inside the two tunnels. These ribs were solid steel, arriving on site in straight sections 23 feet in length and six inches in diameter. It was our task to bend them into perfect 180-degree shapes (semi circles), by the use of our 'legs'.

Our labour would be used to erect the reinforcing steel bars for the two 'water gates' that would control the water intake into the tunnels, which would be 185 feet high structures and some 50 feet wide.

I was quick to learn during my tenure the average daily temperature would exceed 105 degrees Celsius, nights just a 'tad' cooler.

'Paddy' put us to work without ceremony. A crane delivered the straight sections of steel for the tunnels, we were handed a foot pump and the workplace was a section of recently bulldozed land, in the middle of nowhere. We had to measure and draw a chalk line on the round bars and then by placing a 'clamp' type fitting on the end of this hydraulic pump, we took it in turns, using our legs, to exert the necessary force to slowly bend the steel.

Within a few seconds we became aware we were in the company of 'the scrub locals', extraordinary friendly and thirsty little creatures called flies. They were fat, large, lazy and very tenacious characters. They lay in ambush for you as you alighted from the 'bus' each morning and accompanied you on the bus back to camp each evening. Between dawn and dusk they were your constant companions. If a man stood still long enough the back of his shirt - some did not bother wearing shirts - became infested, in fact so infested that the flies covered the back completely so the garment or his skin on his back was invisible.

We invented a game that required a man to bend at the waist and remain still. Hordes of flies would immediately land. Another man would swipe the open palm of his hand across the top of the person's back and then with his other hand, as quickly as possible clap his two hands together. A small black cloud would rise. The man who had the highest number of dead flies on his palm was the winner. How many, you ask? The figure of 25 rings a bell.

We would soon meet the American steel boss. We observed a very large American sedan (one of those vehicles, when you buy them, you order it by the 'yard'). The ground we were working on would eventually be the bottom of the Dam so his approach was visible for at least a mile, dust rising high into the air, the pace of the vehicle very slow. He pulled up next to our location, his window lowered automatically and the cool air from his air condition was a pleasant, if only a fleeting relief.

He was a large man, his safety helmet sat snuggly on his head. The right arm flopped onto the open window ledge. A large diamond glittered from what I supposed was a gold ring on his right ring finger.

No introduction was made, his first words were *"You men need anything?"*

*"No,"* was the unified answer.

*"Put some more mother \*\*king beans into the work, we ain't got all day".*

With that he pushed the automatic window button, and slowly accelerated away. Within days the Aussies had nick named him 'Beans'. To the best of my memory his words to us over the next few months remained much the same, *"put some more beans into that".* The only digressions were the expletives and I must say he had an extensive repertoire, many of them quiet colourful, covering the limitless spectrum of politics, race, religion, sex and social incorrectness.

We were to soon meet another 'larger than life character'. He arrived one day driving an extraordinary large mobile crane. He was another Irishman. Now if I thought Paddy was 'big' then I was on a steep learning curve. Big Joe was just that – the largest man I ever met. He had to stand six foot nine maybe 10 inches. His shoulders were two pick axe handles across. His neck started about an inch below his ear lobes, and went directly to the edge of his shoulders. I estimate his thighs were the same size of an average man's chest, his calves, probably a tad smaller than my thighs. His biceps had to be 25 inches around. There was not an iota of fat on him.

I was fairly close to where he stopped his rig, and I noticed he extended his rig legs out. For those who may not be familiar, the crane has four legs to stabilise it when lifting. It carries a foot for each leg.

As he was clambering off the rig, he said to me, *"Give me a hand mate, put the feet on."*

Thankfully, I had been on sites prior and knew what he was talking about. He walked towards the closest leg, so I darted around the opposite side of the crane. I found the foot on its rack. It had a steel bar on either side of the top, the shape of a pyramid so it could be carried with two hands. I lifted it off the rack with both hands, it was that heavy I could not keep it in the air. It fell to the ground. Then using my leg and back muscles along with both arms I lifted it up and staggered towards the leg. Joe appeared, I tried to give him one of those, 'she'll be right mate' smiles but by this time the foot was hanging between my knees, and progress was less than swift and problematic.

*"F\*\*k me,"* he said, *"Where do they find these "f\*\*king" wimps? Put it down."*

It was just about there anyway, so I thankfully dropped it.

With his left hand he wrapped it round one handle, walked on to the next rack, picked the next foot up with his right, then walked back and dropped both feet in position.

I have no idea of their weight, but they looked like small toys in his hands. I was astonished by the man's strength.

I became friendly with another Irishman, also employed as a steel fixer who arrived in Australia after working in Nome, Alaska, where he had been employed underground in the mining industry. He claimed the only time they stopped work was when the temperature dipped to 40 degrees below. He was ex-British Army and in exceptional physical condition. About six foot tall and as strong as an ox. A man with a ready smile he drank like a fish, and when he was drunk (more nights than not) he burst into song, his favourite was 'The Wild Colonial Boy'.

Though I chose not to drink, I was saving up for 'the big day' and my future as a 'married man' I did patronize the bar on some occasions. Initially I received abuse and was derided for drinking non-alcoholic beverages. *"He's a bloody queer bloke, don't drink none, reads f\*\*king" poems and draws pictures."*

It had caused some unpleasant scenes, which had resulted in 'stepping outside' to resolve our differences. Thankfully the really 'big boys' were never involved. I had a fair amount of experience in 'dispute resolution' of this kind and frankly my thoughts are there are never any winners. One thing I did experience in the Ord was being sober when 'resolving' an issue. With someone who is drunk the sober chap has an enormous advantage. So thankfully, after a few such 'determinations' I was left alone.

I also initially received some criticism for being a Head Office stooge and 'rooting the boss's daughter' but with time and a few 'dispute resolution exercises, thankfully, it faded away.

Within a few weeks of our arrival the bulldozer drivers and management got into some dispute over working conditions. Australian Head Office people were sent to arbitrate and failed. Work stopped, not for any others just the dozer boys. I was walking out of the canteen one morning when 'Beans' called me.

*"Can you drive?"*

*"Yes sure I can."*

*"Well then drive me to the airstrip."*

Quite why I was chosen I shall never know. A small charter plane landed and out stepped what I thought was a Hollywood extra.

Tall, thin man, with jeans and long, leather cowboy boots (carved), a decorated shirt and a string tie, with a large black ball around the neck and 'yes Sir' a white Stetson 44 gallon hat. I could not hear their greetings as they walked over and both got in the back.

In a most amplified southern drawl I heard the visitor say to 'Beans', *"Now we have a small labour problem the Aussie can't fix."*

*"Yes the dozer boys won't agree with our offer."*

*"Well, how to we deal with these Aust-tral-ians?"*

*"Just like the niggers back home man, just like the niggers."*

The discussion turned to domestic issues and company gossip. I dropped them off at the office and got a lift down to the bottom of the dam. That night a chartered plane arrived and removed twenty bulldozer drivers, and returned the following morning with their replacements.

Whether this would be achieved under today's industrial relations climate I am not sure.

\*       \*       \*       \*       \*

## PERFUMED LOVE LETTERS,
## IMPALEMENT AND HOSPITALISATION

I have no recollection of how many ribs can be fitted in a 1,200 feet tunnel. I felt like I went to the gym each morning, and stayed there the whole day. I swear blind my thighs were increasing in size daily. 'Paddy's' boss was a small, short, thin little Czechoslovakian, whose boots always seemed bigger than his body, I always envisaged him sliding down into them and disappearing. The 'rib bending pump' frequently broke down and replacements were flown in from Sydney or Melbourne. The Czech and our team were standing around waiting for a new pump to arrive from the local 'stores department' on site when 'Beans' chose that exact time to drop by on his usual patrol.

Same routine, the window rolls smoothly down, the arm flips out, the diamond sparkles and, *"Do you men need anything?"*

Somebody explained, *"the pump was f\*\*ked again"*.

'Beans' addressed the Czech, *"Where are you getting the replacement pumps from?"*

The answer: *"Sydney."*

*"Well I want you to get the best c\*\*k sucking pump in the world, and now,"* with which the window went up and 'Beans' slowly meandered across the dam floor in his air-conditioned comfort. The long and short of it was 'Beans' found us, a few days later in exactly the same state, strangely again with the Czech 'foreman'.

The pump was f\*\*\*\*d again.

*"What is the name of that f********g pump?"*

A steel fixer picked it up and showed 'Beans'.

There was a slight silence.

He pointed at the Czech, *"I told you to get the best pump in the world. This is the same old Australian crap – take this back to the storeroom, pack your belongings and get on tonight's flight out, you are "no f**king use to me, or the project."*

A pump was flown in from the USA - it never broke down in my time. Most of us found the site helmets uncomfortable and very hot, causing sweat to run into our eyes thus attracting the flies. This generally pissed everyone off. The flies had a distinct similarity to the Mopani Budgies we were all too familiar with in the Rhodesian *'gungen.'* Out in the open, it was not compulsory to wear helmets. The Aussies claimed it was good fortune not to do so, allowing an opportunity for the 'Blue Bird of Happiness' to defecate on your head. I do not recall a direct hit or even a near miss but then the Devil makes work for idle minds.

On the domestic front everything was running smoothly, just like clockwork. I was saving over $100 a week – and paying off the car as well. It may not seem much, but as a labourer in Perth, my take home pay was about $50 a week. Daily I received an envelope, sealed with the letters S.W.A.N.K, and a large, deep red lipstick kiss mark. On opening the letter, the pages were drenched in perfume. She had sent a photographic portrait of herself, mounted in a white frame, expressing her undying love and desire. She discussed her plans for the two of us - most romantic and uplifting - doing my battered 'ego' a power of good.

I was transferred to work in the tunnels. Now, this was interesting work, only from the viewpoint that blind Freddy could see it was littered with gins, traps and a multitude of ambushes, hidden from the view of the unwary and amateur players. Safety harnesses were not issued. Steel capped boots and helmets were compulsory.

We fixed small iron rods into the sides of the tunnel to hold the ribs in place until such times as the concrete was poured. The roof was always the scariest part. We used some insecure, wobbly, tubular steel scaffolding, fitted with wheels, which obviously did not work on the rough, dynamited floors. One had to stand, legs astride on a piece of plywood. This was reasonably secure until someone on the rig moved and then your balance was thrown.

Once there were iron rods to secure the ribs on, that is what we did. Once the two bent ribs had been welded together forming a perfect circle, the crane would slowly manoeuvre the ribs, hold them in place and we would secure them with the 'saddle knot'. Not a lot of grey matter needed in this job.

Once the ribs were in place the 'carpenters' would erect the framework, leaving holes here and there. Then the concreters would take over and pump concrete in through the holes at high pressure. Sometimes unseen, 'Beans' could be heard urging you on in his amenable fashion. The 20 feet diameter holes were reduced to 14 feet 5 inches in diameter.

We had finished the concreting of the first leg of the first tunnel. We were now preparing 'the elbow'. Ladders were position on the lower level, which allowed movement between the two levels. As the photo shows, there is any amount of equipment on the floor, electrical cables running everywhere to provide light to work in and not only are there a lot of human beings, but everything was done in a hurry, always 'more beans'.

On the lower level steel fixers were using oxy-acetylene torches to cut steel bars to appropriate lengths. These bars were only quarter inch in diameter, cut to a sharp point and resembled lines of arrows pointing upwards.

To this day I have no idea what caused the next scenario.

Somebody started shouting, *"She's going to blow."*

Followed by others screaming, *"Get the "f**k out of here."*

Panic set in and people started to run out of the tunnel at both ends. I could smell rubber burning, but could not see the source. I turned to run and two men ran past me in panic, knocking me off the top level. I fell feet first. When I landed I felt this sickening pain in my left leg. I felt weak.

*The hydro tunnel where the author was knocked down in the emergency exodus.*

I tried to move but I was stuck. The lower section of the tunnel was empty but for a few making exit through the end. There was a deathly silence. The lights were still shining. I looked down to examine my right leg. A steel bar entered the lower section of my leg just above the boot and came out below the knee. I had been impaled.

I heard screams, *"Put the fire out, if those bottles explode the mountain will come down!"*

It appeared I was the only one left to the mercy of the collapsing 'hill top' nearly a quarter of a kilometre underground. I just could not remove my leg. I was stuck hard and fast. There was nothing else to do, but wait for the explosion and the roof to cave in. I do recall thinking, Christ I hope I am killed instantly – I suffer from claustrophobia, and the thought of being buried alive was less than appealing.

I had obviously not killed enough Chinamen, because someone put the fire out, there was no explosion. When the first person came back in sight I asked for help. Someone examined my situation, and disappeared. Three or four men, stood around me, and attempted to lift my body off the stake. I passed out. When I came to I saw a couple of men swinging from a crane jib. They secured me, under my arms, with leather straps, and told me the crane was going to lift all of us up onto the top level.

The last I heard was, "OK Mate?"

I felt a lifting sensation and passed out again. I came to with medics bandaging the wound, I was stretchered off and an ambulance delivered me to the camp clinic.

I was lucky in more ways than one. There was only limited damage to the external part of the bone and some loss of blood. I was back at work within two days. No overtime pay if you are in sick bay, great incentive to get people back to work!!

One lesson I did learn - 'sissies' need not apply!

\*       \*       \*       \*       \*

*You have to learn the rules of the game.*
*And then you have to play*
*Better than anyone else.*
**Albert Einstein**

## THE IRISH FIST FIGHT
## DEAR JOHN & THE ALL BLACK BAR

O ne Saturday evening, with the following day a rostered day off, I thought I might change my company from Russian to whatever was in the melting pot. I took a stroll to the pub. As I walked across the empty outdoor cinema lot I heard the dulcet tones of an Irishman singing 'Wild Colonial Boy'.

I entered the bar, cigarette smoke revealing a resemblance to a smog filled day in an over populated Chinese city. I ordered a 'rock shandy' (not heard of in Aussie) and walked towards the crooner. There were the usual number of 'friendly' insults about the boss' daughter and whether I had lost the 'poems'. At the crooners table someone kindly kicked a spare chair towards me, an old Aussie fella by the name of 'Blucy'. (So nicknamed because he had red hair.)

*"Pull up a stump mate. Rays got the floor".*

How it happened - or why – is a mystery as Ray never spoke of it, but as Ray got up to get a beer a 'blue' (an argument) ensued at the bar. It was between the two Irishmen - Ray and Big Joe.

I, plus a few others moved in close to get a better position.

It was one of those usual drunken arguments that, to a sober person, made little if any sense. *"I said, you said, F\*\*k you, Get F\*\*ked, you'll get yours, you bloody wanker".*

Compared to Big Joe, Ray resembled a short man (he was six foot), it was a no contest, even as strong as Ray was, it was a no brainer.

Then Ray said the dumbest thing in his life, *"You wanna take this further? Step outside."*

Joe turned and walked to the door of the pub, on reaching it he turned and said, *"Everyone stay inside, if I find anyone outside when I have finished with this punk, I'll ......."*

Whatever the threat was it was sufficient to make everyone sit down and continue with their business.

Ray and Joe disappeared even known 'bookies' (the Aussies will gamble on anything) could not find any takers, whatever the odds they offered.

A few minutes passed after which Big Joe walked back into the pub. He made no comment, picked up his glass and drank on. Tom, Ray's friend and I went outside expecting to find a badly damaged friend. We saw Ray staggering towards the bunkhouse, his movements slow, his head lowered. Winners are grinners and losers can do what they like.

In the bunkhouse Ray lay on his bed. He described what had happened. On exiting the pub, when the fresh air hit him, he realised just how much trouble he was in. His bravado deserted him. He decided to try and negotiate his way out of his dilemma. It was agreed that it would be a no contest bout. Big Joe offered a solution, which Ray accepted, under sufferance.

Joe suggested they take one punch at a time, not a fight per se – just a one-for-one. Joe kindly offered Ray to take the first blow. The one who could not take any more would not return to the pub that evening.

Ray reluctantly agreed. Joe readied himself and by Rays account, a trained boxer, he suddenly realised he was in with a chance. He decided to hit Joe as hard as he could, in the stomach, such that he would be winded and take a long time to recover. So with all his strength he struck. He said he might as well have punched a brick wall.

Joe absorbed the blow with ease, saying: *"Now it's my turn."*

Ray tensed his body and Big Joe's ham sized fist that only travelled a few inches, landed on his sternum. Every ounce of air he had was expelled; he fell to the ground suffering a sharp pain in his chest. His legs were weak. Any desire to continue dissipated into the humid night air. He lay gasping for breath.

*"You want a second shot?"* queried Big Joe.

*"No mate, no I'm done for."*

Joe lifted him up by the scruff of his collar and steadied him. They parted ways. Ray suffered a stressed or fractured sternum and had a bruise six inches across his chest for weeks.

Some four months into my sojourn I was well settled, the jibes had lessened and the money was accumulating in the bank. As always, the chickens in the hen house had all found their different roosting levels – peace and quiet prevailed in the camp.

The mail arrived and I knew, as I handled the letter from my 'belle', there was trouble on the western front. There was no SWANK and the bright red kiss mark was conspicuous by its absence. The first thought, she was in a hurry and just forgot. Wishful and desperate thinking indeed! It was a 'Dear John'.

It had all the hallmarks of trying to let me down softly. *"You are such a sweet person, you have a heart of gold, I feel terrible, and I know you love me. Da de dah dah, etc. etc."* Cutting to the chase I realised someone had taken my place. *"I know you will not come back, what do you want me to do with the car?"*

The reply: *"Thanks for the good times, sell the car and buy your new lover a box of chocolates."*

I am not going to try and hide my feelings, all these years later, I was hurt and the old ego was in pieces on the ground. I now had no one I knew or could trust within a few thousand miles. I did have one thing though, a roof over my head, free scoff and a pile of 'the good stuff'.

This affair has an interesting conclusion. Many years later, I had been married for four years, learning how to 'stay alive' in the Hondo I got home after a month out and my wife handed me a letter. Somehow Shirley had tracked me down in Rhodesia.

She wrote, "I made a terrible mistake, I am so sorry, will you take me back?" I wrote back expressing my sympathy, but I was now married.

Even later still, in 1995/6 I lived in Australia, and received a phone call. *"I am now divorced, next time you are in Perth, here's my phone number."*

And later still towards the end of 1998/9 another phone call, "I am in such and such Hotel in Brisbane, on business, come and have dinner with me, just the two of us."

The last time of contact, a phone call saying, "Good luck and goodbye I have married the marriage councillor who tried to repair my first marriage."

Just an interesting piece of human behaviour.

On the night of receipt of the 'Dear John', I lay on my bed, Kipling's words, came to mind;

*Nice while it lasted, an' now it is over*
*Tear out your 'eart an' good-bye to your lover!*
*What's the use of grievin', when the mother that bore you?*
*(Mary pity woman!) Knew it all before you*

In my Oxford Dictionary of Quotations, which I carried in my pack, that quote has my 'belles' name and the date May 1970 scribed next to it.

I retired into my shell. Seeking renewed vigour and enthusiasm. I must go all the way around the world. That was the task we set, that is what must be achieved. As always, when one door closes another opens, one just has to keep wide awake to identify it.

I was about thirty feet up on a reinforced steel bar wall on the water intake structure tying 'saddle knots'. Again!! Ray was on the opposite side, he knew about the 'Dear John'.

In an attempt to placate me he said, *"Don't worry mate, in six months' time everything will be different, it will just be a memory."*

I was annoyed at his apparent lack of sympathy but it was another valuable lesson learnt - he was right. That philosophy has stayed with me ever since. However dark the night, dawn will follow.

Ray claimed to have read in a magazine in the canteen of a place in Australia where woman dressed in bikinis and high heels, walked around the town putting coin into expired parking meters.

*"If they do that what else will they do?"* he asked.

Two days later we had established this town was about 3,900 kilometres away. We put our 'pinkies' in (resigned) and took to the road. First stop, the nearest bar in Kununurra, 250 km away.

In those days, it was a one-horse town on the border with the Northern Territory. We were now deep in the outback, way beyond even 'the black stump'. We walked into the road bar and up to the counter.

The barman, an aboriginal, said, *"No whites allowed in this bar mate."*

Thinking he was joking I replied, *"Where does a thirsty white man get a drink in this town?"*

The answer, *"Round the other side with the white fellas."*

*"You kidding, aren't you?"*

*"You can stand there all day mate, I ain't gunna serve ya."*

I looked around the bar. Ray and I were the only whites. We walked around the other side and sure enough there was another bar, filled with whites. Some food for thought indeed.

We eventually got to Darwin. Those we met discouraged us from hitchhiking across the desert. We were told it would not be the first time a hitchhiker was dropped off at some residence turnoff and either got lost and never found, or was found deceased. We decided to take the next cheapest option, a 'bus'.

There is not much to report when you ride on a bus through the Australian desert. The countryside slowly becomes less vegetated, leading to a total lack of vegetation. The soil is 'red'. You drift off to sleep and when you wake up you wonder whether the bus had moved at all while you slumbered, same scenery. It took about 48 hours.

We missed Surfers Paradise, the town with the bikini ladies by about 50 km's. That was quickly rectified. We had arrived at party HQ, Australia.

\*　　　\*　　　\*　　　\*　　　\*

*You never really lose*
*Until you quit trying.*

**Mike Ditka**

## FIRST NIGHT IN PARTY CENTRAL
## & ANOTHER LIFE'S LESSON

I t was in a bar aptly named the Bird Bar on Caville Ave, Surfers Paradise, where we established 'all the action took place'. So we hired a double hotel room with two single beds, in close proximity. I was soon to learn of another side of my new travelling partner's personality. It was late in the afternoon; we got dressed and even ironed our best quality shirts, shaved and patted our faces with some cheap and nasty aftershave. Ladies beware, it had been a while for both of us and there were some highly dangerous and charged levels of testosterone in town.

Ray divulged his other side – Doug I cannot wait, I am going to hire myself a 'hooker'. Please do me a favour, give me until midnight with her alone in the room, then, 'if you have scored', I will take a walk. I could never see the logic in hiring what was ample and free and what's more, although I had no experience, they would have to be good actresses to make you feel the way one does in those intimate moments.

I agreed and headed for the recommended American Bar, alone. What the hell did he mean, 'if I scored'?

I had a reputation of being a man with charisma and charm and as long as the lights were low, I might, on a dark night, pass for good looking. Well, reasonably. Actually there was an internationally acclaimed adage that pretty girls fell for ugly men; I hoped that followed suite in this town.

With my best, 'see me now' gait I strolled into a packed bar. Putting on my part Rhodesian part Eton accent I ordered a lager in a bottle with a clean glass. (I thought that a natty way around the complex glass sizes and multitudes of brewery beers.)

While slowly pouring my beer I gazed around the establishment. The number of young to mid-thirties women was remarkable. Many of them just drop dead gorgeous. I also noticed men were, most probably, slightly outnumbered. This was promising indeed. Why, I thought, in God's name would you hire a hooker?

I got chatting to some girls who were very friendly and who introduced me to others. After a few hours they suggested I follow them into the neighbouring bar, where music and dancing took place. I mean, well? OK if you insist. That was my play-hard-to-get, I do-not-really-care, eager-not-to-lose-contact act.

In the next bar the girls introduced me to one of the local men who had women hanging off him. I danced - well I can't dance, but gave it my best shot, something between a drunk Shangaan and a 'Bamba duzi waltz' or as it's known the 'midnight shuffle'. I was on a roll – I was buying girls drinks like money was no impediment. Having not consumed much alcohol over the past five months it started to have an effect on me. I was feeling a trifle light headed. I asked one of my, better looking by the minute friends, where does one get a bite to eat. I could not let alcohol spoil this evening and the sure bet I was on. All I had to do now was to cast out the bait and reel in the 'goods'.

My newfound friend said he had to go back to his place for a shower and said if I chose, while waiting I could make myself a steak sandwich. How life has a way of parting the waters. He had mentioned he had a three bedroom flat. Well there was no doubt he was going to score, and I am sure he would not mind me, and my conquest for the night (or by van der Westhuizen's account of life, her conquest for the night - I was easy as long as I got laid, who cared who instigated the move.) Ray could have the place for the whole night!! That's what they call a 'win-win' situation.

We walked back to his place with one of the girls. She had obviously been there before.

While my new mate showered, she helped me find my way round the kitchen, they were not hungry, so I ate alone.

We soon returned to the frivolities and the night wore on, dancing, drinking, and falling over (sorry I just slipped!)

In what I presumed was the early hours of the morning, it was closing time. You would not credit it, in all the fun I was having I omitted to cast out the bait, the room was bereft of possible catches. I had blown my opportunity. My new mate, his girl and I walked out into the cool morning air. I told them my plight with Ray.

"No problem," says my mate, "Stay at my place, don't disturb a man while he is having fun."

That was the right spirit. We walked back to his place and then the girl leaned over and kissed me, "Nice to meet you, hope to see you again." Then she kissed my mate and walked on. Odd, well lovers have tiffs, happens all the time – 'Dear John' indeed!!!

We went up to his flat. That is where I sleep. Choose any other room you like. I found a spare bed, took off everything except my underwear and got into bed. I was soon fast asleep. I had this peculiar dream about someone in bed with me. It was a little hazy. I awoke and the dream did not end.

My new mate, was cuddling up to me and he whispered into my ear, *"I am a good F\*\*k I can make you really happy."*

Mother of Jesus, I froze, *"What the f\*\*k??!!"*

I have never exitted a bed that quick in my life. It was pitch black. I bumped into the wall, found the light switch, gathered up my belongings, he said, *"It's alright, you will enjoy it!"*

Transferring all my kit to my left hand, I let fly a rather wobbly haymaker that found its mark on the side of his head.

I bolted out the door, down the stairs and it was only when I was half way back to my hotel room, running bare foot through the streets of Surfers Paradise in my undies, did I realise, if the police ventured by I would be arrested for public indecency. At least that would resolve my upcoming problem with Ray.

I got to our hotel door, hammered loudly, shouting, *"Let me in, let me in."*

Ray retorted, *"F\*\*k off and find somewhere else."*

I threatened to break the door down and kill him. The door opened, I threw my clothes on the floor.

The girl was striking one of those surprised poses, holding the sheets over her breasts. I jumped into my bed, brushing away a bra, red wig, and a handbag and fell into a deep slumber.

Oh mother of God this is a strange world in deed.

We partied long and hard. We took up residence at 18 Palm Ave, Surfers Paradise an old house on a lot of land. A party financed in the main by Mac and I was nonstop 24 hours a day. I recall one night ordering and paying for thirty-four Chinese take away meals for our guests.

We got employment as builders labourers at the end of the street. We were paid $65 a week. The money soon ran out and as one expects, when the money ran out so did 99 per cent of your 'friends'.

One young lady stayed on, a nurse doing her midwifery at Southport Hospital. Sue Henry. We became friends and lovers and some years' later man and wife.

Mac and I decided we would go back to the 'camps' to earn the 'big bucks' again. Our choices were; a town called Weipa in northern Queensland or the island of Bougainville in Papua New Guinea. We applied for jobs at the latter and were successful.

A few of the girls, who had remained loyal to us idiots, threw a farewell party for us. I went home at midnight with Sue and told Mac not to get into any trouble, as in two days' time we were scheduled to Bougainville.

The following morning I was awoken by a loud knocking on the door: a friend of ours, a lawyer, said Mac had contacted him and wanted to see him. Mac was in custody in the police cells at Southport. We visited Mac, and the lawyer friend offered his services for free.

Mac was placed on remand, for a later hearing. He refused any legal assistance. I left for New Guinea alone. The last I heard of

Mac was a newspaper cutting, with headlines, - 'Mad Irishman pleads he was in Love'.

He had been driving a car, under the influence, on the night of the party and had proffered the occupants of a police car a race down the street. It ended with a fleet of police cars, chasing the drunken Irishman, who then drove over a traffic circle, in an attempt to escape his pursuers and crashed the car. He was sentenced to six weeks in prison. I never saw him again.

\*    \*    \*    \*    \*

*If all be true that I do think;*
*There are five reasons we should drink;*
*Good wine- a friend- or being dry-*
*Or least we should be by and by-*
*Or any other reason why.*

*Henry Aldrich*

# WORKING IN THE JUNGLES OF PAPUA NEW GUINEA

*From 2,000 feet above sea level;*
*In the distance two boats wait to be unloaded*

For a while in my life I worked in the jungles of Papua New Guinea. We were engaged in the opening of a gold mine. The lifestyle was as rugged as the characters that lived there. They used to transport the 'labour' to work sites each morning from a variety of residential camps. There were some 4,000 of us. Troop carriers came in various sizes. One thing common to all, the back area was fitted with two bench seats fixed to the floor and sides. They all had a steel frame over the back covered in canvas. We (the labour) would be assembled at pick up points, the truck would arrive, sometimes with the driver suspected of having recently finished off a 'joint' (known colloquially as the 'Merry–Jew-Anna') and everyone would scramble on, some never bothered to take a seat, and stood for the duration.

One morning I was running late for the assembly point. Running as fast as I could I watched as the transporter arrived, the 'labour' started to clamber aboard and I knew I would make it, if I just ran faster. A few yards from my entry, the driver engaged first gear and drove forward.

Those members in the back, realising my plight, started shouting and hitting the roof of the drivers cab, urging him to stop but he drove on so I increased my speed.

I caught up to the rear of this small transporter and with all the flair and dare-devilry, which is common in idiots I jumped up and grabbed the last section of the steel frame. It was at this precise moment the driver reacted to his passenger's pleas. He slammed on his brakes with force and purpose. My legs had been calculated to have slid down the middle well and by this time were airborne. Unfortunately like so many well-planned maneuvers, theory and practice failed to mesh.

My right leg went under the right bench seat, my left leg managed to get onto the well surface. With the sudden breaking my hands lost their grip on the frame. The result was my body was thrown down left and backwards (that gravity thing Newton spoke of) my left leg entered under the fixed bench seat. Fortunately both knees immediately dislocated, had they not, the only thing left to break would have been my back.

The vehicle stopped and I was hanging upside down, with my back against the number plate. I was taken to the local clinic - no resident doctor and the nurse, bless her, a typical Aussie examined me and said, *"Sorry mate this is going to "f**king hurt."*

Some Aussie girls talk just like that!! Then placing a paperback novel in my mouth, she said, *"Bite down hard on that."*

As she and an assistant started the long process of re-locating the knee joints – first one and then the other, the pain was excruciating, and no, unlike the movies you don't 'thankfully pass out'.

I learnt from her the mechanics of the knee joint and in the unlikely event it should ever happen again, what was required to be done. All I had to do was get a couple of mates, one pulls your shoulders back, one grips your ankle and readies himself to pull, and the third, squats above your knee, and then on the count of three, the last individual 'drops' his arse and weight on the knee, the ankle man pulls like hell, and the shoulder man, hangs on, so your body does not move.

"*Oh and Dougi* (the Aussies always put an 'i' on the end of everyone's' name*) try and bite down on a paperback, the pain will be intense but will not last long. Now... right, off you go to work.*"

Fast forward to Rhodesia, the right knee became a regular problem. There was no knowing when it would 'come out'. Fortunately, when it did I was always with mates. Sometimes the paperback was not available, but we got the manipulation down to a fine art. The only good thing was the sympathy my mates had for me - I always scored a free beer.

This was my last employment of any substance during my world travels. The Island of Bougainville, some claimed it to be the sovereign property of the Solomon Islands, was a disputed territory. I cared not for the politics. I was thinking of returning home. I had maintained correspondence with St Clair, now serving in the Regiment. I revealed my thoughts to him. He replied enclosing a small BSAP document, showing the current salaries of 'all ranks'. I was actually earning more than the Commissioner!!!  I thought it would be of interest for readers to have a glimpse of life in such a remote part of the world and what had to be endured to earn the kind of money we did.

In 1969 the Panguna mine was discovered. The mine had reserves of one billion tonnes of ore grade copper and 12 million ounces of gold. The island was uninhabited, and had many volcanic peaks, thankfully none smoking or rumbling in my time. I got there in 1970. There were about 4,000 European men of all nationalities and less than 50 woman employed. There were many more indigenous people, who by contract we had to tutor in the work we had been hired to do. The indigenous New Guinean people were referred to as 'red skins' because of their skin colour, while the local people from the Solomon's identified themselves as 'blacks', again based on the colour of their skin. The Europeans were simply known as 'the whites'. We operated between a port called Kieta, on the east coast, and HQ, about seven miles inland and then 34 km's into the mountains, at some 3,000 feet above sea level was the mine itself, Panguna.

Ocean going landing craft were used to ferry the construction material on to the island from the South Pacific Ocean. Huge mobile cranes, working on the beaches, lifted the cargo off the ships and placed them on mega-sized trucks that transported them to where they were required.

The road to Panguna was still under construction. Huge bulldozers (D9's and 10's) worked 24-hour shifts carving the road out of the sides of the mountains.

It rained once a day, every day, usually but not exclusively in the afternoon and evenings. Rivers ran down the mountains washing the roads away. I once witnessed a D9 driver jump from his dozer, seconds before a wall of water cascading down the mountain, hit the machine causing it to summersault down the hill, like a dinky toy. Non-existent rivers in the mornings appeared in the afternoon, totally destroying bridges built of steel and concrete (the Yanks called them culverts). I rebuilt one 'culvert' three times. Most artisans worked 12-hour shifts.

We were billeted two to a room. Such rooms could be in rows of ten or twenty. They were known as dongas, with doors facing onto a communal corridor, or if you were lucky, onto a veranda, with showering facilities on the end of each such row. In Panguna the rows of rooms were built on the sides of mountains, so steep were the mountainsides that the floor of the level above you was the same height as the roof of your accommodation.

There could be as many as seven such levels, all interconnected by timber staircases. 'The whites' lived in a separate community to the 'reds' and 'blacks'. I think they were housed in separate compounds. They were always a long distance from 'the whites'. Communal dining rooms were scattered around the accommodation.

Sounds a little like some fanciful and charming history lesson, with a little geography thrown in for those interested in that side of things - possibly the introduction to a romantic tale where Errol Flynn swash buckles his way in.

For those a trifle squeamish, read no further. These are a few of the incidents I witnessed and lived through.

Most if not all Europeans were hired in Brisbane, Australia, where you had to sign a document called the 'terms of employment contract'. Most of the paragraphs were pretty standard. One condition required your removal with immediate effect from the Island should you be become involved in any form of violence, relating the striking of a local, irrespective of circumstances. Another said visiting or being in the accommodation area of non-whites also resulted in immediate removal. Anyone found fraternising with local 'red' or 'black' females also faced the same fate.

Getting to and from Bougainville (whether to start work or on cancellation of contract) was an experience in itself. Those who may have flown around the area will know the air turbulence is frightening.

You have to maintain your seat belt at all times. On my first flight in, the plane dropped out of the sky that quick and that far, the airhostess serving the passengers was momentarily stuck to the roof of the cabin, along with all the plates of food, bottles of drinks, the trolley and anything else that was not tied down.

Once the pilot regain control, the poor stewardess and her equipment fell to the floor. Newcomers learnt quickly the 'real rules' that governed the residence and work place of the 4,000 men. Those rules bore little resemblance to those mentioned in the contract of employment. The work place was heavily controlled by rabid trade unionist, mostly of UK origin.

The accommodation area was run by what I described as criminals. Inter-leading verandas were gambling dens where roulette wheels, black jack and a game illegal in Australia called 'Two Up', flourished.

Dining tables had bench seats, four a side; no tablecloths. I must say the food was excellent, and you could eat as much at each meal as you wished. In my early days at Panguna I was seated quietly at a table, when joined by four Czechoslovakians, on the opposite side.

As I sat eating my meal a cooked lamb chop bone that had been gnawed, landed on my plate. Just as I looked up a second similar bone landed on my plate. I stood up and remonstrated with all four, not being able to identify the culprit.

They all stood up, they were my height and more, two grabbed me by the front of my shirt literally pulling me across the top of the table when I heard the 'switch' or would that be the 'swish' of a switchblade knife, and the third had it pointed at my throat. I remember feel extremely weak. I was helpless. Then all four burst out laughing, throwing me backwards, I bounced on my seat and fell back on the floor, my plate, knife and fork followed me, they walked out laughing, conversing in their own dialect.

At night I kept my own company, taking solace with the poets. The gambling dens were very noisy. Thousands of dollars exchanged hands nightly. There was reputedly one Aussie that ran it all. He was a carpenter by trade, reported to be a millionaire.

He did not actually work so this was contrary to the terms of employment. He was there for the six months of my duration.

Each gambling den had its 'minders'. There were frequent fights. The minders were also debt collectors. The local 'clinic' always had a few beds filled with people who had failed to pay their debts.

I was a steel fixer, working on the main crusher in Panguna, some fifty feet off the ground on scaffolding. At one time I was required to use an oxy-acetylene torch to cut re-enforced steel sections in preparedness for tying and a concrete pour. As I have mentioned most 'whites' were, by contract, required to have a 'red' or 'black' skin working with them, to teach them the work being undertaken. To put it mildly, those attached to us, were poorly educated, spoke little or no English and we spoke little or no 'pigeon' English, a local dialect bridging the two cultures. It was frustrating to say the least.

Constant rain was a 'dampener', if you will excuse the pun. One morning, my 'mate' asked if he could have a go with the oxy torch. In compliance with my requirements but contrary to my better judgement I handed the controls over. Without further ado he began cutting away and then turned to me, I guess to seek my approval. The flame cut across the front of my torso. My immediate and obviously clueless reaction was to punch him in the head.

He fell or dropped on the top section of the scaffolding, and then like one of those spring toys we had as kids that walked themselves down stairs, he slowly fell earth bound, bouncing off each layer of scaffolding, followed by, or in unison with the oxy and acetylene bottles and torch. Thankfully he stopped about 15 feet down.

I climbed down, and by the time I got to ground level I was surrounded by 'reds' and 'blacks', who were baying for my blood. I was protected by other 'whites' who took me straight to my room where I packed my kit and I was driven down the mountain. With the luck of the Gods I was not deported. I was transferred to Staff and went on to become one of the top steel managers, called 'steel bosses' working in the HQ and Port areas. I never went back up the mountain to Panguna.

I was given the job of running the steel-bending yard that operated 24 hours a day.

We were supplied with basic reinforced steel rods, of a variety of diameters, off the ships, and required to bend them into a multitude of differing shapes, which had been developed by onsite company engineers. Irrespective of the amount of rain falling work never stopped.

We had four or five bending machines, with four man teams working on each one – they worked 12-hour shifts. My record for nonstop working was three nights and three days.

The reason was the monsoon rains had destroyed the 'bridges' we were building. As a consequence we lost all the steel and had to re-start the exercise anew.

My roommate was a very proud German, foreman carpenter. His face was literally filled with scars. In time I got to know him well, but was always wary. He had migrated to Australia after the war.

*The steel bending yard, Bougainville – My office is at the back left next to the toilet (the long drop)*

The scars were the result of beatings with rifle butts from Russian soldiers, because he been part of the Hitler Youth, when captured. He quite openly despised Jews and suggested their only worth was to make soap from. His violence on the job was legendary. He claimed to have been working 'the camps' since his arrival in Australia in 1948, he was single and claimed to be the owner of 26 houses on the main land. In each building the tenants were paying off his mortgage.

One day the entire island's work force, including those at the bending yard went out on strike. I do not recall the reason. I refused to join the strike claiming I was on staff, and therefore not bound to Union requirements, and continued to work, albeit very slowly at the 'steel bending yard' at HQ.

Some days went past, and although the company fed the strikers, they did not pay them. I continued to be paid. One night as I was returning from the dining room I was confronted by two Union members, they were known as 'Enforcers'. I was told they were Union 'educators'!! They informed me they came with a message from the Union rep in charge.

*"As soon as you 'down tools' the Union will arrange for everyone to return to work."*

Whatever got into me I have no idea. I hit the first chap as hard as I could in the face. He dropped which caused the second to be confused, so while the going was good, I belted him as hard as I could as well. I walked away. I heard them threatening me, but they never followed. The following morning my boss, a Yank, called me in to his office. With him was the Union Rep.

My Boss said, *"Will you please go on strike so we can get the island back to work."*

I replied, *"I am on strike now."*

The Rep nodded and walked out. I went back to work and the matter was finalised.

The place was filled with some of the most undesirable human beings imaginable. I presume, I have no actual experience it was similar to a prison. Individual knife or other weapon fights, as well as gang fights, were common incidents. Fearful men, as big and strong as oxen many illiterate some of them simply had non-existent table manners, included spitting in the food and on the floor. Hands were never washed. Blatant and overt sexual advances anywhere anytime to anyone they thought a possible conquest. I was lucky, being ugly I was never approached!

Pornography in both written and film form, for which there was a cost was commonplace. Strangely I never came across any drugs. I recall one Sunday afternoon, a young white kid, 16 not much more, God knows why he was hired and sent to work with us, was drinking with a group of Czechs in the next room.

At first laughter could be heard, then begging *"No"*, then screaming, *"Stop."*

I rose to offer assistance, the big German, grabbed me, *"No you might get hurt. Leave him."*

I presume the kid was gang raped. Such was life. It was no place for the faint hearted, the fearful, the timid, or self-opinionated.

For that you received large monetary rewards. My boss had been all over the world on large-scale construction sites, his philosophy on man management.

Make sure you give construction workers, the 3 "M's" and you can do what you like with them - Mail, Meals and Money.

\*       \*       \*       \*       \*

## THE LONG ROAD HOME

F or the next part of my world trip I travelled with Sue Henry, my then girlfriend / amoureux and totally inexperienced hitchhiker. Sue had planned to fly to Canada where she had a work visa organised. Her contacts were two former Sydney nurses now working in the country of the 'Maple Leaf'.

As we sat on a moonlit drenched beach of Surfers Paradise she asked if she could join me on my travels through South America, where I was bound. I explained my experiences in hitchhiking, which necessitated sleeping under bridges and in fields and unused railway carriages, or wherever possible. Also food, when available, was restricted to 'street food' that varied greatly in quality. She found my experiences romantic, and cashed in her one-way ticket to Canada, purchasing one to Santiago, Chile.

On submitting my discharge from Morrison Knudsen in New Guinea my steel boss Fred Mead made some very attractive offers, including setting me up in married quarters with Sue until the end of the project – another 12 months or more. Sue declined. He then offered me work in Chile and Canada, with the same company, although he was unable to influence Immigrations Departments to provide the necessary work permits. That was my problem to resolve. I thanked Fred and bade him farewell.

I returned to Brisbane, picked up Sue - her father had brought his suit to Queensland, expecting there to be a quick wedding – she explained we were travelling together as 'mates'.

He replied, *"He is not a bloody mandrake you know."*

I suggested to Sue she should dump her suitcase, fancy dresses, hats and all clothing that was not dark in colour and purchase a haversack, in readiness for the journey. She did not heed my suggestion.

We flew to Fiji, Tahiti and Easter Island before landing in Santiago, Chile.

I was fascinated by the Moai Statues on the Isla de Pascua (Easter Island) - there are a total of 887 of them, all monolithic, averaging 20 tons and 20 feet in height, built by the Rapa Nui people between 1400 and 1650 A.D. The current residents numbering about 5,000 live in the most isolated human settlement on earth.

*The remotest place I visited. Isla de Pascua (Easter Island) Closest Continent (Chile, South America) Distance 3,512 kms*

On our first night in Chile, we agreed it was the last night in a cheap Pension (Hotel). The following morning I asked her to discard all the 'fancy gear'. She refused, dressing in short high heels, with a pretty yellow frock, matching hat and carrying a large suitcase.

I assured her I would not be carrying the suitcase and the shoes were totally inappropriate. She told me she would manage.

Whilst resident in London I had read in an issue of the Times magazine the only statue in the world to Che Guevara was under construction in Santiago. It was always my intention to see it. In the 1960's Che was an icon for the youth of the world. For goodness knows what, fighting against the establishment maybe?

He was a freedom fighter to some and a terrorist to others. A mercenary from Argentina, a medical doctor and from all accounts a very vicious and savage person. I tore out the article and promised myself it was one of my 'targets'.

*Che Guevara*
*Freedom Fighter or Terrorist?*

I had a few other places on my wish list: The Tierra del Fuego, the Pampas in Santa Fe and Buenos Aires, Argentina, Lake Titicaca and the old Inca ruins of Machu Pichu in Peru, a visit to Uruguay (where legend has it many of the German Nazi high command took refuge at the end of World War II) and also the towns and fields where the Mexican revolutionary Francisco "Pancho" Villa fought, in particular his place of assassination Parral, Mexico.

In life things don't always turn out the way you hope for. Regrettably as it was, Sue was unable to come to terms with the 'hitchhiking lifestyle'.

As we walked towards the main bus terminus she constantly stopped, saying she was uncomfortable and tired. It was clear then as it had been from the very beginning this lifestyle was not suited to her.

We sat down on the street and I told her the best option was to return to Australia and then fly to Canada or fly direct from Chile to Canada. I offered to pay her ticket. She refused. I was now stuck with a major dilemma.

It would be irresponsible of me to 'leave her', she had never travelled and was quite naive by nature – she was to my mind 'very vulnerable'. I explained my thoughts, and while she refused to accept them I had to move on.

I walked into the next travel agent I came across and asked the manager to give me the price of an air ticket to Australia. I put the money on his desk and told Sue I was leaving, and she should go back home. I walked out of the building, turned south and headed for my next stop, the Tierra del Fuego, the most southern tip of South America.

I heard Sue shouting to me, turning I saw her running down the street towards me. She promised to try harder. She returned my travellers cheques and asked me to find a store where we could buy a rucksack. On doing so she ceremoniously discarded her suitcase, high heels and a few of the lighter coloured clothes in a waste bin.

We never went to the southern tip of Chile, South America. We travelled to the town of Pucon, the location of the Villarrica Volcano, the world's most conically shaped mountain, and Peru's most active volcano. I compromised and we hiked to Argentina, over the Andes Mountains, via the Southern Lakes District. The journey took us over five lakes, all interconnected, but strangely all different hues, then over the top of the South American Andes Mountains down on to the Rio Negro in Argentina. The distance was 1,680 odd kms.

*A narrow valley on the top of the South American Andes*

One incident of interest occurred, while hiking across the Rio Negro, in Argentina, we were picked up by an old man in a very old car, as always we were thankful. My Spanish was limited to enquiries of transport and food. Slowly very dark clouds of an approaching rainstorm enveloped us. Not seen since my days in Africa and not unlike Africa, day turned into night, and the mother of all storms, with loud thunder and sheet lightening engulfed our lives.

The driver lost control of the vehicle, we spun off the road, first fish tailing, and then spinning in 360 degrees circles. We came to rest in a field. Thankfully there were no injuries. We tried to wait out the storm before getting out of the vehicle, which tested our patience. Firstly, the driver and I alighted, then Sue came to see if she could help. Eventually Sue took control of the driver's position and the old man and I heaved, slipped, shoved and swore until the wheels found some traction and Sue directed it back onto the main road. All three of us were saturated and covered from head to foot in mud.

The old man drove on and through his mixture of Spanish and English he offered us his house for a clean-up and sleep. We were most grateful. As in life, the storm eventually passed. We drove with the setting sun behind us and a clean, fresh, warm aroma filtering through the open windows. Night had fallen when the old man parked outside a house and called us in. There were lines of different coloured lights hanging on the veranda. A number of young males and females were sitting drinking and chatting on the veranda as we walked passed. The old man talked to a lady, presumably his wife, and presto, our clothes were removed - not only those we were clad in, but the contents of our rucksacks as well. We gratefully accepted the offered hot water shower and some spare clothes. Soon after two plates of meat soup/stew and some bread arrived that tasted like a 5 star hotel meal. As I sat sating my hunger, I observed my surroundings.

I worked out the predicament we found ourselves in. Dog tired, after the meal, a double bed was offered and we lay down. Sue remarked to me the old lady had a lot of daughters, and we seem to have gate crashed a party. I suggested we were sleeping free of charge in a South American brothel!!!

At breakfast I was able to confirm my thoughts, we shook hands with the 'madam', her husband and some of the 'girls of the night' – we were soon on our way to the capital city of this vast country.

On arrival in Bueno Aires, the relationship deteriorating rapidly, I again compromised and we flew to Lima, Peru.

While walking down a street on a sightseeing trip we received verbal jeers of 'bloody gringos' and we were pelted from windows above, with water balloons (well I hope they were- and not something else they could have been).

It was unpleasant and we hastened our strides. Suddenly out of a side alley we were confronted by three youths who looked menacing and, I thought, intent on doing us harm. Two were brandishing knives.

I told Sue to run back. I stood my ground. They were very vocal and antagonistic. I carried a 'flick knife' in preparation for just such occasions. I took it out of my trousers pocket, extended the blade and had I been religious would have said a 'small save me prayer'. Thankfully the three fled and I beat a hasty and welcome retreat back to our Pension.

Sue was nervous and scared. She wanted desperately to leave, which we did, flying to Mexico City. So long to the Machu Picchu and the Inca civilisation, lessons in life.

*Mayan Pyramid de la Luna (of the Moon) Mexico*

I have for as long as I can remember been interested in previous civilizations and cultures. The pyramids in Mexico were built by the Mayan civilization that existed between 1800 BC and 900 AD. The area was visited by the Aztecs centuries after the structures were abandoned.

Modern day scholars believe 'over population', 'overuse of the land' 'endemic war faring' and 'drought' led to the demise of the two civilisations.

Certainly has a familiar ring to it, does it not! Ironic similarities to current civilizations!!! They say, 'history repeats itself' and yes they also say 'we seldom learn from our mistakes'.

Sue had no interest in historic matters so we flew direct into Toronto, Canada. I thought I would leave her in the safe hands of her 'contacts, make some more money, as I by now I was desperately short.

I then intended returning to South America to complete my education at the University of Hard Knocks.

On arrival in Toronto we had come out of the summer in the Southern Hemisphere into the middle of a Canadian winter. We suffered through lack of appropriate clothing.

We located Sue's contacts easily enough, only to be confronted with a situation quite alien to me. Sue was made most welcome, but I was refused entry into their flat. Sue came back out and advised her two contacts were lesbian and had a rule no males allowed within! I had never been associated with lesbians before, well not to my knowledge. I found some less than desirable digs in a very ugly and suspect part of town.

In the hitchhiking game, as I have mentioned previously one relies on local knowledge and contacts within the system. I was bereft of both. I knew not a living soul in Canada, I was broke and if I did not get an income soon, I would be homeless on the streets in mid-winter.

With a lack of local knowledge I made my next mistake, which I paid for dearly. I secured a position in the security industry, which was provided on condition the authorities gave me permission to work. I applied to the authorities for a work permit, submitting my confirmed work application. That was the mistake. The authorities refused and gave me a week to leave the country. The reason, I had lied on my document seeking entry claiming I was on holiday. When clearly, as it transpired I actually intended seeking employment, apparently an offence for which I could be deported.

Sue had obtained permanent work and residency and told me she did not wish to continue the relationship! What relationship?

I was tired of the new life that was the old. The road had been too long and too hard - the nights too dark. The idea had become stale. I returned to England, with the financial assistance of my mother, and then flew into Kenya. My mother was taking my sister to Zambia for a hockey festival. I joined them on the drive south through Tanzania to Zambia.

I was dropped off on the northern side of the Chirundu Bridge and walked back into Rhodesia.

I was home in one piece. I was penniless, homeless and unemployed. The epitome of a vagrant, vagabond or 'bum'. But I owed no man, and while it had been at times a hard life – it was an amazing experience and a wonderful education.

Of everything I learnt in my world travels, this actuality remains the most significant lesson of them all; however important one may consider one's self, and however important we may be to those around us our existence in history is nothing more than a micro blip in time and irrespective of our achievements, in history we are less than an insignificance. This realisation is just a simple reality check. I am content in that knowledge. Hopefully I could relate some of the stories and score a free beer here and there.

Fate played an odd hand. I married Sue in 1972, and had two wonderful children with her. What she may have lacked as a hiker, she made up for in our married life. She was an excellent mother, a good provider and good wife. She proved a most resilient person during the war we endured. She helped build a home in Rhodesia that we lost and helped build another in Australia. Unfortunately Rogan, our son was born with a terminal condition and died at 22 years of age. Our daughter Natalie is married, has been extremely successful in life, and is the mother of two young boys. Sue passed away from cancer in March 2011, just after we retired.

## MAY SHE REST IN PEACE.

\*　　　\*　　　\*　　　\*　　　\*

*There are no secrets to success.*
*It is the result of preparation, hard work,*
*And learning from failure*

*Colin Powell*

# WHATEVER YOU DO – DO NOT RE-ATTEST!

I s it truth to say 'birds of a feather' and 'old habits die hard'? Well I thought so – I hiked from Chirundu to Salisbury. If true to form, my friends would knock off at 4.30 pm so 30 minutes was by far sufficient time to deploy to the pub, a well-known hotel close to Avondale. I walked into an oft pre-frequented watering hole at about 1700 hours.

As I waited I sat sipping my cold Lion Lager, the first in over three years. Being most mindful that I had started to spend, my now exchanged US$200 - my total worldly assets. Experience over the past three years demanded as the sun started to fall, I make pre-emptive plans for my night's repose. A few lessons learnt, had bade me well on my travels; always bed down after dark, make certain you are not being watched, if no rain was imminent, culverts and storm drains were ideal. Haystacks, bridges, parked railway carriages, dense foliage and abandoned residences were also effective. None of these were applicable in my current situation.

I was sitting quietly, rucksack at my feet, propping up the bar. I watched as well-dressed business commuters of varying ages, slowly filtered into the bar. En route, no doubt to their homes in the leafy well-groomed suburbs; their houses monuments to their achievements in the world of commerce and industry, servants for cooking, gardening and house cleaning. Living the life of the landed gentry in the colonies.

Some I guessed drowning their sorrows, others avoiding getting back to 'the battle axe' too early. One or two maybe fortifying themselves before the evening onslaught for a variety of failures they had achieved on the domestic front. One or two no doubt savouring their thoughts of a soon to be continued, illicit love affair. A few smiles, a little laughter and much deep discussion.

I could see I was the focal point of discussion, in many of the groups that had formed. It was obvious from their sideways glances, with looks of distaste, disapproval and disgust, with the glare and exaggerated shaking of the head, letting me known of their disapproval. I realised this returning prodigal son was not of the standard expected of this fraternity.

What they were looking at was a 25-year-old, 6'4" European male. Emancipated, dark brown in colour, hair receding in the front and unattended shoulder length at the back, with possibly four or five days' facial growth.

Clad in an unironed and probably unwashed shirt, a pair of denim jeans, fraying at the pockets and on the turn ups, sun bleached to a white/cream colour, with patches of dirt, or was that old stains embedded so deeply that no end of washing could remove them. And for those observant enough, wearing a pair of shoes made from a hessian type material, rather than leather, with no socks. Guarding a scungy canvas bag.

A bum no doubt, a slob, poor bastard had fallen on hard times, an undesirable, most probably an alcoholic. Who the hell let him in? I don't know, the standards in this country are deteriorating rapidly. Had they known the truth the man who was the focus of their attention was homeless, unemployed and a vagrant; that actually qualified him for arrest under, I think it was, the Miscellaneous Offences Act.

Time marched on - no signs of any of my comrades. I was wrong, out of touch, things change and we change with them. To preserve my most important asset I left the bar and sat outside on the veranda near the pub entrance, watching and waiting. Half past ten came and revellers, now forced to return to their billets, staggered from the premises. Some unpleasant remarks issued forth; "get a job", "pull yourself together", flowed back to me as they disappeared into the night.

Avoiding an area lit by street lights, and where experience guided me, I bedded down for the night, my rucksack my pillow, my cash hidden under some grass and stones, close by but sufficiently far away that if mugged, my assailants would fail to find it. Placing it in a roll of socks or wearing socks and hiding the money between foot and sock (if you owned any) was a well know hiding place, in Europe anyway. That was presuming their efforts would be successful. I felt confident in my ability to repel an attack – I drifted off to sleep, pondering my next move.

One always gets up early when billeted as I was. It is the lack of comfort, I had learnt to dig or scrape a hip hole, but it was always uncomfortable. The early morning light acted as nature's alarm clock, the birds, always noisy before dawn. The dreaded dew, if sleeping in the open, helped one wake up. A new day dawned, life was good, but I needed to get my act together. A morning wash and shave, even teeth cleaning were unavoidably impossible.

I knew my best friend's parents were resident in Avondale. Tony St Clair , had been a Squad mate, an associate and accomplice in crime in Fort Vic District, one of the subjects of Insp Cavey's riot dress punishment in Mashaba and my comrade for the first year overseas, one of the *Three Must-get-beers*.

We shared the adventures of the running of the Bulls in Spain; were members of a sub-contract steel erection firm in Peterborough, UK, where he was registered on the contractors books as Lardner Burke, along with others like myself, namely Jack Musset, together with an ex Gwebi chap by the name of Cliff DuPont and even Ian Smith, an ex-tobacco farmer from Mtoko.

The British tax department would have had difficulty recovering unpaid taxes from those fellows. We did well, the average wage in England at that time was a poultry 12 pound something a week, which was taxed. We earned 60 pound a week, untaxed so to speak, working on a Rhodesian system known as "gwaza". It worked well in Rhodesia and even better in England, after we had manipulated the assessing process.

We had enjoyed incredible experiences, beyond even the wildest dreams of the District Trooper. St Clair had fallen deeply in love with a gorgeous Rhodesian blonde, absolute top drawer stuff, whose father was a well-known and extremely successful businessman.

With heavy heart he broke the news to me, he was abandoning our venture, as true love, and not lust had overwhelmed him. I had learnt one valuable lesson in the first year of travel; all males, suffer from the same anatomy dysfunction - periodically, our brain descends about a metre, positioning itself firmly between our thighs resulting in some fairly reckless, ill-defined and at most times decisions contrary to our best long term interests.

They planned to marry at home. If possible could I make it back to be his best man? At that exact point in time, I was unemployed, sleeping on 'carpet space' on the floor of an unpaid, dirt cheap Earls Court flat, with little more than the cost of a beer as my total assets, his request was respectfully and regrettably declined.

He was flying home immediately, intending to re-attest in the Regiment, so her father would know he was a good prospect. She would return home on a leisure cruise, going through the Mediterranean, via the Suez Canal and down to Durban. I am not now and I wasn't then a 'Dear Abby' type when it came to advising on affairs of the heart. However, well knowing the lifestyles that we had all lead in the Swinging Sixties in England, something told me, something was amiss - blind Freddy could see that. I wished him well on his departure.

I knew not the address of his parents (his father was a former Member of the BSAP) and became a successful Insurance agent.

An address was available from the phone book in a telephone booth; alas I had no map to guide me. As always time was on my side. So I walked around Avondale in the hope I would recognise something from the past. Eventually, before nightfall, I found the house. Mrs St Clair opened the door, in response to my knock.

She looked at me, and said, *"Yes, may I help you?"*

I retorted, *"Mrs St Clair it's me, Doug Stanyon."*

She burst into tears, threw her arms around me, hugged me tightly, yelled for her husband and dragged me inside.

*"You look like you need a good feed and wash Doug, where have you been?"*

St Clair's old man made a phone call and within minutes a black and white Austin pulled into the driveway, out stepped Detective Patrol Officer St Clair– the only insurance policy I ever had.

He whisked me off to the CID Mess he was living in, strangely within a mile of the pub I had waited at and near my previous night's sleeping place. There was no blonde, nor was she mentioned. There was however a young lady in his life. There always was, he had some charm that I always threatened to discuss with him, sadly for me it never transpired. I met and renewed acquaintances with other Members and met their civilian Mess mates. They provided a bed and offered food and shelter. We drank long into the night, telling lies, stories, yarns and jokes.

*"Whatever you do Doug, do not re-attest. It is no longer the outfit it was. We will keep you for free until you get a job. Oh s\*\*t!! We have run out of beer and the pubs are closed. Oh well we shall just have to drink Rum or Brandy. Now that's tough."*

Some things never change. I knew I was home safe and sound. Life was good.

\*　　　\*　　　\*　　　\*　　　\*

## THE GOLDEN JOURNEY TO SAMARKAND

*We are the Pilgrims, master; we shall go
Always a little further: it may be
Beyond that last blue mountain barred with snow,
Across that angry or that glimmering sea,*

*White on a throne or guarded in a cave
There lives a prophet who can understand
Why men were born: but surely we are brave,
Who take the Golden Road to Samarkand.*

*Sweet to ride forth at evening from the wells
when shadows pass gigantic on the sand,
And softly through the silence beat the bells
Along the Golden Road to Samarkand.*

*We travel not for trafficking alone;
By hotter winds our fiery hearts are fanned:
For lust of knowing what should not be known
We make the Golden Journey to Samarkand.*

*James Elroy Flecker*

# BOOK THREE

T his covers the period between 1971 and 1980, the latter being the year when a political settlement of the hostilities in Rhodesia was reached. The hostilities were referred to as a 'war', an incursion of 'freedom fighters' or a 'terrorist infiltration'. To the British aristocracy and members of England's Parliament it was most probably nothing more than one of those 'fracas' out in Africa, where some awfully belligerent whites are blind to the realities of the future of Africa. McMillian is famously quoted, in 1960 as saying:

*"The wind of change is blowing through this continent and whether we like it or not, this growth of national consciousness is a political fact. **And we must all accept it.**"*

Rhodesia's problem lay in its unilateral non-acceptance of the last sentence.

Let us leave the politics aside. The following 'tales' recount some of the more interesting situations I found myself in during this turbulent time in Rhodesia.

Most European civilians resident in Rhodesia during this time were by law required to act in defence of the Nation which eventually was required every second month. Permanent members of the Army and Air Force spent the majority of their lives involved in the conflict. Certain members of the BSAP were also required to contribute towards the 'war effort', with many of them spending alternative months in anti-terrorist operations. During their 'off' month they carried out their policing duties, as normal. A small number worked constantly in the prosecution of the war.

Depending on where one was stationed, and what ones normal police function was, dictated the amount of extra time one spent at what was known colloquially as 'The Sharp End' or 'Hondo'.

The following 28 stories, all based on truth and fact, reveal the times I spent in anti-terrorist operations and affiliated circumstances.

We were not highly trained military operatives; our main task was an attempt to maintain law and order, from a policing point of view.

Some of us occasional took a wrong turn!!!!!

## RE-ATTESTATION

J ob seeking was engaged in for a few weeks, most jobs I thought I could do, appeared to be dead end streets – no real excitement. The Police offered work I found very easy to do. While I realised the law was an ass, investigations and docket preparation came easy to me. Dealing with the public and criminals alike, again was something with which I had little difficulty and at least I would be outdoors, not cooped up in an office.

Excitement would be minimal (how wrong did I get that bit!) but I had had my fun, sown my wild oats, now I needed to get my nose to the grindstone. I was slightly behind the eight ball as far as promotion was concerned. Some former squad mates were now the equivalent or close to the old Crown Sergeant.

There were long and serious discussions with my associates. I was flat cold broke living off their charity. I tried to borrow money from them to get back overseas. I had written to my former boss in New Guinea. He replied, the company would hire me only from Brisbane Australia. He did however confirm immediate employment and offered me three postings – one in Chile the other in Canada or a return from where we met. They would fly me from Australia to any one of these locations. I could not access funding anywhere. I bit the bullet.

I phoned the BSAP Recruitment Officer, located in Police General Headquarters. We confirmed a mutual date for an interview. He assured me he would recover my Record of Service from the archives in the meantime.

Suddenly I realised I had no decent kit to wear to the interview. I had not given that a thought. For 36 months I had lived a life where literally no one, including myself, cared how I was dressed. Everyone in the Mess offered to loan me clothes. We managed to get a very clean well-ironed shirt and tie. A pair of good-looking calf length short socks. I was treated to a haircut and borrowed a razor, and shaved to the 'Depot standard'

I remember Staff Inspector Tacky McIntosh, the Depot instructor, would look at your face and say, *"What did you shave your face with? A f\*\*king bus ticket? You useless \*\*\*\*\*\*."*

Oh! The recruitment officer had advised, if successful, I would have to spend my first three months in Depot and then back to driving school!!! Some things just don't change.

My problems circulated around long trousers and shoes. The elastic in my underpants had frayed or stretched that much that it was my trousers that stopped them from falling off. At least we considered that would not be visible. One civil mate was just a tad shorter than I. However, a problem was highlighted. His 'girth' was larger than normal; mine looked like someone from Biafra. While I tried on other long trousers, there was always an unsightly view of the socks, some three or four inches. We went with 'Ma Garbage's (what kind of a nickname was that?) trousers. They at least were dark. Try as we did, there was nobody we could find that wore size 12 shoes.

On the big morning I had to parade in front of my peers'. Dressed up to kill I was. We had to add some pleats and a very tight belt to the top of the trousers. This caused them to 'scrunch up'. I could not help but notice the suppressed mirth amongst my cronies. I looked in a full-length mirror on the front of one of those old timber wardrobes. My shoes, made from hessian material, resembled a pair of 'tackies' that had just been trampled on by a herd of cattle. They had frayed, discoloured and frankly resembled the most unregimented footwear conceivable. If Tacky had seen them, God knows what he would have said.

I was dropped off outside PGHQ. I paused outside for a while, gathering my thoughts. My father being ex-police had maintained contact with a number of his associates. Now 35 odd years later a few of them had retired after service within the ivory tower I now stood in front of. A few were still working inside this hallowed monument that had witnessed the saddened end to the careers of some Chief Inspectors and Chief Superintendents, who in their mind had been transferred there with prospects of further glory.

Alas it was the promotion graveyard for some, so I had heard, whilst my father sipped a few beers with old friends.

The politics here sometimes outweighed the need for the right people to be in the right place. I never really understood all this – but I did know there were uniformed policeman of all ranks in this building who had never investigated a crime, nor been on a patrol, never interviewed a witness, directed traffic, attended a Sudden Death, nor attended a traffic accident.

Well so be it. Such is life. I stepped through the gates of 'Police Heaven' - where the 'top policeman' delivered his orders.

I was directed to an office, the door of which was open on arrival. Seated at the desk was a young Superintendent. I did not recognise him. An extremely polite man, he proffered a seat. I watched his eyes to see whether he noticed my untidy waist or hessian shoes. I noticed he wore a single medal ribbon on his chest. It was not a second world one that I knew. On a small desk aside was a lever arch file marked PO STANYON 7158. So PGHQ also had those stencils we had in district to mark the backs of files.

The discussion was most amiable, very respectful both ways. I thought this man had not long been promoted. After about half an hour of chitchat that had little to do with my re-attestation or at least my application therefor, he eventually broached the subject.

"Mr Stanyon, I have retrieved your previous RS. You certainly had a colourful four years in your previous service."

I knew he was not referring to some of the glorious sunsets, or magnificent vistas I had enjoyed. He did not really look like the 'arty' type either. Now the truth of the matter is in all of my 'boisterous behaviour' (a description Cavey placed on my 1967 AEC, which you may recall, I had refused to sign, until he mentioned the alternative description.

I had never been charged! I had in fact never been warned, cautioned or given 'a last and final warning'. Did these people write reports without our knowledge, or maybe this young and fine upstanding man, destined for the very top, had contacted people like Cavey and Saul, Hedges and Worden? Heaven knows, some of them may now have been commissioned?

*"I am afraid,"* he continued, *"It is unlikely we would consider your re-attestation favourably."*

Bloody officers' talk, neither this way nor that. Maybe he meant they would re-hire me but not think favourably about their decision?

I was taught to call it as you see it, in plain simple language, no flowery beating around the bush stuff. I replied, *"Are you going to re-hire me or not?"*

I fired off my second question, *"If you reject my application, are you the absolute authority on this decision?"*

*"Well,"* he said, continuing that 'diplomatic talk', *"If you can convince me you should be re-attested, I can give this matter further consideration."*

Jesus! I thought - the boys were right, the first man I speak to is not the same. Where did they find this guy? I offered him a suggestion that I thought we could or would no doubt accept as a final and acceptable outcome.

*"Yes and what might that be?"*

I informed him after I had resigned and was working my three-month resignation period I received three separate letters. As a matter of academic interest I have two of those documents to this day. Obviously typed off a template, as they are almost identical.

In all of these letters I said, there was one common thread – 'should you ever wish to re-join the BSAP, please do not hesitate to contact me and I shall provide any necessary assistance'.

So I said to the Superintendent, *"I will give you their names, and you contact them one at a time and advise them of my application."*

I gave him the names; Asst. Commissioner Gaitskell, A/Comm Van Sittert and A/Comm Sherren.

It turned out the first man had left on pension, the second was still serving but out of the city, however, the third was a lot closer.

*"We will need to make an appointment to see Mr Sherren, he is the current Deputy Commissioner (Crime and Security)."*

I asked that he be contacted or if he had a secretary, she be contacted and at least inform him I am attempting to re-attest and that I am in the same building at this time. I shall thereafter abide by his requirements.

He spoke to the secretary who said she would phone back. Less than two minutes later his phone rang.

*"Superintendent 'so and so' speaking,"* then that all too familiar, *"Yes Sir, No Sir, Right away Sir."*

Standing up, he reached for his hat and cane. *"I shall take you up to see Mr Sherren."*

The quick glance down the tunic; buttons in order, the careful placing of the hat, ensuring the hair was neatly tucked in at the sides, a quick wipe of the toes of each shoe on the back of his stockings, just to remove any dust, a little fiddling with the Sam Brown and we were on our way. Somethings just never change.

I do not recall whether we went up one flight of stairs or two. There was some serious 'brass' on route – I did not recognise any one. People all looked very busy, head down, walking briskly along the corridors and between offices.

As I walked behind my escort I mused, *"So I walk among the Gods, along the hallowed Corridors of Power."*

The escort walked into an office, spoke with a lady, she got up and walked into a closed adjoining office. A door opened, there he was, the man with two different coloured eyes. The man who gave me one of the greatest dressing downs of my previous career - I never before then or after heard a bad word said about the gentleman.

*"Thank you Mr 'so and so', hello Mr Stanyon nice of you to drop in, would you like a cup of tea?"* I hoped the Superintendent would still have been in earshot, I wondered if maybe some re-consideration was occurring.

We talked of times in Victoria Province when he was the OC. He asked me to tell him what I had been doing over the past three years.

Then, *"So you want to re-attest? Is there anything else I can do for you other than that?"*

*"Well Sir, now you mention it, if I am accepted, they want me to spend the first three months in Depot. I honestly don't think that will achieve anything useful."*

*"I did not know that, a bit silly really. Anything else?"*

*"No Sir and thank you for your time."*

*"Just leave a phone number where I can contact you, no need to come back here."*

*"Yes Sir."*

A few days later, nursing a hangover of mammoth proportions the phone rang, *"Is there a Mr Stanyon there?"*

*"Yes Sir it's me."*

*"I shall be brief and to the point Stanyon,* (loved it - no flowery stuff here) *there has been some opposition to your re-attestation. I want you to give me your word there will be no repeat of your wild ways. You have one thing in your favour - the police force is very hard up for recruits right now. That has worked in our favour. I have been able to convince them of the quality of your work and abilities as a policeman. I am afraid I do not have sufficient authority to negate the three months in Depot - you shall just have to do that. Just phone the Recruitment officer and he will arrange everything. Good luck."*

I never stepped foot into PGHQ again.

That night we drank late into the night, telling lies and stories of old.

Little did we know we would soon be fighting for our country, we would be losing comrades in arms. Some we thought we could reply on in tough times failed us; others we considered of little value, proved hard working and gallant operatives. We were to witness the best and worse in our fellow members – human conflict has a way of revealing the true characters of participants.

I was one of the very fortunate ones, I was to be blown up, mortared, and shot at. I survived an aircraft accident, misread my maps and wandered across international boundaries. I worked with the very best men Rhodesia had to offer. It was my honour, a distinct privilege. I shall never meet the likes of them again.

I re-attested in the force on 10th May 1971, one of the few who actually had three interviews to join the Regiment.

I was required to complete a shortened course of three months in the Training School, which by comparison with my first two stints was little more than a number of laughs and a waste of time. The most significant issue that occurred during this time, was the arrival, unbeknown to myself, in Rhodesia of my last girlfriend Sue, from Canada. She was immediately employed as a Nurse in Salisbury. On advice from Chief Inspector McBride, and with his assistance, I was posted to Southerton Police station in Salisbury South on 31st July 1971.

Given my previous experience I was immediately transferred within that station to the Enquiries Section. A much sought after section for new Policeman, who in the town branch, anyway, usually commenced their careers by walking the beat and doing other less than mind taxing work. From my perspective, all I was doing was investigating petty crime, all the interesting cases were taken over by CID.

The force had changed, well the personalities at least, the life style in the "town police" was also very tame and uninteresting. In an effort to spice up my working life, I applied to and was accepted by the CID. I started my year of probation on the 1st August 1972 by being posted to Store breaking section.

Investigating the same crimes day after day, was not my cup of tea – and my thoughts turned to travel again. For those uninitiated, the CID probation, is an opportunity for the senior members to assess the probationer's quality and ability to fit into the CID mould.

Some of my peers failed to make the grade, not because they did not have the ability, but their personalities were deemed "unacceptable" for CID work. I had signed on for three years, and did not have the money to buy myself out, so I was stuck with my lot. On the 6th December, 1972 I was transferred to the Residential section of CID – an even more boring place, stuck with investigating Housebreakings!!!

As has always been the case in my life, at the oddest times and in the most peculiar situations Fate played another card unannounced. At 3.00 a.m. on Thursday the 21st December, 1972 communist trained terrorists attacked Altena Farm in Centenary. On the 23rd December, 1972 a second attack, on Whistlefield Farm, Centenary. Now this was a surprise to most people in Rhodesia. I have on good authority from my friend DSO Peter Begg (former Special Branch Officer) that it was not a surprise to Terrorist Desk Mashonaland, who had been reporting a probable "incursion" for months prior to the first attack!! As no troops had been deployed, the mind boggles as to why?

All personnel in CID Salisbury were summoned to the PCIO's office, I do not recall the date, but it was within days of the 21st December 1972. We were briefed and volunteers were called for – every man took a step forward.

My life would never be the same again – I am, pleased I was one of the men that took a step forward, I was sent to Bindura on operational duties soon after.

I last saw and spoke to Mr Sherren on his farewell tour as the Commissioner. I just don't recall which Mopani tree I was under at the time. There were a few wild times, and some 'confrontational issues' which were all resolved amiably, so to speak.

$*$ $*$ $*$ $*$ $*$

*A man travels the world over*
*In search of what he needs and returns home to find it.*

**George Moore**

## UNDER INVESTIGATION
## FOR FRAUD

In early 1973, after having compiled many of the dockets against captured terrorists and those people who had assisted them, the 'powers that be' decided I should be delegated new duties, one of the reasons I think was that we had filled up all prison facilities in Salisbury and surrounding towns as well as Bindura.

I was the investigating officer of the first terrorist to fire a shot in anger in Operation Hurricane and therefor 'the war'. He was a well-educated man, and although I cannot recall his birth name, his terrorist code name was Joshua Misfire. It was he who wounded the female farmer in the arm in Centenary – the shot that started the war. I remain in his debt for some of my education.

I asked him whether he wished to make a statement under caution. He elected to do so. I asked him whether he wanted me to type it out, or would he prefer to write it himself.

He elected the latter and asked, *"how do you want me to write the statement in capitals or cursive?"* I did not know the word cursive!!! He was found guilty and was one of the first terrorists hanged in Salisbury after 23rd December 1972.

One of my jobs entailed the perusal and acquisition of certain information that could only been gleaned from Police Station Crime Registers. This information centred on contraventions of the Law and Order (Maintenance) Act.

To accomplish this, I was given a Land Rover. My Officer in Charge informed me there was no need for anyone to go with me, as long as I did not travel after sunset I would be fine! I had to leave Bindura, go to Mount Darwin, Centenary, Umvukwes, Concession and back along the railway line through Glendale and back to Bindura. Those were all the Police stations in the 'Sharp End' at that time.

Apparently there were rules to this incursion, we, that's the good guys, moved during the day and they, the bad guys, at night. I set off armed with an FN, one magazine with twenty rounds, three pens, two notes books and a plastic pouch to ensure the documents did not get dirty. The Land Rover was fitted with full-length doors, no mine proofing.

*Mines? Oh there were a few of those here and there but stick to the main road Stanyon you should be fine.* Your FN rifle was placed barrel down, between the driver's seat and driver's door. No camouflage for the CID, we were crime fighters not soldiers! It was just a pair of those short shorts, veldskoens and your cleanest dirty shirt.

I was to find out dismounting from the vehicle at each station required a contortionist act which made Houdini look like a rank amateur but it was not long and I could exit a police Land Rover with three fixed AK's blazing away, fully armed, faster than Dick Turpin.

The incursion, war, fracas, rebellion, conflict, campaign or *chimurenga* was commonly called simply 'the Hondo' or 'The Sharp End'. People were having the devil's job trying to find common terminology. There was no doubt that 'police speak' was altering in leaps and bounds, just about every corner one took, someone was using unfamiliar language.

There was the Daily Sitrep, large amounts of 'int' was being collected, collated, compiled and disseminated to 'JOC' and 'others' (not necessary to be too specific on this point). A lot of the disseminated 'int' was typed on A4 paper with coloured ribbons down the centre, red and blue and maybe even a green.

New terminology like, TOP SECRET, CONFIDENTIAL, FOR -specified ranks or positions - EYES ONLY. There was a series of codes applied to the 'Int' – 'A1' 'B2', 'F5'.

One District Code had survived the new way - 'File 99' - the rubbish bin -always useful when no other file could be thought of.

Being very much on the sidelines of these people, it was a very busy time. Panic, astonishment and disbelief are words that would adequately describe the mood I found.

*'Where the hell did they all come from?' 'What was SB doing?' 'Why have we got Ground Coverage?'* (I had never heard of the unit)

I arrived right on lunchtime. At either Centenary or Mount Darwin.   My enquiries about a meal led me to a caravan with a long line of men standing patiently. Most were dressed in camouflage, some in deep low whispered conversation. I picked them as the super sleuths, the SB.!!! The food was being served by the always cheerful ladies of the Police Reserve.

I noted once you received your meal, there were a number of benches, where people ate hurriedly and left.  Having got my meal I looked around for somewhere to sit – and lo and behold there was a face there, an adversary, I had not seen for a while - old Section Officer Eric Saul. He was now commissioned, as I had learnt from his discussion with me about my driving.

He was sitting alone at a large table. I asked if I could join him, he nodded approval.  I sat down and asked how he was doing in the war.

He made some diplomatic reply and then said, *"Stanyon, you are heading for a lot of trouble. I have checked and you knowingly made a false declaration in your application to re-join,"* and without waiting for my answer, he continued, *"I am aware that you were married in Australia. I have read your re-attestation application, you clearly state 'never married'.*

I pondered for a while on two points. One - how would he know anything about my life, whilst I was in Australia?  Secondly, why would he have gone to the trouble of perusing my application for re-attestation?  It may seem strange, but I do not think Saul was a vindictive person. I do know he was fearless in his determination to ensure anyone in breach of the law was rightfully prosecuted.

I told him his information was erroneous and I had never married at any stage in any form. I said it was possible and most likely I had skipped the marriage ceremony and gone straight to the consummation of the relationship.  However in legal terms that did not constitute 'marriage' so my application form was, as I had submitted it, correct in every way. The matter was never raised again.

I hope he did not waste much of his time on the matter. There was a war to fight and while he was a most capable man, he really needed to concentrate on the important matters. I do not think I ever set eyes on Section Officer Saul again. For his sake I am, pleased to report he is recorded as having left the Police Force as an Assistant Commissioner – and all said and done, he would have been very good at his job.

$*$    $*$    $*$    $*$    $*$

*Build me straight, O worthy Master!*
*Staunch and strong, a goodly vessel,*
*That shall laugh at all disaster,*
*And with wave and whirlwind wrestle!*

*Henry Longfellow*

# CID
## OPERATIONAL INVESTIGATIONS

*Army Co-operation, Spouse Incident Advice & Incident reporting to both HQ's*

Y ou might be surprised by what you read. Life is full of twists and turns with things that go bump in the night!

Anyone resident in Rhodesia in the early part of 1973 will recall the tragedy that occurred when the RBC broadcast to the nation, *"with regret we report the death of...."*, and named the person. Unfortunately the spouse and family had not been notified in advance and first heard of their loved one's demise on National Radio.

Members of CID Salisbury were gathered together and informed this deplorable situation would not be repeated. In future we were told to tell our families, should the unthinkable happen to one of us, a Commissioned Officer would be despatched immediately to the next of kin, notify them and provide any necessary support required.

On my return to residence I advised my wife, although highly unlikely should I be killed on Operations, a Commissioned Officer would advise her in person and provide whatever assistance she needed. We then shared a pint bottle of Lion Lager, as was our custom (no money see!) and went about our business.

I continued my 'month in month out' duties, each night I was on Op's, by mutual agreement, I would phone my wife, tell her I loved her and all was well.

Throughout the war I never discussed my work with my wife – one policeman in the house was more than enough, also some of the duties I was required to carry out would have been depressing for any sane person.

On the morning of Wednesday the 19th September 1973, I was in Mount Darwin. D/Insp Ted Painting instructed me to get organised, we had two farm attacks to investigate. Instructing me to drive, we left Mt Darwin for Centenary. We had with us D/Sgt Nyenya and D/Const Ndhlovu. For reasons I am unable to recall we also had a PO Campbell.

Painting navigated us to the first scene - unfortunately I do not recall the name of the farm. There had been no injuries and we went about our normal routine procedures. I was approached while so engaged by a person who identified himself as an army engineer.

*"Greetings and can I help you?"*

*"I want to know who was driving that police Land Rover,"* he said pointing to the CID vehicle.

*"I was,"* I said, thinking 'and what the hell has it got to do with you?'

He then shifted into the official military talk, "Don't you know you need clearance from us before you travel on these roads!"

Now I was busy! We had detained some men so I had work to do and what's more I still had a second scene to attend. I do not recall my exact reply, but do recall thinking - do not be rude – so I told him we were the BSAP, we did not need anyone's authority to do anything, anywhere or at any time.

He said, *"I am warning you. In future before you attend any more attacks, contact base and find out whether we have cleared the road of landmines so you can do your job safely."* His persistence was starting to fray my nerves a trifle.

*"Yes, sure,"* I said.

*"Now what do you want me to do with this TMH46 land mine you have just driven over? You flicked it out of the ground, it was lying exposed when we were clearing the road."*

In his hand was the first TMH 46 anti-tank mine I had seen – and I had just driven over it!! I felt cold.

My mind went blank, "Sorry what was the question?"

*"What do you want me to do with this TMH?"*

*"Would you be kind enough to place it in the back of our Land Rover please?"*

Knowing he had me against the ropes he left with these parting words of wisdom, *"Ja youse okes should know the gooks always leaves behind a mine, after an attack, that's why we are working in the Sharp End."*

He had won.

*"Thank you,"* I said with diffidence.

We finished the scene, placed the four employees in the rear of the Land Rover and told one chap to keep his foot on top of the mine to stop it moving around. We departed with Painting saying that we had to go via the Centenary East Club to Kachipapa Farm – I informed him of my discussions with the Army.

On arrival at the Club, Painting said, he would radio base and ascertain whether the road to Kachipapa Farm had been cleared. We were stationary, with myself seated in the driver's seat, next to him. I heard the entire conversation.

Painting, *"Confirming the road from the Centenary East leading to Kachipapa Farm has been cleared."*

You can always hear when the radio operator becomes agitated, *"Yes that's – affirmative."*

Painting instructed me to drive down the road, instructing me to travel very slowly and where possible to place one wheel on the centre hump and the other just off the road. To achieve a better view of the road, I lifted my buttocks off the seat by pulling on the steering wheel, I was ignorantly looking to see if I could spot if a mine had been laid!!! (Some years later I received instruction on how mines were laid, and thus should not have bothered with my vigilance. I cannot imagine why I was attending that lecture.)

Travelling no faster than five or six miles an hour we slowly crept towards the next scene. What happened next is etched in my memory for life. My next recollection was I was positioned so my head was lying on the floor of the front passenger's seat. Facing up towards the radio cradle. My legs extended upwards and folded over the backrest of the seat. There was a loud ringing in my head, like a million busy musical bees. My sight was blurred, flashing between sight and blindness. There was a deathly silence.

I could not hear the engine running. No external sounds. I looked to my right and saw part of a leg, a thigh it was European, covered in blood. It took me a while to realise I was actually viewing the leg through the vehicle window. I was conscious of some pain in my chest and arm.

All of a sudden I was back in normal time - my thinking cleared and I found myself standing outside of the Land Rover. I looked down and saw the vehicle was lying on top of Painting. He was conscious. I could only see his head. I spoke to him and asked where he had pain.

He said he could not feel his legs. Looking around I saw the two African policemen and PO Campbell. Our four detainees had given up on the war and had vanished – I presumed they would now be at full tilt running through the maize fields headed for the hills.

The vehicle was either precariously balanced or Campbell and I found some super human strength, we grabbed the roof of the vehicle and 'tossed' it up and forward. Thankfully it stayed put and I was thrilled to see Painting was all in one piece.

Realising he needed medical help I leant in through the front left window, grabbed the radio microphone and called Base. No answer, I called a number of times. No response. I asked for any call sign receiving my message to respond. Silence. With some choice words I left the microphone hanging on the edge of the window. The weight of the microphone pulled the cord with it and it hit the ground, it was unattached. I looked inside the vehicle and there was no radio at all – nothing, just the cradle.

I grabbed my FN and started running down the road in the direction we had been travelling, it would take me to the farm, from where I could get medical assistance. I had not gone far, when a turn in the road revealed armed men, Gooks! Coming to finish the job. I ran, stumbled fell into the maize field.

A European voice shouted, *"Don't shoot, SF."*

I thought, *"Thank F**k!"* I had had enough noise for one day.

It was a response team from the farm homestead that we were travelling to. Little did I know but the explosion could be heard for miles.

I requested a doctor be brought in with the medivac. I also requested a few rolls of film be brought out, because in the mayhem, I could not find my spare rolls, I had used all the film in the camera at the last scene.

Thankfully the chopper was soon on the scene – the medivac team promptly attended to Painting. CID was required to photograph the scene, measure the depth of the hole, the diameter of the hole and dig in the hole to recover fragments of the device for identification. I did all this, except the photographs.

Now I cannot recall the identity of the CID Officer in the front of the chopper – I recognised him and walked towards him, he was obviously not getting out to give me my film. He waved frantically – stop, no stay away! He then lifted his arm up, and displayed a roll of film between thumb and forefinger.

A smile and a nod to me, which I presume meant, we did not forget your request son. He then drew his arm back as though he was going to throw the film to me.

Now it was my turn to frantically wave. The noise of the chopper blades still rotating did not allow for meaningful communication. I gestured I would walk in to collect. He shook his head, smiled and threw the roll of film. I stood there, with confetti falling all around me. Realising his error he shrugged his arms and shoulders, as if to say, *'That's the way it goes!!'*

Miraculously he produced a second roll of film – I started to walk forward. Madly gesturing but not waiting for me to gesture back, yes he did, he did indeed, he threw the next roll of film as if I was attending a second wedding. I turned to walk away, when one of the African police told me to look back. Well you never know your luck in a big city – there is his hand was a third roll of film. I ran towards the chopper, ducked under the blades and grabbed the roll of film.

The chopper departed with Painting. It was lucky I got the roll of film because one of the photos I took that morning has been re-published a number of times. Officially known as the Painting Mine, it can be found in 'The History of the BSAP' – they had it as occurring in '72, rightly; one of the first police incidents. In Blue and Old Gold, again '72 but the vehicle was recorded as being driven by DI Hart".

I have seen it in a number of other publications – that photograph is possibly my only real contribution to the history of Rhodesia.

The Painting Mine, Kachipapa Farm, Centenary Sept. 1973.

Map Ref: US 313539

During the examination of the land mine scene, I became aware of something unusual in my camo jacket pocket – examination revealed a piece of engine shrapnel, later identified by a CMED mechanic. The Land Rover had no mine proofing at all. This piece of steel must have ricocheted around the interior of the cabin and then when everything settled down found refuge in my pocket – it sits in my bar at home: a reminder of the luck you need to survive.

I completed the scene of the mine detonation – never giving the first land mine in the back of the vehicle a second thought. I have no idea of its fate. I walked down to the homestead and started carrying out a CID Scenes of Crime examination. The African Detectives (A/Dets) were speaking to people in the compound.

I was measuring, photographing, writing observations, taking statements and asking questions. *"Now do you feel certain the cook would not have ….? Do you believe one of these terrs may have been a previous employee?"*

What other stupid questions could one ask of someone whose life has just been turned upside down? *"Did you see his face?" "Did he have any scars or tattoos?" "How tall was he?" "Describe his build."* All the old familiar questions and procedures were laughable in their irrelevance.

Then a familiar voice from behind me, *"Were you the driver of the truck that just got blown up?"*

I turned around and bless my soul there was the army engineer we had met at the first scene. Now the boot was on the other foot.

So in my best official policeman's voice with just a tinge of cynicism, I replied, *"Indeed I was, and presumably you are the person who clears the roads of land mines so we can get to do our work safely?"*

Stick that up your jumper, I thought, now squirm your way out of that Sunshine.

*"Yasiss (Jesus) you okes! Man, we cleared the top road that was the one you should have took, you took the bloody lower road, and we had not cleared that yet. Man, you have got to get your act together or you will get killed."*

And with that last punch, which I thought was well below the belt, he walked away shaking his head. I am not certain but I think I heard *"Bloody Fuzz…"*

I have no recollection of how PO Campbell, the African staff or I returned to Darwin, but we did. I went straight to the 234 Club and began to celebrate in earnest. I never needed a reason to drink, but now I actually had one.

Unbeknown to me, there had been other movements relative to the incident. There was a loud knock on the front door of my house. My wife answered. There stood a sombre looking gentleman, clad in a suit. She thought possibly a door to door salesman or insurance agent.

*"Are you Mrs Stanyon?"*

*"Yes."*

*"I am Superintendent 'so and so' from the CID. I have some bad news for you."*

My wife felt faint, she tells me it was all she could do to make it back to the chair in the lounge. The CID Officer followed her in.

*"It is your husband, he has hit a land mine and we have no idea what has happened to him. We cannot get any information, I'm sorry."*

*"But he is OK isn't he?"*

*"I am afraid I cannot say that with any certainty. We shall notify you as soon as the matter is clarified. Is there anything I can do, anyone you need me to call?"*

*"No thanks."*

*"Thank you Mrs Stanyon and good luck."*

With that he was on his way.

Back at the 234, the party was firing up – with each beer my pains subsided, I was now walking at about 45 degrees, with a slight sway or would that be stagger. My usual phone time to home was at 6:00 p.m. However at that time I had still been on the road. After a few too many beers, and telling lots of lies and having a great joke and laugh at the expense of the 'confetti officer', time slipped by. I walked out of the bar to relieve myself, and in the clear sobering star lit night I realised I had not phoned the wife.

I immediately went into my office and phoned home. I decided not to tell her about the mine, she would only worry unnecessarily. She answered and in my best, drunken, slurry voice, I greeted her and asked how her day had been. She was sobbing. My God something had gone wrong at home, she is in trouble.

*"What's wrong?"* I asked.

*"You are in hospital I can tell."* She was a nurse. The confusion just escalated. *"A CID Officer visited me and said you hit a land mine. You said they would only come when you had been killed. You have obviously been badly injured, you are not talking clearly or have you just recovered from the anaesthetic after surgery. Tell me you are alright."*

*"No I promise you, everything is fine, I'm just drunk."*

*"Don't lie to me, tell me the truth, how badly injured are you?"*

*"No I'm fine,"* I said attempting to sit on my desk top, unfortunately at that very moment, I misjudged my seating and fell onto the office floor. The phone cord had not been long enough, so the handset fell away and the main phone cradle hit the floor as well. I recovered as best as I could.

*"Hello are you still there?"*

*"Get me the nurse Doug, just get me the nurse."*

It went on forever – in the end we agreed that if I was injured it was not serious and we went to bed. The following morning I was able to clarify the situation. She never did hear from Supt 'so and so' again.

So one would expect that to be the end of that and onwards and upwards with the war effort, but no, not in the BSAP and, as it turns out, not in ZANU either. The BSAP needed to have a report, from me because I had been driving a police vehicle that had been damaged.

Whether a Traffic Accident report book (TARB) was filled out or consideration was given for me to re-sit my driver's licence - in compliance with Standing Orders Section xxx – I shall never know.

The demand came from INTEL SBY (who in God's name were they?) in RADIO GAM 489/73. They had to have a report detailing the circumstances in which this vehicle had been so extensively damaged. My report dated 4th October 1973 refers. (I have a copy) That was two weeks after the incident. Now, surely we could put that behind us and get on with fighting the war.

No we needed more paperwork. You can detonate a land mine but don't for a minute think you don't have to explain yourself. The paper work had not been completed.

On the 29th November 1973 (over a month later) the PCIO (Salisbury and Mashonaland) demanded a report on the incident – so once again I submitted a two-page report detailing the incident.

Now the date escapes me, but it was after my last report. D/Insp Stanton (SB Terrorist Desk) an extraordinarily talented anti-terrorist operative, who should have been Commissioned to further the prosecution of the war effort, but alas never was, telephoned me.

He said, *"I have a terrorist's note book here in which it is reported you were killed when you detonated the land mine at Kachipapa Farm. I shall forward you a copy."*

I do not recall whether Mr Stanton had the perpetrator alive or not. I never asked.

He added, *"Were you one of three Europeans digging graves just south of Mount Darwin on such and such date?"*

I had been on many grave-digging expeditions. The disposal of terrorist bodies killed in action fell on the CID Department and continued until the end of the war. I am not sure what happened in other arenas. The policy demanded only European police attend to such duties. The purpose was to conceal the locations from all Africans, so the final burial place could not be re-located and treated as dedicated martyrs' ground. I was unable to confirm the dates he provided.

He then described one of the Europeans who had wandered off from the main group, shooting guinea fowl with a shotgun.

It was my Member in Charge D/Insp Painting. I asked how he knew. He told me he was currently interrogating a capture who described all of us and every move we made. They had been seated on a small rise, less than 100 yards from us.

The luck of the Gods sit in weird places at times, I am thankful they did not shoot us.

A copy of the terrorist notebook reporting my death is reproduced for this tale. I learned ZANU also had to produce 'paperwork' to finalise their own.

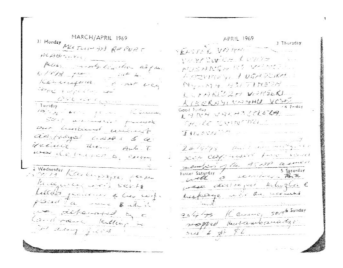

*Copy of terrorist notebook reporting the death of the author*

While difficult to read, it reflects in part:

MUTUMBA REPORT

*18/9/73   Kachipapa Farm. Knegwagwa's Sect.*

*Killed farmer and his wife. Placed a landmine that was detonated by a Land Rover killing 4 SA Army Officers.*

Authors Note: Not only sad that it was my epitaph, but that I had been demoted to an SA Army Officer in death.

There is a difference of opinion as to the date the incident happened. I am willing to argue the point with the gook if that is deemed necessary.

It also reports: captured two secret members of the BSAP armed with a revolver both were destroyed. *Mlinzhire* (sic) and *Mapayne*(sic) were the names.

By 1974 finally the ordeal was over – all the paperwork done on both sides – the vehicle sent to the scrap yard. I am pleased to report I visited Painting in hospital; he was expected and did in fact make a full recovery, although I believe he suffered some hearing loss. He went on to get his Commission and retired from the force as a Chief Superintendent. I remain unclear what ever happened to the land mine in the back of the truck. Hopefully someone recovered it or it may be sitting in the fields today waiting for some poor tractor driver to detonate it.

My marriage remained intact and possibly the only time in the 38 years of my marriage, did my wife not show any displeasure at the fact I was inebriated at the time of her call.

It is highly unlikely there would be many other police forces, worldwide, that faced the same obstacles during crime investigations as the BSAP.

\*       \*       \*       \*       \*

*I Laugh at Life: its antics make for me a giddy game,*
*Where only foolish fellows take themselves with solemn aim.*
*I laugh at pomp and vanity, at riches, rank and pride;*
*At social inanity, at swagger, swank and side.*
*At poets, pastry-cooks and kings, at folk sublime and small,*
*Who fuss about a thousand things that matter not at all;*
*At those who dream of name and fame, at those who scheme for*
*pelf…*
*But best of all the laughing game – is laughing at myself.*

# FIRE FORCE

I have told a few yarns about my experiences in the Hondo, the more observant reader will have noticed a scarcity of my involvement in full-blooded combat. Some may recall the fictitious statement now etched in the history of the Vietnam conflict:

*I love the smell of napalm in the morning.'*

I recall the film and thought I might involve myself in some plagiarism, and offer a Rhodesian CID version of it. Those who saw the film will remember the character removes his tee shirt before delivering the line.

I decided to omit that bit, as it was most likely I would have been bitten by so many Tsetse flies, I would have ended up with Trypanosomiasis (African sleeping sickness). I knew a few police operatives incorrectly diagnosed with 'Trips'- they were actually, work-shy, inactive or lethargic.

Now where was I – Oh the title of my war exploits? It was either to be: 'In the abortive pursuit of Gallantry Awards' or 'I hate the smell of cordite at any time'.

In Mtoko circa 1973/74, someone decided a CID/SB rep would be a worthwhile addition to the 'Fire Force'. The idea was that if during a 'contact' a terrorist was captured or wounded, a chopper containing an Acorn (I thought they were meant to be wise things?) would fly above the skirmish and just below the Commander in the 'G' Car. The chopper would drop into the contact, the Acorn rep would bale out with his interpreter, take control of the gook from the soldier, start interrogating him, thus allowing the soldier to get back to fight the good fight.

I am not sure if the 'men of wisdom' thought this exercise through as that actually meant we would be interviewing/interrogating (dependent upon whether you are talking to the left or right wing of life) this chap while the 'contact' was still in full swing.

Now I do not have much experience of these things, but the few 'contacts' in which I found myself, there was no front line, so sometimes there were people shooting at each other all around one!

This meant while we were engaged in questions like: *"What is your Chimurenga name?* (code name). *Real name? Kraal head? District? Where have you come from and where are you going? Commissars name? Where is your RV point? Where were you trained? Etc, etc, etc…"*; the sweet, acidic aroma of cordite was wafting through the air the whole time. If you did not have 100% full concentration you would sometimes wonder whether one of those whizzing or whirling noises may not in fact continue past into eternity, but come to a sudden halt in your person.

For my sins I was always placed in the front left seat of the chopper. As you may be aware, there are no doors. The pipes located just below the doorframe, used as a step, were positioned at just the right length for my lanky legs. All went well for a few trips. Sometimes we flew for twenty minutes or so and then landed somewhere in the bush, thankfully usually on top of a small kopje. We would remain there for the duration of the day, whereafter, with nothing reported, we returned to base. On other occasions the fire force became involved, however there were seldom any captures or wounded, so once again we all went home.

One morning as we were flying, I was advised of a capture on the ground! I realised this was to be the acid test. To say I felt uncomfortable would be an understatement. Before I could make any meaningful verbal contribution our chopper dropped down like a hawk onto its prey. He found a spot where I was to be deployed.

Picking his place and time, the pilot said whatever they said, meaning *"Get Out"*.

I looked down, out of the door and two things immediately struck me; beneath me was elephant grass, sure some of it had been flattened by the down draft of the blades, but it was unclear what lay beneath the grass! The second thing was the height the pilot expected me to jump from – now you might think I am exaggerating, but so help me God it did look like 100 feet or more!

I know it was close to the ground but I said to the pilot, *"Can you go down a little further please?"* I thought if he did I could get a better view of what I was going to land on.

From his language and demeanor in response, I was not left in any doubt - he intended throwing me out if I did not jump. I jumped.

I had no idea where the capture was! When we had been 100 feet up, the pilot had pointed into the bush – I had seen lots of good guys and bad guys running around, but to say I was disorientated would be an understatement.

As I went through the elephant grass, I hit the deck and, guess what – my right knee dislocated. I was not equipped with a radio nor was my interpreter – I think the plan was if I found the army, they would have any communications means necessary.

The chopper flew away, and the grass returned to its normal height, I found myself enveloped in this beige coloured shroud gently swaying in the breeze. I was stuck between a rock and a hard place. I could not move, I could see nothing, the noise around me was deafening – people were shooting at each other, interjected with the occasional loud explosion.

Eventually, with the assistance of the African detective and a cessation in hostilities I was casevaced from the scene by chopper.

I think they were a trifle annoyed I had not been wounded or engaged in some other 'action' that may have resulted in consideration of at least a mention in dispatches. The medics were also a trifle surprised when I directed 'operations' to re-locate the knee and once done I walked away.

The war meandered along. It was to take another six odd years.

\*      \*      \*      \*      \*

# A POLICE LADY
# IN THE LIFE OF RENEGADES

M ay I commence this humble contribution by apologising to the fairer sex of the BSAP, for your apparent exclusion from my police career. The reason is simple and much to my personal loss, I only ever served with one of your fine company.

Having said that however, I must say at the outset, whenever I was CID Nights in Salisbury, I came to know the Information Room Police women by their voices. So on my weeks night shift I was always pleased and thankful when a woman's voice came over the radio *(sorry chaps – they were better organised, quicker to respond correctly and were able to keep all the 'issues' they were juggling with in the air without dropping them.)* I was going to use a common term there, but in the context of whom I was referring to it would have sounded rude. CID Nights duty fell to a single individual, for a period of a week of night shift. It was this person's task to make assessments of all serious crimes reported between 4.30 p.m. and 7.30a.m. He would determine actions to be taken, inclusive of "calling out" appropriate persons with the expertise to investigate such crimes, preservation of the scenes of crime, acceptance by CID for further investigation of the crimes or not, in Salisbury.

It was a most grandiose title which had many junior Information Room and suburban Station Members, either very mindful of their P's and Q's or those with more experience thankful, when CID Nights 'took the matter over'.

The very experienced uniform policemen, when observing the CID Nights character, was nervous and those with limited experience tried to con him into taking responsibility for 'a matter'. I might add also I was doing CID Nights (Salisbury) for the last week of Rhodesia's existence, i.e., on the 13th April 1980. Those who were in and around Salisbury and elsewhere I guess, will recall it was busy, "bloody busy."

The only woman detective I was ever stationed with was on CID Crimes of Violence, Salisbury. That lady, she really was one, was WDSO Daph Morrison, I can provide no other regimental detail – she was senior to me in service and I presume rank (we were both SO's) I always treated her as my senior. A quiet, almost reserved, lady-like personality, I never mixed socially with her, but over the years on the section we became 'good buddies'.

Daph or Daphne used to get most of the crimes involving 'females', accused or complainants. We helped each other out when requested. I recall her entering my office one day telling me she was investigating a rape - white on white. As I recall the accused was a male tourist from RSA.

She told me she felt certain he was responsible. As in many rape cases, (DNA not as prevalent and advanced as it is now), the circumstances always ended up his word against hers. He was claiming it was consensual – forget about forensic hair transfer etc., always a difficult defence to deal with.

Daph was in a bit of a dither. Her questioning of the accused had exhausted her and been fruitless. Would I be able to help? She did say he had a 'smug attitude' (I think that was the term). He was in the cells.

"Sure," I said, "I shall have a word with him."

I read all the information available and took a walk across to the Charge Office cells. I interviewed the man in the cells. We had a long, meaningful and constructive discussion. I escorted him back to the Crimes of Violence offices and handed him over to Daph, advising her he had seen the "error of his ways" and wished to tell her the truth.

His family, including his wife returned from whence they came without him. If my memory serves me correctly, I think at his trial he was acquitted.

On another occasion I had a well-known PO from Traffic, as a probationer on Crimes of Violence.

We were given the task of locating an errant Magistrate from Botswana, who for reasons unknown, had emptied his official safe, helped himself to the cash contents and entered Rhodesia under false pretences.

The chap I had under my wing was DPO (he may have been an SO I am not sure) Gordon Greenwood. He was, to put it mildly a 'wild bit of gear', a tireless worker, keen as mustard, but when you let him loose, he was like the seven winds all blowing at once and in differing directions.

The exercise to locate and arrest the errant Magistrate was simple enough, and while we had worked long and tireless hours in the 'Vice Mile', information received was he had a preference for ladies with dark coloured skin. I am not certain we made the actual arrest.

Daph had been in our company the following morning at about 10.00 am when we decided to go for quiet celebratory drink. Greenwood and I took a company car and drove out to a small hotel on the Fort Victoria road, which we knew was not frequented by anyone who could make life uncomfortable for ourselves.

We fell into the age-old trap! Was it willingly? I guess that had to be possible.

*"Let's have another one, just to balance up the first."*

*"Why not!"*

*"There's not a lot on, those two tasted quite fine. Should we sample a third?"*

*"Good idea."*

*"What about one for the road?"*

*"Yes, that was just what the Dr. ordered!"*

*"It's a long road, maybe just one more!!"*

*Etc. etc.*

There was a phone call for a Mr Stanyon – there was absolute amazement on the faces of the two, now somewhat intoxicated upholders of the law. Who knows we are here? We scanned the bar, for someone up to no good.

It was Daph on the phone.

The OC had called a meeting in his office of the whole section, to congratulate DSO Stanyon and Greenwood on their determination and persistent investigations. It has been postponed to three o'clock.

*"You two better get back."*

*"Thanks Daph."*

From the police entrance on the corner of Railway Avenue to the Crimes of Violence offices, one had to walk the entire length of the south wing of the CID building.

The first hurdle was a simple one, a Constable normally. We passed that one, with flying colours. The second was the PCIO's office on your right. We knew if seated at his desk our passing would not be detected. As luck would have it we passed his door without mishap.

At times we had to use the walls to steady our gait.

The next trap was the SWO's office (The Senior Warrant Officer - DCI), not someone one needed to meet on a good day, let alone when travelling with three sheets in the wind and positioned at 45 degrees to the vertical. Passed there and done and dusted. A few less difficult and threatening hurdles, Members in Charge Residential and Stores, just young bucks, newly appointed D.I.'s.

The second last hurdle was the Office of the OC Property Section. Now this did present a quandary of some magnitude. His desk was so positioned at the base of the steps going up to the offices of 'sunglasses and raincoats with large lapels' - The Special Branch!!!!!! Movement along this section was in full view of the one and only Supt 5265 Angus Ross, a dour and cranky Scot, no nonsense man, who did everything at the speed of light, with steely, uncomfortable eyes.

He had recently questioned me at length in Mount Darwin regarding the sudden and unexpected death of a witness who had been assisting terrorists. Just in case, some might choose to tarnish my good reputation, I was not the suspect in the case. If Ross saw us, our fate would be unpleasant to say the least. As we staggered past, the luck of the Gods were with us, he was absent. We had cleared the minefield, with 30 minutes to spare.

Daph had been hovering around, waiting. We were seated in my office. She entered and said, "Oh no, the smell, look at the two of you, you look awful, go into the toilets and wash your faces and rinse your mouths out."

As we respectfully obeyed, she said, *"And try and walk straight!"*

On our return she claimed, *"I can still smell the alcohol a mile off."*

She left returning with her handbag and taking out one of those spray bottles she said *"close your eyes,"* and then sprayed both of our faces and shirts.

Now I have seen drunken men in brothels before - for the righteous, no, I have not partaken of the forbidden fruit. I just knew that was what we must have resembled and now smelled like. Why did the OC choose today to do this?!

She said, *"I am going into the OC's office."*

Times flies when you don't want it to!

*"I shall make sure no one sits on the chair, next to me, follow me a little later, and one sit on the chair and the other on the arm rest. Try and look intelligent."*

She disappeared. We waited then walked out of my office and witnessed other members entering the OC's office. As I entered I put on my best 'casual look'.

Greenwood had obviously, without consultation decided he was sitting on the chair. I stood between him and Daph, who was also seated on a chair.

The OC opened his address, *"That's everybody then – well welcome, I have taken this unusual step to applaud the work of two of our members Greenwood and Stanyon ......"*

At which point I started feeling a little faint. I extended my hand down to feel for the armrest and felt Daph's hand grab mine and move it to the armrest. Now there was some lack of planning and proper research - in my defence - there were two chairs. One can only place one cheek on one armrest, I knew that! But regrettably I placed the wrong cheek on the wrong armrest. The result was I totally misjudged my move and unceremoniously landed on my arse, lost my balance, fell backwards and hit my head against the brick wall. I was moderately dazed and my next recollection were the words,

*"Thank you that will be all."*

Thanks for the memories Daph – you were a champion – hopefully we will meet on the other side.

\*     \*     \*     \*     \*

*Life is not about,*
*Waiting for the Storm to pass,*
*But learning to*
*Dance in the Rain.*

# THE ART OF ANTI-TERRORIST OPERATIONS
## *According to 'Gentleman Jack'*

On the 31st October 1973 I was drafted to complete my two years commitment in CID HQ. Everyone in the CID was required to complete this posting. By that time I, as had many of the others who started their two years admin stint at CID HQ had acquired varying degrees of experience in combating terrorism.

The wisdom of posting experienced anti-terrorist operatives to work 8am to 4.30pm in offices totally divorced from the war effort, remains, to this day a mystery. Alas in hindsight, it was yet another example of how ill-equipped our leaders were to deal with this incursion. What had worked for so many years was blindly followed, irrespective of circumstance.

As always I chose to see the glass half full. I was more fortunate than the others - I got the plum job of Forensic Science Liaison Officer. My experience in this regard dealing with some of the 'leading lights' in the world of science in Rhodesia brought some interesting observations. I took over from the previous incumbent, who in a day or two explained my requirements and informed me I reported to the Deputy OC CID. He did say it was highly unlikely, unless I saw a need to talk to the Deputy OC, that he would approach me.

For those readers who may be unfamiliar with BSAP CID HQ, it was a cluster of very old, single-storied buildings surrounded by a ten-foot high cyclone fence, with rolled barbed wire on the top. All the buildings surrounded a small, square, concrete surfaced courtyard. It was positioned within the Depot grounds next to the farrier's shop and horse stables. Hidden from public view by thirty-foot high pine trees, it housed the Fingerprint Bureau, the Firearms Registry, Mashonaland Scenes of Crime staff, the Handwriting Expert, and the Records of Service of all members of the CID.

Outside of this complex, directly across the road leading to the stables, was an equally old building housing the Police Forensic Science Laboratory, Dr Thompson and Mrs Coates his able assistant, a lady typist and the FSLO. The complex also housed the Black Museum and some rudimentary scientific apparatus.

I had held the position for a couple of months with minimal contact with either A/Comm Jack Denley or Snr Asst Comm Peter Allum (OC CID). My main task was to ensure all 'exhibits received for scientific evaluation' were correctly labelled and presented and ensure the requests from investigators were specific to their needs, wishes and intentions. I had to evaluate which scientific 'boffin' was the most appropriate for the work required to be done and to arrange with that person for the work to be carried out in a timely fashion and ensure the chain of evidence was maintained in terms of legal requirements.

I also had to accompany Dr Thompson to all scenes of crime countrywide when his presence was requested. One major plus for a hard up DSO, newly wed, was that I was issued with a Renault R12 motor vehicle for both private and company use. Dr. Thompson made his name working on 'heavy water' during the Second World War, which was, if I remember correctly a pre-requisite for the Atomic Bomb. I played a lot of chess with him and we raced each other to finish the daily crossword in the morning newspaper. He kept me amused with stories of the 'antics' on Friday nights in the Officers Mess of which he was a member. No one ever actually came and checked on what I was doing.

So you can imagine it came as a total surprise when I was walking across the courtyard one morning and was approached by A/Comm. Denley. *"Mr Stanyon, may I have a word with you please?"*

*"Yes, Sir."*

We were standing in the middle of this open space. In full view of I know not how many wretched souls doing 'time' and in the blazing sunlight. There stood an A/Comm. and a DSO. No one would have been close enough to hear our conversation.

*"I understand you have some experiencing in fighting terrorists?"*

*"Well, no Sir, I have some experience in carrying out criminal investigations, inclusive of scene examinations and exhibit collections in which terrorists were obviously the accused. But fighting. No Sir. No fighting."*

*"My understanding is you detonated a land mine."*

*"Yes Sir that is part and parcel of the CID investigators lot when attending scenes on Operations. If you don't see them and run over them in the vehicle you can be unlucky when they detonate."*

*"Do they not all detonate, Mr Stanyon?"*

*"Well in my limited experience Sir, not always. At one scene we attended we dislodged a mine, which a follow up army unit then located and we placed it in the back of our Land Rover as an exhibit, Sir."*

*"What happened?"*

*"Well Sir we went to the next scene of crime, a few hours later, and that's when we detonated a land mine."*

*"Mr Stanyon I am going to give you some very useful advice in combating terrorists. After you leave CID HQ you will undoubtedly return to the war."*

*"Yes I hope so Sir, sooner if possible."*

*"You must understand Mr Stanyon I was one of six members of the BSAP seconded to the Kenya Police during the Mau Mau emergency."*

I did not tell Mr Denley as a child of a Kenyan farming family I too had been in Kenya during the Mau Mau emergency and that all the adults in my family had actually hunted them for the duration of the emergency. I did not think he would be interested.

He continued, *"Ever been fly fishing Mr Stanyon?"*

*"No Sir. No Sir I have not."*

*"Ah! You see there lies the answer. Fly fishing!!"*

He then gave me a physical demonstration and running commentary on the fine art of trout fishing, explaining that flies must be used as bait. He said imagine the terrorist is the trout fish and you the hunter thereof are the fisherman. He cast an imaginary fly out across the courtyard, into an imaginary stream, then with his left hand pulled slightly out and left applying a slight jerking motion.

*"You see Mr Stanyon that is what attracts the fish, in your case the terrorist, the constantly moving fly on the top of the water. Now, Mr Stanyon what is absolutely critical is patience, plenty of it mind you. Slowly, slowly, draw them into the trap and then"*, with that he flung his righty arm above his head, imitating the striking of a fish on the end of his line, *"You have it, out of the water, in your domain and you have the ascendance."*

I was speechless. With that, the man we called 'Gentleman Jack' or 'Jack the Hat' strode back to his office, leaving me standing alone in the courtyard, bewildered, confused and amazed – he was one of our leaders.

Before leaving the forensic lab on the 3rd January 1975 I acquired a Mau Mau Oathing chain from the Black Museum that was labelled, in part, *'brought back by members of the BSAP seconded to Kenya during the Mau Mau'*.

I had indeed learnt something, but I fear it was not what Mr Denley presumed I had learnt.

\*     \*     \*     \*     \*

*The Moving Finger writes; and, having writ,*
*Moves on: nor all thy Piety nor Wit*
*Shall lure it back to cancel half a Line,*
*Nor all thy Tears wash out a Word of it.*

*The Rubaiyat*

# THE BEST 'GIG' IN
# THE RHODESIAN SECURITY FORCES

F or just over twenty-four months of the Rhodesian War, the Hondo or the second Zimbabwean Chimurenga, whatever one choses to call it, I had had, without doubt, the best 'gig' of any member of the Rhodesian Security Forces - bar none.

Better than all the Generals, Wing Commanders, A/Commissioners, bottle washers and cooks, strategy planners and desk pilots, would-if-they-could-bes and legends in their own lunch times, braggers and misfits, shirkers and want-to-bes.

On 1st February 1976, DSO Stanyon whom National Service PO's who patrolled the valley and those who were seconded to the CID and SB, called 'Uncle' because he was so old, just landed unquestionably the best job in the war.

I was posted to CID Sinoia. This had come about in an unusual way. For the third and final time, I had been approached by a senior SB officer and invited to join Special Branch. He offered me the position of Member in Charge, SB Sinoia. As a former cattle rancher's son, the opportunity to work and live partly in the bush was just too much to resist.

I had observed and gladly did what I was asked to do by some of the most experienced and professional anti-terrorist SB men. I never asked questions and just went with the flow.

Names that spring readily to mind in no particular order, other than by rank – so Regimental do you not think! DSOs Ed Bird, Dewe, Grant, Stewart, D/Insp's Opperman, Hart and Stanton. I had also worked with an SB attaché SAS Sgt 'Stretch' Franklin.

I went to my OC, the renowned homicide Investigator C/Supt Hobley and informed him I would have to reluctantly accept the SB offer, to escape the city environment, which frankly like all cities I have lived in, to my mind is toxic to the soul. The reason for the reluctance was that while the SB operatives I have mentioned and a few others were by 1976 top drawer quality: with the increased work load for this section, SB had lowered its standards by accepting men who were untrained, inexperienced and unsuited for the work they were involved in. I think some 'got off' with the fact they were allowed to wear beards!! I realised it was a means to an end and in a macro management sense there was little else they could do.

In 1977/8 I bumped into people from the Army RIC (Rhodesian Intelligence Corp) – whom General Walls was rumoured to have introduced to the war effort because he thought they could do a better job than SB??? Not the ones I worked with, with all due respect. Good soldier's maybe, they were far from intelligence gatherers: full of unbridled enthusiasm but absolutely no experience at all - a frustration and frankly an impediment to my work.

Hobley's reaction was, "*Give me 24 hours before you accept that offer.*"

The following morning he called me into his office and told me I was being transferred to CID Sinoia and to make all the necessary arrangements immediately.

I wish to remind readers I was not a professional warrior; had I wanted to be one, I would have joined the Army. I was first, foremost and always a policeman with a natural predisposition towards the law, its comprehension and in the case of police work its implementation and prosecution. I found investigations, production of evidence and compilation of court briefs/dockets for court submission, undemanding and elementary – even though the law was, is and shall always be an ass.

So why was Sinoia the best 'gig' in the Rhodesian Security Forces? On arrival I was immediately placed on their roster of month in and month out. On my month out I was stationed at Karoi

– from whence the origin of the reputation of the high quality drunk Shangaan Bar counter dancer.

Part of my territory was the Zambezi Valley from Chirundu to Kanyemba.

The south border was not too well defined, but it hazily amalgamated with Sinoia and the Midlands area. I also had responsibility for the Omay TTL that bordered on Matabeleland. Dropping in at whim to see my old and trusted friend IC, SB Kariba, DSO Ken Stewart, was simple as I resided at either the Makuti Hotel (where often I was the sole guest) or the Karoi Twin Rivers Motel. As you may be aware, only security force personnel were legally allowed to be on the valley floor. Working with me I had two D/Sgts and one D/Const - fine fellows indeed. Was that adequate to cover arguably some 30,000 square kilometres? Give it some thought.

As an ex-'bush kid' I was actually paid a monthly salary, given a free company car and petrol, free accommodation and meals, flown around the area in helicopters and small fixed wing airplanes and travelled free on boats across Kariba, wandering around, unsupervised, over some of Africa's greatest and most natural game habitat, unhindered by any other humans. Now pray I ask you, who had a better Gig?

Some guys just get all the luck … seriously!!!

As I mentioned when starting this tale I am now headed back to Africa (which I miss dearly) and I estimate I am going to pay A$20,000 dollars for my six week visit to RSA, Zambia and Swaziland. Many friends have generously offered assistance, to stay with them, reminiscing, drinking and telling lies will be a joyous occasion indeed. At times I have to hire hotels, pay for car hire fees, feed myself, pay for plane tickets, all of which in days gone by was free!

I cannot bring myself to 'go home'. I could not bear to see what has happened there - I am still in correspondence with old friends, who have adapted to the new environment.

Let life at least allow this ageing dancer's unbroken dreams and memories of a once beautiful country and lifestyle remain.

\*        \*        \*        \*        \*

# RECRUITMENT & TRAINING
# OF THE HOME GUARD

I met my Australian wife in Queensland, Australia, whilst I was hitchhiking around the world. Our romance took us through South and Central America and into Canada where, after a lovers spat, we parted ways. I returned to Rhodesia. Some months later she pitched up unannounced. One thing led to another and we married six months before the war started. Unfortunately after 38 years of marriage she died from cancer, in 2011.

When I was posted to CID Sinoia, being a nurse she was employed by the Alaska Mine Hospital, as the Sister in Charge. The hospital was some 20 or 30 miles from the village, which she traversed twice a day. We occupied a Government residence, which was situated on the edge of the village suburbs. From my work I knew terrorists frequented the local African township (Chinoyi), they also bypassed Sinoia on their way ex Zambia to Salisbury.

I was concerned for her safety and suggested she get a job at the local Sinoia Hospital, as she was vulnerable travelling on her own, sometimes at night. She made a suggestion. Why don't you teach me to use an FN and then I can carry one to work and back and keep it in the house when you are away on Ops.

She had never fired any weapon in her life. She was the progeny of well-to-do parents from a salubrious northern beach suburb of Sydney. Frankly her father was horrified when he met her 'boyfriend' – the man she was going travelling with.

*"Are you going to marry first?* He asked, "He is not mandrake you know."

Folklore has it that the Mandrake plant root that resembles a human figure is hallucinogenic and narcotic. In sufficient quantities it induces a state of unconsciousness and was used as an anaesthetic for surgery in ancient times. Her father was a University scholar!!

My wife is best described as petite. She stood 5'2" in height and was very fit with little or no fat. Being 6'4" and having been involved with firearms since the age of seven, I never gave much thought about training her to use a weapon.

We agreed she would learn all the necessary information about weapons handling; how to strip and reassemble, how to quickly reload ammo into magazines, maintenance and safety. We practised this for a month at least. When we decided she was ready to use the weapon, I approached the police reservist running the firing range. I found a time and date when no one would be on the range and we went up for her initiation.

The Belgium Fabrique Nationale (FN) is 3'7" long and weighs 9.5 lbs (I guess most of you know the weight, having carried the bloody thing for miles!!) That made her just 1'9" taller than the rifle. We went through the standing position, I fully explained about 'recoil', how imperative holding the butt tight into the shoulder was. The recoil lift "up and right" was also explained. We were ready.

She asked, *"Can I put it on automatic?"*

*"No let's start with single shot."*

*"You always spoil the fun."*

*"Maybe so, let's try one at a time and when we have full control and all the confidence needed by all means place it on 'sing' and let fly."*

*"You are such a spoilsport!!!"*

*"In your own time (I learnt that from annual musketry!!!), fire the first shot."*

I was standing close to her right shoulder, maybe two feet away. I saw the adjustment and re-adjustment, she pulled it tight into the shoulder, the finger went to the trigger guard (good girl!) the finger moved off the guard and 'squeeze'!

Her feet left the ground flying upwards as the recoil sent her upper torso backwards. The FN went forward and with a loud and dusty crash she hit the ground butt first. Then she fell back onto her back.

*"Did I do that properly Doug? Gee, it's got a lot more kick than you said it had!"*

As I helped her to her feet she said, *"Let me do that again."*

Three further shots, all with identical results. The Range Master brought the lesson to a close.

The pupil complained, *"Give me another chance please, pretty please."*

*"No I shall have to get you a shorter rifle and one that does not have as much recoil."*

After my next bush trip an almost brand new AK, with night sights and 40 round Bakelite magazines became available, the previous owner no longer had any use for it. Just the job I thought, I know someone who will cherish it.

We went through the same training; stripping, loading, cleaning and security. There was just a slight variation this time: I taught her that there were two different types of ammo available. One was known as a 'tracer' the other 'normal'. I always loaded my magazines with alternate rounds, ensuring the first one/top one was a 'tracer'. After a few weeks she was extraordinarily competent – the range practice was excellent; the recoil had no adverse effect. She got her long wished for desire –After some days of practise she was able to put most of a 40 round magazine into a Figure 11 target.

We had a real Annie Oakley on our hands. Then, as I did each night, both AK's were placed on the floor with one up the 'spout' (is that really the true word? It sounds a bit rude) and safety catch on.   I also emphasised emphatically the folly and extreme consequences of having an AD (Accidental Discharge). In both the Army and Police it was an offence that brought about immediate imprisonment.

*"You must always be conscious of the safety of your weapon,"* I stressed.

Now it was no national secret that sometimes and in some circumstances when the 'cat was away the mouse would play". So my wife and I had an agreement. If through some circumstance, either of us should 'stray' we should have the courage to advise the other and allow the matter to be sorted out as we deemed fit. These were unusual times and unusual things happen.

Induction Training over, armaments acquired, sufficient ammo available to start the Third Chimurenga and new married life was bliss. We had one servant, a dear old Malawian man called John who lived with his family on the property he had been with us since day one.

He was part cook, (the new wife wanted to display her culinary qualities and we both loved to garden) – so John's life was as good as it got. He polished shoes, cleaned the car each morning early and generally did what we chose not to do. The war escalated, but I was living the dream with the best 'gig' available.

One Friday afternoon I returned from what was sometimes called a 'bush' trip. I had been away a month – looking forward very much to sleeping in my bed, if you understand what I mean. My wife was waiting at the office to pick me up and take me to our 'love nest'. I jumped in the passenger's seat and learnt over to give her as kiss – she was cold and unresponsive - very quiet and nervous.

*"What's wrong?"*

*"I have something to tell you, please don't get mad at me, it was not my fault."*

I knew it, I just bloody knew it and the bastard, some filthy grimy bastard had taken advantage of my wife. So help me God, I am going to get his name and kill the son of a bitch.

She said, *"You have to put petrol in the car, I will tell you at home."*

*"At bloody home, I want to know now."*

She started crying.

*"Don't pull the tears thing on me – let's have the details, all the details and now."*

By this stage we were at the service station. She got out quickly, before the attendant had filled the car and hurriedly moved into the office. I sat there and my mind saw the face of a chap I had been in driving school with after re-attestation. His name was Ken Steel, a

30 odd year old late recruit in the police, an ex-farmer from the eastern Highlands. We became friendly. He informed me he had joined as a married man and while in Depot his wife had had an affair. She denied it but was still having the affair. Steel asked me to accompany him on a few nights observation of her flat, which I did, but there was no evidence of his accusation.

Just after I joined CID Steel was stationed in Bulawayo. He had purchased a .303 rifle, driven overnight to Umtali, knocked on his mother-in-law's front door and when she answered he shot her, stepped over the body, found his wife and shot her, killing her as well. He then fled the scene. He gave himself up and after his trial he was hanged in Salisbury Prison.

I warned myself not to kill this bastard, but to injure him for life, divorce the woman and move on.

She returned to the car and all my demands were met with silence.

I followed her into the house, she said, *"I want to show you what happened."*

Is this SOB still in the house, has he moved in? I thought.

Still crying she took me to the bedroom and at the door she said, *"Go in."*

There was no one in the room! I looked around, and then saw the windowpane had been smashed, further examination showed three bricks had been dislodged from the external wall, and the curtain had obviously been burnt.

I turned around and she said, *"Will I go to prison?"*

She continued not waiting for the answer delivering her defence, *"For days I got up every morning and just had this urge. Then a few days ago I took the weapon off safety and was fiddling with it and it went off. John was outside washing the car, the bullet didn't hit him, but he was shouting "No Madame No" and hiding behind the car. The curtain caught fire because I had one of those thingy's in the magazine, and when I put out the fire, I saw I had knocked the bricks out of the wall and had smashed the window."*

The relief I felt was palpable. They say make up sex is the best. I concur with those sentiments. The Home Guard was up and running.

\*     \*     \*     \*     \*

# DISTURBING THE
# UTOPIA OF THE OMAY TTL

M ay of 1976 was my month out, again! Ah yes, Makuti and Twin Rivers Hotels, odd drinks at the Jam Jar in Kariba, swanning around Mana Pools and along the valley to the Angwa River, I'll drop into Mashumbi Pools, see the lads there – what a lovely war. I hope no one finds out about this job I have been given.

The member in charge casually called me in to his office:

*"Doug, I forgot to mention there's been a slight change in your deployment."*

*"Oh really, how so?"*

*"You are to spend the next month in Siyakobvu."*

*"Where?"*

*"It's in the middle of the Omay TTL."*

*"Where is that? "*

*"It's on the banks of Kariba.*

*"Big dam that, whereabouts?"*

*"On the border with Matabeleland"*

*"You have to be kidding right? What happens there?"*

*"Not sure really, Salisbury wants you to go and have a shufti and see if you can pick up anything, something about a possible terrorist R & R area. Someone in Karoi will know the route in.*

*Sgt Fani have you been to Siyakobvu?"*

*"Kwete Ishe."* (No Sir)

*"Do you know it?"*

*"Kwete Ishe."*

*"Have you heard of it?"*
*"Kwete!"*

I studied a map. Ah! There it is 50 miles south of the Bumi Hills Hotel. Not exactly close enough to drop in for a quiet one at the end of each day! In Karoi I was given directions and some excellent advice by the resident SB Det/Sgt Nemberi, one of the men I most respected in the police force.

Travel west through the Urungwe TTL, continue across the Rengwe TTI, keep right and follow the road to Siyakobvu. In SB we had a cash reserve called the SB Float. The money was used to pay sources/informants and to buy gifts to win hearts and minds! It was strictly audited.

As I was checking the books from the chap I had taken over from, the D/Sgt informed me, *"No good taking cash Sir. Go into town and buy bags of salt, mealie meal, fishing hooks, also fishing line, cash is no good in the Omay."*

In my world 'you don't have a dog and bark yourself', this D/Sgt was amongst the smartest operators I knew. I followed his every word and suggestion. I had enough stuff in the back of the Land Rover to pass as a regular trader!

Fani and I left for the new world. He drove. I enjoyed the freedom of not having to concentrate on the road. I pondered if we might bump into Dr. Livingstone or even Stanley – or maybe some lost Portuguese traders, with beads and mirrors.

As we drove, I was trying to think when and why I had heard of this Omay – I mean what kind of a name is that? Then it dawned on me - The Pearce Commission – 1972. The British Government chose a judge called Pearce to test the acceptability of the Constitutional Settlement signed between Smith and the British Government. One of Pearce's representatives had visited the Omay TTL.

Legend had it, this Englishman stood in the blazing hot sun on the banks of Kariba, dressed in a white safari suit, (and I presume a Pith helmet!!) perspiration running off his red cheeks and lily-white skin as he addressed a crowd of the local Batonka tribesmen. The story tells that this civil servant, presumably a product of one of the better education facilities in the UK, explained in great and technical detail about the settlement reached between Ian Smith and Douglas

Hume, the pros and cons of accepting or rejecting the agreement so reached and the consequences.

The tribesman obediently sat and listened to the translated dialogue.

They appeared enthralled by the information being passed, nodding, and twisting of heads, elders coupling hands to ears to ensure better hearing, periodically at the appropriate times murmuring in agreement or showing dissatisfaction by a shake of the head. After an hour or more the Englishmen finished.

*"Any questions?* He asked.

Now those who know the African know there has to be consultation amongst kraal dweller and their kraal heads, after which the kraal heads gather and consult with the Chiefs. Only then will the elected spokesman be able to voice the collective will of the people. Tis' been that way since time immemorial and the very dawn of time itself. Eventually an elder tribesman stood up. Respectful silence swathed the crowd. He spoke with sincerity and deep thought.

The interpreter, from the District Commissioners office, who had been so employed for many such meetings, listened.

Then interpreted what had been said:

*"We thank this man for coming to see us. We hear what he has said. He is a wise man. We only have one problem here, when is he going to come and kill the elephants that are destroying our crops?"*

Welcome to Africa, Englishman, take that back to Lord Pearce.

In due course we arrived at the Siyakobvu base. It consisted of a few outbuildings enclosed by cyclone wire fencing and what I was to establish was the District Commissioner's residence when he was visiting. In the old days we called it a DC's rest camp. It was an idyllic spot, next to a river, and beneath some high cliffs covered with dense foliage. There were a couple of Patrol Officer's going about their business – I introduced myself.

*"Why have you come here?"*

*"I am not sure myself to be honest. I have to stay for a month."*

*"Have you brought any rations?"*

I always carried four cartons of 'rat' packs in the back of the Land Rover, one of each kind and an extra - I am not sure now but I think there was an A, B and C and maybe even a D 'rat' pack

–I forget how many were in a carton – enough to keep this place going for a while.

No. They ate fresh scoff – they had a cook, bottle washer, cleaner, batmen, beers, fridges and deep freezers. These lads were well organised. No electricity! Who cared? Now to be honest I just do not recall what their job was – but I hope they were usefully deployed.

It did not take long to identify the alpha male. Not always the senior man I might add. In conversation I pointed out how vulnerable we were to attack from gooks, who could sit on the cliff top and pick us off one by one.

*"That's the thing,"* he said, *"no gooks here!"*

I found myself a piece of floor, threw my kit down. Fani and I took a ride, and then walked around the perimeter of the camp. We were sitting ducks. The bush around the fence had not been cleared. Even the road that entered the compound came down from a height, maybe a couple of hundred yards away from the gate.

*"Do we have any Claymores?"*

*"No"*

*"Do we have any trip wires with sound devices attached?"*

*"No"*

*"Did we have guards operating at night?"*

*"No, no need."*

Just a regular 'colonial weekender,' where for years I bet after 'white man' first came by horse and cart and then car, they stayed while hunting in darkest Africa. Maybe he even had a floozy with him. The old devil!! *What Ho!*

*"How far away was the closest clinic?"*

*"Not one."*

*"Oh, then the township?"*

*"None."*

*"Well then there must be a mill?"*

*"No."*

*"How frequently does a bus travel through the area?"*

*"Never!"*

*"Many locals have cars?"*

*"None."*

*"Where are the locals from here?"*

*"A long way, most of them live on the banks of Kariba – anything between thirty and fifty miles away."*

Now I was sent there for a month but after 30 days I was told my replacement was having domestic problems at home, could I just hang on for a week or two and they would find someone else.

At the end of the next 30 days, they were so sorry, but no replacement had been found and anyway, it was now my month out 'in the bush again', so I would just have to do the next thirty days, as well, which I would have had to do anyway.

*       *       *       *       *

## PRESS ON

*Nothing in the World can take the place of Persistence.*
*Talent will not.*
*Nothing is more common than unsuccessful men with talent.*
*Genius will not;*
*Unrewarded genius is almost a proverb.*
*Education will not;*
*The world is full of educated derelicts.*
*Persistence and Determination alone are*
*Omnipotent.*

*Calvin Coolidge - 30th U.S. President.*

# THINKING ON YOUR FEET:
# AN ESSENTIAL REQUIREMENT

M akuti, in Rhodesia's northern region was just a magic spot to be in whilst engaged in a war. For the majority of my time, the war must have passed us by. Sure there was the odd land mine, one or two wayward terrorists, who got lost, an attack on Moro Ngoro and Mana Pools, (the latter most regrettably taking the life of a good friend of mine) and an attack on the Bumi Hills airfield. We got mortared once, causing me to run through the valley, watching trees falling over as a result, made me think things were getting fairly serious. This was war – it was, is and will always be evil, it is said that old men start wars and young men fight them.

There are however always positives in life, it's a personal choice, you can complain or cheerfully accept the glass is either half full or half empty, it is your call. I found one became innovated and cunning, devious with a great aptitude to think whilst 'dancing'. None of that has anything to do with fighting. No, all those newly acquired personality traits/talents were required to keep operational.

Those in charge, mainly oblivious and inexperienced to what was happening on the ground, maintained steadfastly. The 'rules' that had served the Regiment well for years, 'pre-war years' – that's the bloody second world war had to be obeyed and maintained.

This is the story, where we outfoxed, outsmarted and outplayed 'the system'. This will be the first time this ruse will be divulged. I know that the statute of limitations applies and will provide a sound defence, if facing any Regimental discipline! During a particularly quiet period in the Hondo, I was twiddling my thumbs as the Acorn rep at Makuti. Each night we closed up shop in terms of normal police working hours, at 1630.

Fani and I had an arrangement, which had worked for years. He drove me from the police camp to the hotel. He then took the Land Rover and picked me up the following morning, after breakfast. We had an agreement, no drinking and driving.

There were three fixed and loaded AK's in the Land Rover, one in the engine facing forward, and one on each side immediately behind the front cabin. If we approached a nonoperational area we were required and always did, stop and clear the weapons, each weapon was fitted with 40 round magazines. If you hit the 'red' button on the dashboard, all three firearms would discharge - there was no means of stopping them, until the ammo ran out.

Makuti and surrounds was considered an operational area, so we never cleared weapons. High risk, given that the cabin had no doors, and if someone fiddled with the dashboard it resulted in the expenditure of 120 rounds. In the bush it was a godsend, as Acorn reps only travelled in pairs, and the normal terrorist group consisted of a minimum of six people. We needed all the help we could get.

When Fani dropped me off, I would amble into the Makuti bar, as Neil Diamond serenaded the clientele. Ah! Yes the melodic sounds of; Sweet Caroline, I'm Alive (I always thought that enigmatic.) Holly Holy (some chaps eventually went that way) and my favourite, Beautiful Noise!!! (Lots of that from time to time!)

It was never long before we locals were joined by someone travelling from Kariba to Salisbury or ports in between, or the odd tourist, sometimes to the amazement of the single P/O's or Wildlife chaps, some unattached young ladies. Most evenings, whoever was in attendance, or as it was commonly referred to as, 'on parade', the games would start; Liar Dice, 7: 14: 21, Top shelf, Bottom shelf, any bloody shelf. The odd game of Bok Bok and Dead Ants usually provided some bruised and painful bodies the following morning. It was a distraction from the war I think and a small release of the pressure valves in each operative.

At times some idiot gave a drunken and wobbly demonstration of Shangaan dancing, much to the amusement of waiters and barman, who must have thought - what chance had we of winning this war?

The pub would close and I for one and usually the only one would stagger to my room.

As the only person in the motel, it was obvious the location of my room could be easily identified by vigilant terrorists or 'employees' assisting the terrorists, so I never slept in the same position within the room on consecutive nights. Windows always closed and curtains drawn. I figured I needed as much time as possible to repel an attack. Thankfully it never happened in 24 months.

Each morning, I would sit in the dining room, every table immaculately laid and I the only guest, waiters in crisp snow-white uniforms ready to take my order. I always wondered how management ran the business so efficiently, with such limited custom.

So it was one morning, I stared at my breakfast of bacon, eggs and tomatoes, with two slices of toast - not forgetting I was not one of Rhodesia's professional warriors, just a policeman doing his bit. Crisp, white table linen and silverware cutlery, a white napkin poised elegantly on my lap, one might be forgiven if some passing guest had presumed I was a VIP or high ranking Officer rather than a person, one step up from the lowest rank in the Regiment. I often wondered what the Army chaps thought of us CID/SB operatives living in the lap of luxury!!!!

The inevitable hangover thumped relentlessly, causing temporary sight malfunction.

The waiter approached me and said, *"The Sgt wants to see you."*

I looked out the glass doors, and as usual the Land Rover was parked, with him leaning on the bonnet.

*"Ask him to wait, I have not finished breakfast."*

He knew the setup. Hell we were not going far - a mile maybe then another day of thumb twiddling and navel gazing.

The waiter returned, *"The Sgt said it was very serious."*

Suddenly the cogs in the brain turned a lot quicker – there is a problem, and it has to be major. Tread carefully Doug there are many gins, pitfalls and traps on the road less travelled and many a slip between cup and lip. Had the war come to the motel? Was he being held hostage? His wife and kids held hostage maybe? Shit this is all too much so early in the morning. I stood up and removed my 'rifle' from the grey cloth bag, I took the safety catch off, then slowly and with eyes as wide open as my hangover would allow, I approached Sgt Fani.

His normal jovial self was not apparent; the ever present smile and smoke drifting from his mouth not visible. I did not leave the confines of the building - I was now positioned some fifteen yards from him.

*"What's the problem Sarge?"*

*"It is bad Ishe."*

*"What?"*

*"There is a big moswa. It is not good Ishe."*

I could not read into what he was saying. I was expecting some encrypted speech (maybe too many James Bond movies!).

*"What has happened?"*

*"Come and see Ishe."*

*"You have to be kidding! Tell me what has happened."*

*"The Land Rover is buggered."*

*"Looks fine to me"*

*"No come this side."*

After a cautious survey of the area, I walked past him, initially much to my relief until the situation clarified itself. The whole left-hand side of the vehicle had been seriously damaged. We travelled without doors, however there was very little resembling the front mudguard and the back panel of the pickup area, was in need of some major panel beating.

I checked the left rear AK, it did not seem to have been damaged, although I think it had been pushed backwards.

*"What the f\*\*k happened?"*

*"Ah Ishe, I hit the side of the Mountain."*

*"Which f\*\*king mountain?"*

*"The one on the way to Kariba."*

*"Why were you going to Kariba?"*

*"No Ishe, I was coming back to Camp, from the CMED camp, at the bottom of the mountain."*

*"Why were you in the CMED camp?"*

*"Ah sorry Ishe, there was a beer drink there."*

*"So you were pissed?"*

*"Yes Sir, too much doro."*

He was most repentant, feeling very sorry for himself. The wrath of the Gods was about to descend upon him. His career was over. He knew I would have to suspend him from driving. The consequence was devastating. He would have to re-sit his driving test (Section 123 of Standing Orders had that sewn up) the waiting list for African police to re-sit, extended beyond 18 months.

An African detective with a drivers licence was highly sought after, those without were dime a dozen. This would most probably mean a transfer from Sinoia to one of the larger cities. His admission to drink driving was the death nail. As we used to say, he was 'up shit creek without a paddle'.

I told him he was suspended from driving.

*"Yes Ishe."* He was forlorn.

I sat in the shotgun seat and told him to drive down to the station.

*"But Ishe you have suspended me from driving."*

*"Yes I know just don't let me see you driving."*

A small smile flickered across his face as we drove to start another day of war. Fani took his place outside my office. I began typing. Always typing in the war. I typed out a two page statement in great detail, read it once, then twice, I was satisfied it would pass muster.

*"Fani."*

*"Yes Sir."*

*"Sit down here and read your statement, if you agree with it, sign it."*

He finished. I could see his eyes watering. *"This statement Ishe, it says you were the driver. That's not right."*

*"I am about to phone the Member in Charge and tell him I pranged the car yesterday when returning from patrol. You will need to back me up – I was sober and the other facts are pertinent."*

*"Tantenda Ishe – zakanaka. Kwazo."* (Thank you Sir, thank you very much) He signed.

I phoned the Member in Charge, reported the accident. He told me he had no alternative but to suspend me from driving and asked for a full report. I requested an immediate replacement with AK's mounted, and assured him Fani would drive until I re-sat my driver's licence test.

A day later a replacement vehicle arrived, the wreck was removed and a phone call from the Member in Charge informed me, after consultation with the PCIO, they could not afford me not to be driving, so I had been re-instated.

Fani and I shared a beer outside the Makuti Hotel that evening. He took the truck and departed as I walked into the bar to be serenaded by Neil Diamond singing, '*He ain't heavy, he's my brother*'.

Life was good, we had beaten the system - how good did that feel?

And the war rolled on.

\*       \*       \*       \*       \*

*For you who have drunk deeply*
*Of the waters of this African land,*
*Will find an aching thirst to quench,*
*And return to drink deeply of it once again.*

*Susan Cook-Jahme*

# DEPLOYMENT OF
# THE NEW HOME GUARD

T his is the first and not the last deployment of the New Home Guard to the Sharp End.

As previously mentioned, I had done my month out. I was 'required' to do the following month and thereafter the following month. I would phone my wife whenever I could. Those wives who suffered the absence of their husbands being in the bush will be able to sympathise with her feelings, when told, after a two months absence, I was to continue serving another stint.

*"That's not fair. You always do your bit and now …. Why you? There are hundreds of men in the police? What's so special wherever you are? I'm all alone - even the dogs are missing you. If you can't come home I am coming to see you."*

*"That's not possible, I am on the Matabeleland border, a long way away."*

*"How come Ken (Stewart) has seen you and I can't?"*

*"To get to me you either have to drive through a lot of terrorist infested territory, or come halfway across Kariba, it is not possible, also, there is nowhere for you to sleep, or bath and the food is not all that flash at times."*

*"I can drive to Kariba! Then Ken can take me by boat to you. I think that is fair. We used to sleep anywhere when we were hiking we can do that again.*

*I am going to phone Ken and see if he can help!"*

Sometime later I got a message from Ken saying he was arriving with Sue, at such and such a time, on this date. Please meet me at Bumi Harbour, so I went to see the caretaker staff at Bumi and asked what the chances were of a room if nothing else. They were very kind, arranged a room, food and bath – all on the house.

At the given time and date, a boat travelling at high speed came across the lake, it docked at Bumi, my wife got out, she was dressed in a full bright yellow dress, yellow high heels, with a matching yellow handbag – in her right hand she carried a grey cloth bag about the size of an AK!!

She ran up the boat ramp as I approached and threw her arms around me, we embraced. I became aware of clapping and shouting. Looking around I saw a group of SF members cheering us on. I felt humbled and proud of her. That weekend we spent on our own, we frequented the well-known veranda and swimming pool of Bumi Hills Hotel, two AK's lying next to the chairs, sipping beers and watching the elephants, doing what they had most probably been doing for centuries.

Two days went past far too quickly and her departure was as dramatic, in the same yellow outfit, as it had been when she entered. Maybe not as many men, but those that were there gave her a rousing ovation. As the boat, with Ken at the wheel disappeared, I thought, the training of the home guard was excellent, but I must advise her to wear clothing less conspicuous and maybe some slacks would be more appropriate in these circumstances.

## Second Deployment of the New Home Guard

Many months later I was at home in Sinoia telling my wife about the delights of the Valley floor and Mana Pools. Of the huge variety of game and the rhino I had nicknamed 'Khali' (Swahili for cross/grumpy). She asked whether she would ever get to see the sights.

*"No one but SF are allowed on the floor dear, that's the rules."*

*"Oh, and when did we start obeying rules?"*

*"True, however there is always a risk of hitting a land mine or being ambushed, and we don't want you involved in those shenanigans."*

*"You take those risks everyday, it does not seem to worry you."*

Then, with respect to all ladies reading this tale, the 'nagging' started so after a few days I thought, why not. I know the chaps from the Parks and Wildlife Department had graciously showed many of the fairer sex the 'hot spots' of the valley.

With partial plans laid, on my next trip I went to see John Stevens, an excellent fellow, at Mana. I told him in confidence of my plan. Excellent he said, pick me up and I shall show you some sights.

The day came, my wife stayed the night with me at Makuti. Early the next morning Fani, my wife and I in the front of the Land Rover drove to Mana. I had suggested she make a list of all the game she saw. We met John, who drove ahead showing us the way. John used roads I never knew existed. The highlight was when we arrived at a saltpan like clearing. In the middle was a herd of Cape buffalo, the size of which I had not seen since the mid 50's.

Now the reader may think I have joined Ripley's Believe it or Not, or possibly my old age has shadowed the facts. I estimate we were parked on the edge, I mean no more than 100 yards, from the herd. I assisted my wife to stand on the roof of the vehicle, followed by Fani and then myself. Stevens, tall, blonde haired, sun tanned, clad in a Parks &Wildlife shirt, shorts and *veldskoens*, slowly walked towards the buffalo.

To my utter astonishment and trepidation, the herd started parting, dust was welling up between their bodies, their heads lowered in that threatening position that they are renowned for just before a charge. Stevens kept walking slowly he must have gone twenty yards into the herd. They appeared confused, but none ran. Stevens turned around, his arms raised and this huge smile came across his face. If only I had had a camera, no one will ever believe it.

I later took my wife on a tour of some of the less frequented areas of the Valley, less likelihood of any untoward activity. We returned to the Marangaro/Makuti road by 1700 Hours and were in time for sundowners at the Makuti Hotel.

How many species did we see? I still have the list in my records. 30 is the answer plus a cheetah kill. Just as an aside the 2015 Mana Game count, revealed no cheetah and only found 28 species. I hope there were more. We never did see Khali – maybe he was shy of women.

That was the last deployment of the New Home Guard.

Our war trundled on – same old, same old.

\*        \*        \*        \*        \*

*A Blessed thing it is for any man or woman,*
*To have a friend, one human soul*
*Whom we can trust utterly,*
*Who knows the best and worst of us,*
*And who loves us in spite of all our faults*

*Charles Kingsley*

# THE BUMI HILLS
# AIRSTRIP ATTACK

M y research suggests terrorists attacked the Bumi Hills airstrip on 5th June 1976. I shall accept that date. On that evening I was spending the night at the police base camp at Bumi, it was located on the top of a hill, on the south side of the Hotel. If one faced south, you looked over the airfield, and across the mostly peaceful Omay. The airfield was obscured from sight, due to vegetation. One of the aspects of the 'Hondo' years that I really enjoyed, was it produced some real characters. Human conflict certainly sorts out the wheat from the chaff, and quickly.

From 1976 onwards, many men had found important jobs to do: flying desks, ensuring the finances were correct, ordering this and distributing that, submissions of reports and returns, AEC's, writing important circulars, which clearly would have taken many committee meetings and consultations. With experts springing out of the woodwork, like borers subjected to insecticidal fluid.

At Bumi on the night of the attack, were two much larger than life characters: Supt John HICKS and SO Eric Kruger. It was fairly early in the evening, when we heard automatic fire on the airstrip – we were seated having our well-earned 'sun downer' at the time. We all stood up, beers in hand and peered into the darkness. Instinctively, I thought 'retaliation'; to have driven down, would have been futile if not suicidal. So without further ado, I placed my beer on a table picked up my rifle and fired, towards the noise – a very calm hand grabbed my arm, it was John Hicks.

*"Don't waste your ammo, you are achieving little."*

Realising his point was well made I cleared my rifle, put it down and picked up my beer. The result, the following morning those pilots that could fly out, did. Others hired aircraft to pick them up. Within 24 hours, Bumi Hills was silent. Over time service was slowly reduced to accommodate the dwindling guest list.

I only ever made up the numbers, but was honoured to have worked with many really good men.

The only other incident that comes to mind, involved 'Eric the Red' Kruger. Ground coverage guru of high or ill repute, dependent upon your point of view - a fearless operative.

Like most of us, he did not mind a beer on a hot day, nor after he had experienced a long hard day at 'the office'. In the Kariba area, those days were as common as the sunrise each morning. Camp beds were positioned wherever a floor space occurred – there were no bedrooms.

We were having a quiet beer one evening, not the 5th June. Eric and others were lying on their beds, others were seated or standing. Unbeknown to any of us, Eric had drifted off to sleep, exhausted from his efforts that day!! He had failed to extinguish his cigarette. We became aware of a burning smell, and realised Eric's bed was on fire. He, oblivious to his predicament was sound asleep.

I recall someone walked over and quietly poured the remnants of his beer bottle over the flames. The effort while essential was insufficient to douse the flames. Realising the fire was intensifying, a few of us, very charitably, followed the leader. Now with six or more fire fighters on the job, not only was the fire doused but Eric was rudely awoken.

He lay there, dropped his right arm onto the floor, clutched his beer bottle, sat up, took a long deep mouthful and asked, *"What was that for?"*

And our war went on unabated.

\*        \*        \*      \*      \*

*However long the Night,*
*The dawn will break.*

*African Proverb*

# S.B. GAMES OR PLAIN & DANGEROUS INCOMPETENCE

I was seated in my office at Sinoia, as usual not doing anything of much consequence. If I was in town my friend and fellow CID operative DSO Mabin was on his month out – in the bush again! He used to work the Angwa Region, along the PEA border, out of Sipolilo. The Member in Charge Det/ Insp. Looker was on a visit to Kariba – I am not sure what for. This left the Member I/C SB, also a DSO and myself, as the only ranking plain-clothes police on station.

CID D/Sgt Fani came to see me and said two SB African police members requested to speak with me. That may seem odd to the reader given that I worked in an SB capacity for six months of the year. SB, I found, had some very odd, confusing and unpredictable attitudes, dependent upon each individual you came across. In Sinoia, SB occupied the same building as CID. There was a common entry point, to an enclosed courtyard. SB had a steel grill erected across the common veranda, which incorporated a lockable door. This barred entry of any personnel inclusive of CID.

We had to request permission to enter and give a valid reason. Needless to say Mabin and I never bothered to try and enter. As I have also previously said SB, in my mind, had some high quality operatives in the anti- terrorist world, I had the honour to have served with their best.

I have no knowledge what else 'the Branch' did for Rhodesia. I am certain they were a great asset to the security of our Nation.

Unfortunately they had, I guess like most organisations, people with varying degrees of ability and competence. In my opinion Sinoia was stuck with two SB reps, poorly suited for anti-terrorist work, the Member i/c SB and the Station Member in Charge (CID/SB). Neither was anywhere near fit enough, nor agile enough for operations and neither were sufficiently orientated towards the local populous or had sufficient experience for survival in the bush. I presume they had other talents, which did not concern me or involve my working in those areas. Fortunately there was minimal terrorist activity in the Sinoia area.

That being said I asked these two SB African staff members to sit down. One was a Malawian who operated along the Angwa area: he wore dreadlocks and frankly no one would ever have picked him as a member of the police. They reported that information had come to hand of the presence of a fully armed terrorist in the local African township. They had determined the exact address where he was staying, had carried out observations and knew he was wearing civilian clothing. Informants had advised he had an AK, magazines and hand grenades.

I was confused as to why they were telling me when their Member in Charge was seated in his office, a few yards from my office. Being extremely respectful, they informed me that they had told the member in Charge SB, exactly what they had just told me. He had told them he was far too busy to attend and dismissed them.

I sought entry into the SB area and approached the Member in Charge. He had headphones on and appeared to be listening to some tape recordings. I asked what could be more important than a fully armed terrorist, in our African township and why if he had not gone to arrest the man could he not have passed it on to the Uniform Branch and they could organise who knows, PATU or whatever else that was available to them.

He repeated to me he was too busy to attend – someone else will have to sort it out. I was flabbergasted. Who I asked is responsible for terrorism? Someone else he said not him. I felt something was amiss.

Had he planted this guy, maybe a policeman, a 'turned' gook or one of those Rhodesian Government trained terrorists who were popping up out of the woodwork now and again.

I asked him to advise me if all was in order, that if it was part of an SB plan, I would never mention the matter again.

He assured me it was not an SB project. Now I had heard that before, only to find it was. I pressed him. No he knew nothing of it.

So I gave him an ultimatum – I will give you 15 minutes to think about it, if you have not contacted me I shall personally go and arrest the 'terr' myself. I warned him there was a possibility it could go wrong and we would shoot the terrorist, if we could not take him alive. Therefore if he was an SB operative he should stop me. I walked out. 15 minutes passed.

I sent Fani out to commandeer an African taxi, test to see the engine was functioning properly and if necessary place fuel in the tank and drop the driver off at the CID offices. I sent the Malawian, D/Sgt Chilumbu out to keep an eye on the house. He knew we would be driving around in a taxi and would see Fani driving.

The terrorist was described as being clad in a bright orange long sleeved shirt and between the three of us we agreed on the smaller, but just as important details of the unfolding event and how it would be executed, if you will excuse the 'pun'.

The taxi arrived, thankfully a large American type vehicle. I had a shotgun and lay on the back seat. We moved off with Fani driving and providing a running commentary of proceedings. The taxi stopped and I heard the Malawian and Fani talking in whispers at the driver's window. He said the terrorist, periodically entered the one room house and was currently standing in the doorway, sunning himself. He was in full view of our position. Fani identified him.

The plan was working. Fani drove away, and a few minutes later drove slowly back, towards the location of the gook. He told me to unlatch the back door, which I did, keeping it closed. He kept me abreast of developments, the distance between us and the target, what to expect, in terms of buildings, the number of steps up to the door and general comment on the surroundings (one would be excused for criticising our plan, me going in blind so to speak but time was of the essence) it was a bright sunlit morning and the chances of me studying the scene as well as escaping detection was minimal.

Why did I not consider, using PATU or Uniform Branch personnel? Time was one issue; getting people together would take hours, then a briefing, and then transporting them to the scene. Also the important consideration - collateral damage!! Did we really have to kill innocent people? This was not soldier/warrior stuff, this was a policeman's common sense thinking – the aim was to get this gook alive.

They were worth much more alive than dead.

We were now approaching the target, *"Very close now Ishe, he is leaning on the doorway, I see both hands he is not holding anything, I cannot see a gun on his side."* Then the pre-determined signal, which Fani gave believing he was positioned so I could have maximum effect.

He spoke directly to the terrorist, *"Mangwanani Mamuka sei?"* (Good morning how did you wake up?)

I pushed the car door open, got out as quickly as possible, saw the target, who while surprised at the activity, was not reacting to it. I hit him on the head as hard as I could with the butt of the Browning. He staggered back into the room and I jumped on top of him. Like all African huts the only window had been closed and draped with thick blankets.

The door had swung closed. It was bloody pitch black inside, not anticipated at all. Not good! How many others are inside? I needed a Plan 'B' and fast. I had eight rounds of buckshot. I was on the floor on top of someone who was not moving. I lay still and waited for the first sign of movement. If that occurred who or whatever it was, I was going to start shooting.

Everything was in slow motion – I recall thinking, what if he had a 'lady friend' with him? Collateral damage? Suddenly the door was flung open, the two Detective Sergeants entered. The opening of the door provided enough light to reveal one battered semi-conscious gook and thankfully no one else. A search produced a new AK and three hand grenades, two magazines, some 'terr' literature and one of those little ZANU/ZAPU badges some of them carried.

Something was just not right. I felt it in my water. The gook was handcuffed, a blanket thrown over his head and we all headed back to the office. We gave the driver a few dollars and returned his car to him, with a warning not to use it as an illegal taxi again or he would get arrested.

The gook was in the SB office area.

I spoke to the SB DSO, *"You can have the gook now to interrogate."*

He again said he was too busy. I could not help but think – what game is this SB bloke playing?

We gave the gook enough time to come to his senses and I started talking to him. As normal he came out with the same SH One T that most terrorists I had interrogated had. I applied some pressure and he started to talk.

He claimed to have recently come across below Chirundu Bridge with at least 200 other gooks!!!! They were headed towards Matabeleland, he had gotten lost.

There was something amiss! In those days and in that place there was no history of mass crossings. I phoned one of the experts, D/Insp Vic Opperman, a top quality operative and told him the whole story. No he knew of no SB operation where this chap would have been involved.

He suggested I take him on indications, because 200 people would have left plenty of evidence of their presence. I phoned the man in charge of CID/SB Sinoia. I told him that we had made the arrest and what I intended to do.

He instructed me to hand the gook over to the SB DSO – it was his job! I informed the Insp. that the SB chap was incapable of carrying out the requirements, he was physically unfit, incapable of climbing up the escarpment and it was likely the gook would escape and on top of which he had been too busy to become involved with the arrest.

I continued to argue and was threatened with disciplinary action if I did not follow orders. I transferred the call to the SB office.

I lay the gook down on the back floor of the Peugeot. I placed him in two sets of handcuffs, securing his leg irons to the handcuffs on his wrist. I placed the indications rope noose around his neck and wrapped the 'follow rope' around his body. A hood was placed over his head.

It was late on a Saturday night – I went home to bed. The following morning at about eleven o'clock my wife and I were playing a game of singles tennis on the tennis court inside the police camp, local members of a nearby church could be heard singing hymns and praising the Lord. When the OC Lomagundi, C/Supt Ian Hogg, a first class leader, approached the tennis court.

*"Doug can I speak to you?"*

*"Sure Sir."*

*"That terrorist, you arrested yesterday, escaped this morning on indications. He is believed to have made his way back to Zambia."*

The African staff involved were never thanked or congratulated by the member in Charge or Officers responsible for their supervision. I thought it poor man management on their behalf.

The SB DSO was never charged for allowing a prisoner to escape. Nothing was said – like it never happened.

One whispered rumour on the streets did come to my notice: the D/Insp. was pending an interview for promotion and thus kept it quiet, so as not to jeopardise his chances. He did get commissioned and the DSO was promoted to D/Insp and remained in SB.

The story has been provided in some detail, for the reader to understand firstly the complexity of the exercise, not only of the arrest but the nagging attitude and refusal of SB to get involved and secondly, the dangers to a number of human lives, if shooting had started. It was no war hero stuff, it was part and parcel of CID work – while it may appear dramatic, in essence, we had a known suspect, with reliable information available, he was armed and a danger to the community – his arrest had to be affected.

The questions one has to ask is: was it an SB operation that went wrong and they did not care whether the terrorist (or whatever he was) was killed during the arrest?

Knowing they could release him if arrested alive did they let him go while on indications? Were they all serving the same flag? How did they make a judgement so soon that the gook had made his way back to Zambia? Why had a uniform policeman been advised of this occurrence? Did they not care the gook might have shot, killed or wounded those involved in the arrest? Was it possible that SB Sinoia were blatantly incapable of involvement in anti-terrorist work?

I spoke to a Detective Sergeant who had been on indications and was the person allegedly holding the rope. He claimed they were climbing a steep incline when the terrorist, who had had his handcuffs removed, lifted a large rock and struck him on the head. He was clearly suffering a recent wound to his forehead – which had not been visible on the day they left for Kariba.

I have spoken to two people who were later stationed at SB Sinoia and requested they scan records to try and clarify the situation. Both, independent of each other, informed me records held at SB Sinoia before April 1980 showed the terrorist arrested was not a plant and formed no part of any SF exercise or operation.

We shall never know. We know how records can be amended, to suit circumstances. From a personal point of view – I had learnt a lesson - I knew who not to work with thereafter.

I never did.

.*       *       *       *       *

*The most important example of real courage*
*Is having the strength*
*To pursue our dreams in a*
*World full of obstacles and excuses.*

# JUST ON THE EDGE
# OF 'C' SQUADRON S.A.S.

W e all suffer regrets in life for deeds done in haste or through lack of forethought, regrets too, for opportunities lost when they presented themselves.

I, like most, have experienced my fair share of regrets for a multitude of my life's endeavours. One of my greatest regrets was not working with the elite of Rhodesia's Security Forces. It would never have happened, I was not trained to their standard, and I would never have passed their selection course. Even if chosen to work in the capacity for which I was trained and possibly reasonably successful at, I acknowledge that I would have been more a liability than an asset.

I did however become fleetingly involved with the SAS 'C' Squadron on two occasions; both times I was left with indelibly imprinted memories.

## Mushumbi Pools

I was instructed to meet some members of the SAS at Mushumbi Pools, while operating out of Makuti. It was an oddity, as Mushumbi was the patch of the Acorn rep from Sipolilo. D/Sgt Fani and I drove across the valley floor, presenting ourselves at the given time. It was relatively quiet and not difficult to locate the SAS representative, a Capt. whose name escapes me. Unfortunately, I am at a loss to recall what I was needed for.

We chatted for a while, until I heard the arrival of helicopters coming in from PEA. They landed not far from where we were, troops alighted, and scampered into the surrounding bush in different directions. One soldier approached the Captain, addressing him as Sir'.

He placed his enormous pack on the ground, rummaged inside, producing a small primus heater and a canteen mug. He filled the mug with water from his water bottle and lit the primus. Remember this man and the others had just flown in from an external operation. It transpired this chap was a Sgt. I noticed he had a TMH 46 attached to his pack.

The Captain gestured toward the mine and said something like, *"still got it?"*

He answered, *"Could not find a good enough target, will try again."*

The water boiled, he dunked a tea bag in it then offered it to me, *"Do you take milk and sugar?"*

I was humbled and honoured, I declined, saying he needed it more than I. He then offered it to the Captain, whose response was similar. The Sgt, doctored his tea, drank deeply clearly enjoying it. We then got down to whatever our business was.

Those who know the desire to quench a desperate thirst, will understand. The Sgt was more than deserved and entitled to drink his own tea, given his recent predicament, rather than offering it first to (a) a complete stranger and (b) a colleague who could have consumed in safety any amount of tea. I also wondered how many soldiers not finding 'the ideal target' to lay the mine, would have bothered carrying it back, remembering they weighed 8.5 kgs, rather than lessening his load and burying it, knowing someone would eventually detonate it."

Say what you will, no great act of heroism, but certainly a level of professionalism hard to emulate. I was deeply impressed.

## Kanyemba

The second occasion was on the morning of December 31st. My boss called me saying intelligence classified as 'A1' had been received stating Kanyemba Police Station was going to be attacked with an aim to totally destroy the camp. The attack was planned for the night of the 31st.

Now if my memory serves me correctly, I think the Zambian army, who maintained a base and mortars on the opposite side of the Zambezi River were going to be involved. The boss informed me such was the quality of the source of the intelligence that a number of SAS soldiers were being deployed by Dakota that afternoon to assist in the defence of the Police Post.

Kanyemba was my 'patch' and being a 'lover' and not a 'fighter' from a combatant point of view, I told the boss I would be ready to go up to Kanyemba just as soon as the dust and cordite had settled.

He told me there was a PRAW aircraft on standby for Fani and I at the Sinoia airstrip. We were to pack for a week's deployment. I was instructed to be there prior to the SAS, to meet them and liaise with Capt. 'Whoever'.

I gave the wife a big New Year's Eve kiss and told her I would be back in a week's time.

We flew to Kanyemba, where we were picked up at the airstrip and taken to the Mess. I just do not recall who was there at the time. I drove down to the airstrip; the incoming Dakota having advised its ETA. The Dakota landed, taxied to the end of the strip and as it was turning to come back I noticed a number of soldiers disembarking and disappearing into the bush. By the time the Dakota got to my position only one man, a Captain, exited. He waved up at the pilot, who turned the plane around, taxied and took off.

Back at Kanyemba a number of trenches had been dug, prior to our arrival. The sun soon dropped below the Zambian skyline. As darkness settled in I became aware of the missing soldiers milling around, quietly going about their work. The Captain introduced me to a Corporal and indicating one of the trenches said, *"The three of you can have that one."*

The Corporal was equipped with, amongst other things, a hand held radio. Soon quietness enveloped the camp. We cooked our evening meal (Rat packs - glorious Rat packs) and settled in for the night. It was so hot that sleeping bags were not unpacked, just used to make seats to soften the hard ground. Muffled sounds of conversation were audible. In our trench we chatter about nothing in particular.

Unbeknown to us, well certainly I did not realise, the stars disappeared. Quietly, ever so quietly large, black clouds had drifted over our position. At about 10:00 p.m. there was a bolt of lightning that seemed to audibly hiss as it lit up the night sky followed by an extraordinarily loud clap of thunder that, like so many of Africa's storms, rolled into the distance forever. Slowly those very large, but widely spread drops of rain started falling. The beautiful aroma, of fresh rain striking the dry ground wafted through the air.

I made the understatement of the year to my two companions, *"We are going to get f\*\*king wet."*

At that precise moment the mother of all storms bucketed down on us. The lightning and thunder was simultaneously blinding and deafening.

Within ten minutes the trench started filling, our attempts to build small walls of soil to divert the water running across the ground and away from the trench where futile. The water entering the trench was slurry. Within about half an hour the water had reached a level just below our chests.

I am not now, nor was I then a military strategist but I recall wondering if that point in time would be an opportune time for the opposition to launch their attack. We endured the pounding rain for two hours. Any conversation was impossible.

Just before 12 midnight I swear on the life of my mother the rain stopped abruptly. I instinctively reached for a cigarette; they were saturated. No one had dry cigarettes in the trench. It was then that I was party to one of the most moving and heart wrenching occasions of my seven-year war.

Drifting across the eerily quiet night, firstly one ever so distant voice followed by another and then others, crackling through the radio, our Corporal adding his voice - the SAS soldiers were singing their rendition of AULD LANG SYNE. I closed my eyes and listened, it was particularly moving and poignant.

They say big boys don't cry. If watery eyes define crying, then I say maybe that adage is not correct. Two days later we all went home – Kanyemba was never attacked. It was what we referred to as 'a lemon'.

Such was life - one took the good with the bad.

*　　　*　　　*　　　*　　　*

The Day we Die

A Soft breeze shall blow
and
wipe out our footprints in the sand.

When the wind grows silent,
who will tell the timelessness?

That once we walkede this way.

In the Dawn of Time.

**A BUSHMAN'S SONG**

# CLEANING UP MY OWN
# BACK YARD FIRST

S upply of any sort is the life blood of any organisation. Terrorist organisations are no different. In fact in the war that raged between 1972 and 1980, certainly in the North of the country it was a major logistical problem. Terrorist gangs were normally deployed six men at a time. There is a finite amount of "equipment" a man can carry at any one time. Their largest hurdle was of course the Zambezi River, while issued with small rubber dinghies, this stretch of water was a great benefit to the Rhodesians. We were aware Zambian based terrorists used to ferry arms across and leave them stock piled on the banks of the river on the Rhodesian side. I have enumerated two abortive attempts at recovering arms caches, in this book – this is a story with a different ending. I was whiling away my time at either Karoi or Makuti – I lived in each place so often, that unless I had a detailed diary, it would be impossible to remember. It matters not. I received notification a terrorist, armed with a "snipers rifle" had surrender to the "caretaker" at the Selous Scouts training camp, known as Wafa Wafa, on the shores of Lake Kariba. I instructed my caller to pass the information on to the SB Offices at Kariba for their attention and action. It was essentially an SB job and the surrender had occurred on their patch. The answer was that SB Kariba, no name was available, could not deal with the matter and suggested I was the next best bet. Not wanting to get involved in a domestic dispute between the plain clothes departments, I would handle the matter.

On arrival at the camp, I was handed an extraordinarily emancipated human being, he was so weak he had difficulty standing. I was also handed his snipers rifle, I had not seen the likes of it before. It was of 7.62 calibre, but all other details escape me, He was an AmaNdebele from Matabeleland, Russian trained. This was another first, I had until then only dealt with the Chinese trained Shona terrorists, so it all made for a more interesting day than usual. Thankfully Det/Sgt FANI was able to converse with him. He told us his story. He had come across the Zambezi for the first time "x" days ago. He and a number of others, had spent a few days and nights ferry arms and equipment across the river and hidden all of it as best as possible on the Rhodesian side. Their seniors had supervised the transfer and after a given period of time, instructed they proceed on foot, across the valley floor, over the escarpment, and then head South East towards Matabeleland. During the first evening he had become separated from his fellow terrorists. He became disorientated and was not sure of the duration. He had wandered on the floor for a few days, running out of both water and food. Although weak, he had managed to ascent the escarpment. He avoided making contact as best he could, until he found this lone individual, where we were situated. After many hours of observations, he decided to seek assistance. How unlucky can one get? Everything must have looked kosher. Only to find he had stumbled across the training camp of some of the most feared Rhodesian fighting forces there were. It was standard practise all captured terrorists were to be transferred to the SB Fort at Bindura immediately. I was aware of these rules, but as they seldom if ever returned, I decided not to report the situation to anyone. I had not introduced myself to the "care taker" and thought unless he was "wide awake" – it was unlikely he would have taken note of my vehicle registration number. I thanked him, and drove back to Makuti to formulate a plan. I knew word would filter back to Bindura, they would know the identity of the Acorn Rep, and it would in all probability be either DSO's Stewart, Pretorius, or Stanyon. It was most unlikely the caretaker would "on report", feeling satisfied he had placed the "gook" in the hands of Security

Forces. The only other people to "spill the beans" would be either Stewart or Pretorius. I decided to vacate Makuti, where no one was aware of my prisoner. I drove north to Chirundu. I had provided our capture with water – but no food. The uniform member in Charge at Chirundi was a South African chap, whose name escapes me. He had a solid reputation for efficiency and hard work, he was also capable of keeping his "mouth shut" – just the sort of collaborator I need, for the next 48 hours. I made sure I entered Chirundu after dark. With assistance from the Member in Charge I detained our prisoner, again without anyone seeing him, under a false name, for the crime of Housebreaking and Theft. The D/Sgt had used a false name as the arresting and detaining detail.

Sitting in the bar that night, the Member in Charge had a quiet word with me in private. He had received a phone call from C/Supt. McGuinness (SB Officer in Charge of the Fort at Bindura), enquiring whether the Member in Charge had seen me. He denied it. The following morning before sun rise, we travelled down onto the valley floor, with a stick of NSPO operatives. It was my intention to have this terrorist, locate the arms cache, recover same and then inform Bindura.

As beautiful as the Zambezi valley is, there is "nothing like a free lunch" I had the terrorists hands cuffed behind his back. An indications rope, issued from the Fort at Bindura, had the slip knot noose round his neck, and some 100 yards back, I held the other end. Rumour had it these ropes were designed, because someone had been "on indications" with a capture, who lead them into an ambush. Keeping a distance from the capture appealed to me, although in reality, I guess the chap holding the rope was just as vulnerable from 10 yards as he was from a 100 yards. The valley temperature hovered around the 100 degrees mark, the Tse Tse flies were constant, numerous and I swear could sting through your shirt, and jacket, as well as the "veld skoens" I wore on my feet. They were not nearly as irritating as what were affectionately known as "Mopane budgies". These tiny flies lived in vast swarms, and were desperate for moisture. The eyes, nose, ears and open mouth of humans wandering on the floor, were an attraction they treasured and spent the entire day attacking. Along the banks of the river, the grass was high and robust in growth. The floor uneven. The trees and local flora grew with gay abandon, so visibility was limited. If this was not enough, it was similar to searching for a needle in a variable hay stack. There were numerous elephants, going about their daily business. Other residents included Rhino, Buffalo, Hippo and Lion, which if one was unlucky enough to meet any with an objectionable attitude, could make life a little lively. Then of course there was the off chance you might bump into a stick or two of fully armed terrorists.

Such was the scene, as our small group followed the near dying terrorist in an ever apparent abortive attempt to locate the illusive arms cache. Of course it may all have been a major hoax! He may have thought it provided a chance to stay alive, that I would not kill him, if I knew a chance of arms recovery was on the cards. He might be able to walk past a known camp site on "the other side", who may react, and provide him with a chance to make good his escape. 12 hours of walking, being stung, tripping, swallowing flies by the hundreds, the heat enveloping our bodies like stifling blankets, the air sparse, causing one to take large gasps, and of course more flies. Each dense section of foliage, offering the ideal spot for an ambush – or just maybe an angry Lion or Rhino. Or certainly in the early morning a Hippo late from his nights grazing, trying to get back to the safety of the river, and finding you his only obstacle. As the sun started to set, I called "stumps" we would now have to drive back in the dark, a very high risk activity. On arrival back in Chirundu, I arranged for the gook to be fed by Fani and acknowledged two messages had been received by the Member in Charge. McGuiness had called again. Again he received a full denial of my presence. DSO Pretorius in Kariba, wanted me to call him a.s.a.p. Pretorius was appraised of our failures that day, and the fact we would be starting anew early the following morning. He suggested he would like to join us the following day, to which I agreed. The more eyes and guns the better! That night, as I once again sipped the nectar of the Gods, the phone rang, the African Police Constable from the Charge Office, said there was a call for a DSO Stanyon. One of the P/O's handed me the phone. The penny dropped. I quickly found some paper and wrote, 'DSO Stanyon is not in Chirundu". The P/O dutifully said, *"Sorry Sir, DSO Stanyon is not on station"* Yes Sir I *will do. Goodbye." "Who was that I asked?* The reply was, *"a Supt Mac.*

*Something I did not catch his name. As soon as you get in, he wants you to phone Bindura"* You have to stay wide awake at all times. The following morning, as we readied ourselves to leave, DSO Pretorius had not arrived. In my world 0500 Hours is 0500 Hours, I left word for him to follow, when he arrived. We headed back down the valley for another days "cache searching". We had only travelled a few miles down the Ruckomechi Road, when a relayed radio message advised us Acorn Kariba (Pretorius) was a few minutes behind us, and requested us to wait for him.

As his convoy of two Land Rovers pulled up, I immediately noticed, of the four personnel, including Pretorius not one was armed!! I was furious and made my feelings well known. His excuse, they had simply forgotten!!We continued the search. At about midday, I was angry. I thought the terrorist was stalling for time, whatever his motivation. I threw my end of the rope over a large tree branch, and threatened to "hang him", unless he came clean. While holding him on his tip toes, I reached for a cigarette, I lost my footing and landed flat on my derriere, with my coccyx striking a large stone. This made me angrier. I attempted to remove the stone with my right hand. It would not budge. Removal of grass and closer examination, showed I was sitting on a TMH 46 Land Mine. It was the arms cache! Further search revealed the necessity to order a five ton Bedford from Chirundu to move the cache. It may well have been the largest arms cache uplifted from the valley floor.

On our return to Chirundu, I contacted C/Supt McGuiness, who was angry to say the least. After he had calmed down, he sent a fixed wing aircraft to Chirundu. Fani and I escorted our prisoner to Bindura. Mac Guinness asked for an explanation for my ill-discipline. I advised him it was necessary to clean up my own back yard before I offered assistance to anyone else. When the size of the cache was explained to Mac Guinness, he was pleased and appeared to forgive my transgressions.

This story has an interesting conclusion. Many years after the war, probably ten, I received a European male visitor at my residence in Brisbane, Australia. He introduced himself, I forget his name, he said he was a South African businessman, with offices in Singapore. He brought with him the very best wishes of "an old friend Ben Pretorius". Pretorius, he informed me, was now a very senior officer of the South African Defence Force (I guessed their answer to SB). He said Pretorius was offering me a substantial amount of money to act on behalf of the South African Government. I was to monitor the activity of South African dissidents (ANC operatives) in Australia and report accordingly and with further negotiations "any other" requirements the South African Defence forces might require from time to time. I refused and removed the agent from my residence. I contacted Pretorius by phone and asked what he thought he was doing. He said he thought I was "still in the game". I informed him, I was not a mercenary, had no affiliation to South Africa or any of its inhabitants, and not to bother me again.

*     *     *     *     *

*Life was meant to be lived.*
*Curiosity must be kept alive.*
*One must never, for whatever reason,*
*Turn his back on life.*

*Eleanor Roosevelt*

## BUSH LESSON ONE: DON'T GET BETWEEN MOTHER AND CALF

I shall pen what I consider one of the best stories from the Valley and my seven years of 'tap dancing with gooks'.

It is a story that encompasses the work of the oft-neglected NSPO's (National Service Patrol Officers). I had few official dealings with these people. I met a fair few, all young and keen. I do not recall one of them who were not cheerful, enthusiastic and respectful.

However, I do feel the way they were treated by the police administration was very ordinary. The ones I met in the Omay and the Valley (operating out of Chirundu) seemed to be provided with a pointless amount of patrolling. They were not ill-treated or maligned; on the contrary, those to whom they reported were considerate, attentive to their needs and managed them appropriately.

Maybe they were content with their lot, all they seemed to do was walk 'x' number of days north and then the same number of days back south, whether they did two week stints or one I have no idea. It struck me as a fairly boring way to spend a war.

There was a 'stick' operating out of Chirundu, whose lead scout had been nicknamed 'Lemon'. I apologise to members of the 'stick' - your names have long faded in the mists of time.

I sat in the Chirundu Pub (again!!) and asked the 'stick' leader why they had given this unusual name to their comrade.

Allow me to explain to the uninitiated; if a member or members of the security forces were sent out on a mission, with promises of contact with the opposition and on arrival the intelligence was found to be inaccurate or false – it would be referred to as a 'Lemon'. I was told this particular NSPO had been deployed on so many 'Lemons' that his constant description of a pending op was, "I bet this will be another bloody Lemon." This was the origin of his nickname.

So it was I am told, that the 'stick' was deployed along the banks of the Zambezi, their tactical objective to locate terrorists spoor, follow and engage. Or if encountering terrorists entering or egressing Rhodesia, to engage.

As all 'sticks' do, they travel in various formations. There apparently is always a lead scout, who surveys the land ahead and reports back to his 'stick' leader who, I am informed, walks in the middle of the extended line. The reporting back is done by visual sign language and is constant. Each animal or situation seen is reported with the appropriate signal.

The leader assured me they had been together for so long and had come to know the expected behaviour of every species of game, that whichever diversionary tactic was required was automatically taken by all.

On this fateful day 'Lemon' was the lead scout. He signalled back the presence of a herd of Elephants to his right, and kept moving. A short while later he signalled the herd or part thereof was agitated and that a small elephant was off to his left. He continued walking.

Suddenly there was a loud trumpeting, usually accompanied by a mock charge, a warning to the intruder to move away. 'Lemon' knew it was only a mock charge and signalled accordingly. He continued on his way. With no warning, a young female elephant, moving at full tilt, was charging at 'Lemon'.

Realising he was in trouble, he turned to initiate a diversionary move and found that he was facing a large Jesse bush. (For those who may not know of these plants, they are mass thickets of old and new growth that can be 10 feet in height and 15 feet in width. They are impenetrable.) Realising there was no route to escape 'Lemon' turned to face the elephant.  She struck him with her trunk, knocking him to the base of the Jesse bush and flat on his back. He still had his 'pack' on. Most elephants trample their victims by kneeling on their bodies, not by using their feet.

As Lemon was lying there he had the presence of mind to slip out of his pack. The beast kneeled down and realising she was aiming at his chest he moved, her first knee missed his body and landed on his water bottle that was attached to his belt, which in turn was attached to his trousers. Now the whole weight of this beast had him pinned to the ground.

The entire 'stick' by this time was spread in a line watching! Their dilemma; they dare not shoot the elephant as it might collapse on 'Lemon', killing him. The rest of the herd was becoming more agitated.

'Lemon' had the presence of mind to realise if he uncoupled his belt buckle and slid it out of the hoops he would be able to crawl under her body and escape. She was poised to manoeuvre the second knee, to finish him off by crushing his chest. As the second knee dropped 'Lemon' was able again to move slightly, resulting in the knee landing on the ground. The chest of the beast must at this time have been only one or two feet above 'Lemon's' face.

The 'stick' leader was desperate to think of a solution, still fateful of causing the animal to collapse on 'Lemon'. Bear in mind, along with all this activity, the elephant was trumpeting and squealing.

The elephant rose up on one foot and then with an accurate thrust of her small tusk impaled 'Lemon' in the thigh. The tusk was thrust with such force it went through his thigh and into the soil. She withdrew her tusk and manoeuvred for a second thrust. The 'stick' leader recognising a second thrust would probably impale his chest killing him anyway, ordered his 'stick' to open fire on automatic, all shots directed into the air.

With the luck of the Gods, the elephant was so alarmed it rose to its feet and bolted from the scene, following the rest of the herd, which had departed on hearing the shots.  'Lemon' was conscious but bleeding.

Now whatever happened to 'Lemon'? He was casevaced to hospital, examination of the wound revealed no arterial or large vein perforation, no bone fractures, no serious damage to any significant muscle. He received treatment and was back on Valley patrol duties with in weeks.

Do you think his grandchildren would believe this tale? I'm betting on their retort to be: "*Yeh, sure Pops!! Want to play ball?*"

\*　　　\*　　　\*　　　\*　　　\*

*I look down the farthest side of the mountain,*
*fulfilled and understanding all,*
*And truly content that I lived a full life and*
*One that was my own choice*

*James Elroy Flecker*

# TAME GOOKS, LANDMINES
# AND HAEMORRHOIDS

I was getting really comfortable in my role as the Acorn Rep in North Mashonaland. I was as far north as you could legally go in Rhodesia. Green Leader and his cohorts had been further north across the River, but I was more of the stay at home type. I left 'externals' to the professionals.

Life was good. People were very busy, down in my old stamping grounds along the PEA border. There was little activity in my area at all. We travelled 'being two' with my great and trusted friend D/Sgt Fani. We drove the length and breadth of the VUTI Purchase Area, the Urungwe TTL and its neighbour the Rengwe TTL and also to the east the Mukwichi TTL.

We did all the usual police visits, townships, mills, dips, clinics, kraal heads and chiefs. We had what we presumed were credible 'sources', which we visited at night. Leaving the vehicle at least a mile if not more away and walking in – obtaining any information and leaving. Those who have tried this tactic, well know all one has to do to follow the route of the 'skuzapos / mapolisa' or night stalkers, is sit still and listen for the kraal dogs barking.

As one lot of dogs bark fades the neighbouring kraal's dogs start, first one or two inquisitive yelps, getting louder and then reaching a crescendo, then again, the volume and intensity decreases as the night stalkers move through the area – the pattern is repeated over and over again – and everyone in the area knows just where the night stalkers have been – maybe not the exact hut but mark my words, certainly the kraal. About midday, while seated in the 'Acorn office' at Makuti the phone rang. *"This is McGuiness, Bindura."* His reputation had spread far and wide.

*"I would like you to do a job for me."*

*"Yes Sir."*

*"I shall send a plane to Karoi tomorrow morning, which will fly you to Bindura."*

The following day as planed we landed at Bindura. We were picked up by a waiting SB chap and driven to 'the Fort' and Mr. McGuiness. I knew he was the SB boss for the Selous Scouts, a fearsome unit of well-trained army people with a smattering of police personnel. As I walked into his office, I saw a certificate hanging behind him. In big letters it read 'Justice of the Peace'. Surely I thought, a contradiction in terms.

*"Thank you for coming Mr Stanyon."*

*"A pleasure Sir."* It was unlikely that I would have refused.

*"As we speak there is an RIC Unit driving from Salisbury to Karoi, they will meet you there tomorrow morning. They will act as your escort and I would appreciate that you use this exercise as a form of training for them."*

*"May I interject Sir?"*

*"Yes."*

*"What is an RIC Unit and why do I need an escort? We have never used one before."*

Politely ignoring the question, McGuiness continued, *"I shall be giving you a turned terrorist, he will indicate to you a large arms cache on the valley floor. I would like you to recover the cache, give it to the RIC Unit. Once the exercise is over, you will return with the terrorist to Bindura by aircraft. Time is not of the essence – the recovery of the arms cache is. By the way Mr Stanyon the terrorist will be armed with his AK, he is to remain in control of that weapon at all times. Any questions?"*

*"Yes Sir. This AK, has it been doctored or are we not providing him any ammunition?"*

*"No the weapon is fully functional and he will carry as many magazines of ammo as he chooses."*

*"Are you f\*\*king serious, you expect me to get into a light plane with a gook in the back, with a fully loaded AK? Then if I do make it to Karoi, I am to wander around the Valley floor with a fully armed gook?"*

*"Yes, he has been completely 'turned' and to remove his weapon would be a show of no trust – so he remains armed."*

This did not sound good. In fact on a level of dangerous, this was off the scale, unmeasurable.

*"I am not so sure Sir, I don't feel comfortable with the rules."*

*"Mr Stanyon the reason I have chosen you is because of your reputation."*

How he aligned drunken Shangaan dancing with waltzing with a fully armed gook on the floor was any one's guess. Seriously this was f\*\*king bad news. Could this be a bad nightmare I was having, or a very poor SB practical joke?

He reassured me he was certain this chap would be fine. As I drew deeply on most probably my tenth chain-smoked Peter Stuyvesant I thought: you can get killed a hundred times each day wandering around, at least you can keep an eye on this chap.

*"Where do we billet him at nights while in town Sir?"*

*"Just leave him in the SB office, make sure he gets a couple of prisoner's blankets. Also make sure he gets some food."*

I carried an AK myself, always in a grey cloth bag until I was well away from sight of others. As previously explained they were ideal for driving in Land Rovers, they sat neatly on your lap. I was also armed with a Tokarev 7.62 mm handgun, which I wore under my shirt in a shoulder holster.

*"Oh, and the RIC is the Rhodesian Intelligence Corp, a newly formed unit to assist police in collecting and the dissemination of information and other duties, much the same as Ground Coverage and SB."*

*"Yes Sir."*

I took Fani aside and briefed him, he rightly looked nervous. The tame gook was presented, in full East German fleck camo and fully armed. He spoke remarkably good English. We were driven back to the airstrip, the same plane was waiting, the SB truck left as we walked towards the fixed wing.

I stopped and said to this chap, *"You realise those people you have been with fully trust you not to do anything stupid."*

*"Yes."* He said he had learnt his lesson and wanted to fight for us now.

I said, *"I will be honest with you, I don't trust you, if you give me half a reason, I shall kill you."*

Strangely he replied, *"Yes I know that, we will be alright."*

The trip was uneventful, although I think certainly Fani and I most probably needed an underwear change when we retired for the night.

I was at the SB office in Karoi at sun up. For some reason Fani did not come with us but two other African staff, from Kariba I think, materialised and there was also a young European Police Reservist doing his call up, so I planned to take him as well.

The army (RIC) unit arrived. They had a Leopard mine vehicle and a Unimog. There was a Sergeant in Charge and about 12 other ranks.

I could not find any African staff. I wondered how they would converse with the locals in gathering their intelligence. On questioning this matter, they said it was not a concern for this trip.

I noted the Leopard Mine protected vehicle had no passengers and requested we place the tame terrorist in there on his own, otherwise we had to sit three in the front of a Land Rover. Not a good number if you had to exit in a hurry. It was agreed.

The trip down onto the floor was uneventful. The terrorist directed us to the banks of the Zambezi. We started searching. We must have encountered every Mopani fly possible and been bitten by every Tsetse fly we passed. We constantly disturbed the tranquillity of herds of elephant, some of which tested our agility.

There was another problem which had been manifesting itself for days – I was suffering from external haemorrhoids that had formed blood clots. It felt like every minute of my existence, the clots were increasing in size. Walking and sitting was an excruciatingly painful exercise.

We walked all the first day, slept the night and worked the following day. The terrorist was obviously disorientated – I took him aside and assured him no harm would come to him if he admitted he was lost. He admitted he could not find the arms cache, I informed the army and we decided to head back to the main Rukomechi road.

The Army Sgt advised they needed to refill water cans and suggested they would get cleaned up before returning home. Once we had loaded up the water cans and the army felt they were clean enough to head home, I called the Sgt aside.

I told him it was my considered opinion there would definitely be a land mine on the road we were on and before it joined the main Rukomechi road. It was almost certain we had been under surveillance by terrorists and they would have laid a mine the previous night. I suggested if my hunch was correct the Unimog should go first given it had the best chance of surviving a mine explosion.

The Sgt became agitated and said, "*No, make the two Kaffirs go first.*"

To say I exploded would be an understatement. I swore at the Sgt, threatened to do untold damage to him, said he was a disgrace to the Rhodesian Security Forces and that each of those African staff members were worth more than 150 of his unit's men.

I told him I would drive first and the Sgts would drive at the rear of the convoy.

He agreed. One of the Det/Sgts came to me, thanked me for what I said and followed up by saying, "*Ishe, we will drive behind you, let the army drive last.*"

*The Sergeant takes a Zambezi bath*
*The weapon as much for crocodiles as for terrorists*

With the Unimog behind the second Land Rover we headed for the Ruckomechi road. With some experience in avoiding and hitting land mines I travelled slowly, attempting to keep my wheels out of the wheel ruts. I remember taking a sharp, right hand bend when all hell let loose.

There was a massive explosion and automatic fire was trained at my Land Rover. I bailed out, hit the ground, flat on my stomach, and moved as far away from the vehicle as possible. The bullets were whistling above my position, there were bits of branches and debris floating all around. As I was armed with an AK and had no idea where the gooks were, I dared not open fire. I presumed the Army had spotted them.

I manoeuvred to get a better view of the situation. I observed the soldiers on both sides of the Unimog were firing wildly into the bush. I was unaware this was apparently army drill – just in case there was an ambush.

When everything settled I walked back down the road. The Unimog had detonated a mine with the front left wheel. It must have been blown forward, a considerable distance, because the Leopard, which had been following ended up with its front left wheel lodged in the mine crater.

The army had done their thing. Everyone disappeared into the bush.

I went to check on the gook. The back doors of the Leopard were wide open, the gook and his weapon had vanished.

A deathly silence reigned over the Valley – even the birds were quiet. With twelve men having shot off a few magazines each I presumed nothing was living within a couple of hundred yards of the scene.

The Army Sgt came towards me. I suggested we call the Makuti Relay station. Transmissions were not always possible from all over the floor. We got lucky. The incident was reported and now of course we were stuck where we were, because we could not move all personnel safely with the vehicles that were operational.

I asked if they had any qualified trackers – so we could go after the tame gook. The Det/Sgt overheard my request and pulled me aside, out of hearing from the Army. He informed me during conversations with the gook, the latter had claimed he did not trust the army and thought the first opportunity they had, they would kill him. It was the D/Sgts opinion he would not have run away, but would be hiding and watching us.

I felt a cold shiver go down my back. I might have an AK pointing directly at me. I also knew my anus was on fire and the pain was worsening minute by minute. In all the excitement I had forgotten about my 'piles', now they had come back with a vengeance. I had to walk with my legs as far apart as possible. I must have looked like a spastic.

The Det/Sgt further suggested the gook believed I was an honest man, a man he could trust, so the D/Sgt suggested I put down my rifle and walk out into the bush, as if looking for the terrorist. He predicted if I took my rifle I would not find him. Nothing like sending your boss out on a suicide mission, I could have thought of a few of my own bosses I would not have minded sending.

With more than a wing and had I been religious a prayer, I started walking in circles around the scene, increasing the diameter each time.

I had this feeling I was going to hear a burst of automatic fire and that would be the end of the party. I kept walking. The grass was no more than 12 to 18 inches high and relatively sparse. I was looking at the base of trees and thick bushes, which might afford him cover. I thought if he did shoot, I hoped his first few shots would be wide. I still had the Tokarev. It would have been comical watching me trying to remove it from under my shirt, with bullets flying overhead and my arse on fire!!!

I was transcending a large grassy area devoid of trees and bushes, when in my peripheral vision I thought I saw the ear of a small antelope twitch, or maybe a jackal. The grass was no higher than 12 inches. I looked again and then identified one finger of a hand swaying in the grass, about 50 yards from me. Slowly the hand appeared, then one arm and then, a second and there was the tame gook with both hands up.

I walked over shook his hand, and picked up his AK. I handed it to him. He refused to take it. I walked him back or should I say I waddled him back to the mine scene. Once he had had a drink of water he sat under a tree, in the shade.

I asked the Army if they had a medic. No but what was my problem? I explained.

The Sgt, a man with obviously many talents, said, *"Take you trousers off and let's have a gander."*

So there was 'the Acorn Rep' with his pants down, his bare arse pointing to Zambia, with a Sgt, pulling his cheeks apart.

His first observation was, *"F\*\*k that's terrible."*

Not exactly an extract from medical textbooks. He decided to boil some water, and having located a razor blade, he dropped it into the water to sterilize same. Whether he washed his hands or not, I don't know.

Then with no further ado, he made an obvious statement, *"This is going to hurt, you have a number of piles that are infected."*

With that I felt liquid running down the inside of my legs, and frankly the pain immediately dissipated. My newfound medic then suggested he do the rest, and without waiting for answer, I felt further liquid running down my legs. It caused me to feel weak. The Army felt sorry for the 'old man' and provided a stretcher and a piece of canvas for shade.

*ICU Ward – Zambezi Valley.*

With nothing else to do we waited for the 'cavalry' to arrive. In due course two Pookies and a tow truck arrived after which, the much larger convoy limped back to Makuti and beyond.

What had been achieved? One repairable Unimog damaged, an Acorn Rep with a pain free arse and a realisation that the newly formed RIC had limited uses in the world of Intelligence gathering and needed to have a swift attitude change about African staff if they were to stand a chance of being useful.

The tame gook was returned by myself, to Bindura, where strangely enough he thanked me for helping him and said he hoped we would meet again.

\*    \*    \*    \*    \*

*Each morning sees some task begun,*
*Each evening sees its close.*
*Something attempted, something done,*
*Has earned a nights repose.*

**Henry Longfellow**

## RECALCITRANT
## POLICEMAN

M y father was one of the few BSAP men allowed to leave Rhodesia to serve in the Second World War. The BSAP contingent was sent to the Middle East, initially Egypt and later into the Dodecanese Islands in the South Eastern Aegean Sea. A capable sailor since youth he was employed, at one time, as the allied representative on Greek fishing vessels, deploying and recovering British saboteurs in occupied territories.

What you may well ask has that got to do with anything? He was a raconteur of some note. With some amusing stories about his colleagues, some of who became very senior officers in the BSAP prior to retirement. After I re-attested I got into a little trouble with a person senior to myself, miraculously for me, he had been in more serious trouble of his own accord and was instantly transferred inter-Province. I received a 'dressing down', or would that be coarsely described as a bollocking by the OC and from my point of view that was the end of the matter.

It was during this discussion when my father related the words of a senior British Army officer, in the Officers Mess in Cairo. The discussion focused on leadership, man management, discipline, and aligned subjects. While I cannot recall the exact wording, it went something like this. *'If you want to run an efficient command, during troubled times, having a good mix of characters is essential. Never discourage 'recalcitrant men', they may be difficult to control, but are worth their weight in gold especially when the going gets tough.'*

To my mind some of those I served with fitted the definition of 'recalcitrant'. The dictionary defines the word as, 'having an obstinately uncooperative attitude towards authority or discipline'. Possibly those so inclined had compatible personalities. I certainly felt comfortable in their presence.

A former junior Patrol Officer contacted me as I was scribing these lines. Unfortunately with time I do not recall him. He mentioned he had been stationed at Kanyemba in 1976/77. He went on to say he recalled a visit by myself as the SB Rep, on a follow up of some terrorist incident.

He recalled Section Officer Bruce Matthews and I playing cards and drinking beer until the early hours of the morning. Bruce Matthews certainly was one of the memorable characters I met during the war.

He was a free spirit, played hard and worked hard and never got the two prerequisites mixed up. He and I got into a lot of trouble one evening, in the Twin Rivers Motel – we were the only two in the cocktail bar, discussing subjects of common interest, like the rise and fall of the Roman Empire and other short historical antiquities.

He removed something from his pocket. It looked for all intents and purposes like one of those fireworks squibs we set off on Guy Fawkes Night. He asked if I thought it was a good idea to light it. I could see no reason on earth why not, I mean I was three sheets in the wind and would have been hard pressed to remember my mother's name. Remaining seated he lit it and tossed it on the floor, thinking nothing of it and I lifted my glass of beer and sipped the nectar.

This thing went off – there was a frightening explosion. Later investigations made by the uniform branch Chief Inspector revealed it was heard right across the village of Karoi. I got such a fright I actually thought someone had thrown a grenade. Once my addled mind came to grips with the situation I saw Bruce doubled over with laughter. I asked what the hell it was.

He replied, "*one of these*," at which he then lit and threw the next one!!

That one, I found the funny side of and we both roared with laughter as the barman took refuge on the floor behind the counter. Had Bruce had more such items, I am certain they too would have been ignited.

In hindsight, with no constant pressure on life, adrenalin long gone, and no longer in the midst of a 'war', I acknowledge both Bruce and I acted irresponsibly, showed a total lack of consideration for those in the village, who would have been nervous if not scared out of their wits, not knowing that two drunken idiots were responsible. If anyone, reading this tale, was so alarmed, I unreservedly apologise on behalf of Bruce and I.

In my view it is this capacity to act outrageously, to enjoy life in the extreme, not to be self-conscious and not concerned what people will think nor how you may be damaging your prospects of promotion that produces just the sort of character that was at that time Section Officer Bruce Matthews.

It was not long after that incident the he and two fellow officers, found themselves in a situation where the going got very tough indeed. They were awarded The Police Decoration for Gallantry for 'conduct above the call of duty'. I remember congratulating him and he brushed it off, with 'that's what had to be done'.

I don't think he saw his actions any better or worse than throwing a lighted squib, one was play and the other work, in both instances he gave 100%.

I heard a whisper on the streets during the war that General Walls had remarked to Commissioner Sherren, about the disproportionately small number of policemen that received recognition for 'service beyond the call of duty'.

The rumour had it Commissioner Sherren replied, *"They are just doing their job."*

To my mind it is another example of the high standards the Police Force maintained where recognition for outstanding work during the war were few and far between.

Those who were so awarded should rightly be held in the highest esteem.

*     *     *     *     *

# "WHAT'S GOOD FOR THE GOOSE, IS GOOD FOR THE GANDER"

### *A Life's Lesson*

As mentioned in a previous submission, my first journey throughout the Sharp End, in 1972/73 was gauged as being so successful I was sent on a second similar trip, a few weeks later. I presume I might have been getting a reputation as a 'lone wolf operative'.

My second trip was comparatively uneventful; the former threatened investigations never amounted to anything. I would consciously study each station's Crime Register with due diligence, double-checking to make sure each snippet of information was recorded. While realising I was only a minor cog in this machine, which was growing exponentially by the day I quietly felt I must be doing something essential for the war effort.

On this trip, to combat boredom, I had challenged myself to do the entire trip in one day and get back to the Bindura water hole before sunset. Alas I failed, I just made Concession as the sun was setting.

I approached the Member in Charge (with my increased age and life experience he was not scary like C/Insp. Cavey) in fact he showed me some respect, I can only guess it must have been my introduction – *"I am Detective Patrol Officer Stanyon, Crime North Eastern."*

He very helpfully instructed one of his PO's to take this 'CID chap' to the Mess, give him the spare room for the night.

The Station had no end of people going about their business, Police Reservists in their blue overalls, chaps in camouflage, normal police uniforms and again those shady looking characters, long trousers and briefcases! – I guessed SB. Vehicles everywhere.

On entering the Mess I noted a hive of activity. I was ushered to a room, which was more than comfortable – it had a bed and pillow. I dropped my kit and walked out onto the veranda. I stopped one young P/O moving with great haste and asked him what was happening. He informed me I had arrived at the right time and place. There was, he explained, a planned 'shindig' that night. He became very excited informing me nurses and teachers from Salisbury were being brought up for the occasion.

With water dripping from behind his ears and those young bright wide eyes revealing the inexperience and incongruous expectations of youth, he gave this old 'Uncle' a knowing 'wink'!!!

I found the main organiser, realising sleep was not going to be a realistic outcome, well not until late, I offered my services as barman, if such a vacancy was available. He was thrilled and installed me without further ado.

Sure enough the 'shindig' fired up – the ladies (nurses and school teachers) arrived in force and what a sight for sore eyes they were too – dressed up to the 'nines' and ready for the kill. I had some experience in these things. Having been married for six months – my time was over, for all my wicked ways and lack of religious conviction, I believed in the *'I do and I don't, I will and I won't and until death do us part'* thing. I was happy to watch the various players demonstrating their skills in 'wooing' the opposite sex.

I identified one of the male players, a married Salisbury policeman whom I knew well. A charming individual, who from my observation, was making good progress and his partner for the night had him on a string. Once the clock struck midnight they disappeared into one of the rooms. Obviously one of them was suffering a bad migraine and the other was going to sit and comfort them in their time of need! Half an hour or so passed and they returned to the party. My experience and observations showed their exit was a trifle hasty as they were still adjusting clothing and hair on exit – activity not necessarily compatible with someone previously not feeling well, or so I thought!

The 'shindig' closed and I, finding my bed unoccupied, drifted off to sleep. The following morning it was nose to the grindstone, detailed perusal of the CR, my thanks to the boss and back to Bindura – there was a war to fight.

Eight months later I had been transferred to CID HQ – that was the system – everyone had to do two years at CID HQ. The fact that all the jobs in HQ could have been done as well as or better by retired policemen or elderly people no longer fit enough for war service, was an irrelevance.

One day my Concession friend approached me, looking desperate, sad and listless. *"Can I speak to you as a friend?"*

*"Sure. What's up?"*

*"I have just found out my bloody wife has been having an affair with one of my best friends while I have been away fighting the war!"*

He went off like a 'two-bob' watch. *"The bastards this and that ..., unfaithful ..., How can you trust ...? No feelings .... I am going to kill ...., How could she and what sort of friend does that ...?"*

*"Why in the world have you chosen me to tell this to?"* I asked.

*"Well you are a good friend."*

My retort was unexpected,

*"Well my friend, this is the way of the world, some get caught and some escape but in the end what's 'good for the goose is good for the gander'."*

*"You heartless bastard. You of all people! I thought you cared."*

*"Cast your mind back to Concession."*

*"Well, yes, but she did not know about that!"*

Over the seven years or so of my involvement in operational duties I unfortunately witnessed many marriages and relationships placed under enormous strain – these people and the progeny of their unions were in many cases unrecognised collateral damage from the war. Some relationships grew stronger, others faded.

Some lasting the duration only to falter once the war pressure was lifted, replaced by the different pressures of reinventing their lives.

I am no psychiatrist but I did learn many more people were injured in multiple ways as a consequence of the war, not necessarily by direct involvement with the enemy.

\*     \*     \*     \*     \*

*Some favourite expressions of small children:*
*"It's not my fault"*
*"They made me do it"*
*"I forgot"*
*Some favourite expressions of small adults*
*"It's not my job"*
*"No one told me"*
*"It couldn't be helped"*
*True freedom begins and ends with personal accountability.*

*Dan Zadra*

# IF ONLY THE PEARCE COMMISSION
# HAD DESTROYED THE ELEPHANTS

**B**y 1976 we were not required to record diaries or incidents logs, we were not required to contribute to the daily Sitrep (if we were, I was unaware of this requirement). A sitrep was never requested. The 'Hondo' was increasing apace down in the south of Rhodesia and also along the PEA border. No one ever officially inquired what I was doing, which suited me down to the ground. I was never going to change the course of events or history in the slightest.

"*If only*". How often have we either said or mused those lines? Fani and I were back at Siyakobvu, in the Omay TTL. In the dark early hours one morning, well before sunrise the perimeter guard woke Fani who in turn, woke me, there was an elderly man at the gate seeking assistance, he claimed a young woman at his kraal had been trampled on by an elephant while in her fields.

I was weary of these types of reports!! I always suspected the reporter might be freely or forcibly colluding with terrorists. Encouraging me to travel a pre-arranged route on which an ambush had been planned. No terrorists in the area indeed!!! Within a few days of my arrival and swanning around the TTL, we put paid to that line of thinking.

There were very few roads in the Omay and most of our work was done by following elephant trails, or footpaths used by locals.

Having gathered all the information and believing this man had passed all our 'trick' questions (very devious us CID types!), we considered it a genuine report and set sail. Apart from the very few roads, we had no need to worry about land mines – we did not know where we were going or how to get there, neither did the gooks, so the chance of hearing a loud explosion was negligible.

The incident had happened on the banks of Lake Kariba. We were informed the victim was badly injured and unable to walk. Coldly maybe, but to my mind realistically, I considered her chance of survival were remote. The time factor was significant, given the man had walked from his kraal, some 30 odd miles maybe and now with no roads, it was going to take considerable time to get to the scene. Thereafter, I would have to transport her to Bumi Hills and have her transferred to Kariba Hospital by boat.

It was a no brainer – she would never make it. Still we had to try. Driving at an increased speed was not an option. Land Rovers cannot get across small rivers or through dongas and over the tops of heavily wooded hills, as easy as mankind can.

The pace of the war in the Omay was slow and tedious, the chances of accidentally bumping into the opposition was remote. The security forces (SF) were the only people with motorised transport, thus our presence could be heard miles away. A trifle risky from an ambush point of view, but I always lived with the premise 'may the best man win'.

It took us a while to get there, I was sure she would be dead on our arrival. I am not sure what language the Batonka people use, but Fani had little difficulty in conversing with our man.

Told that we were very close I started planning for the disposal of the body. I guessed I would require someone's authority to allow the body to be buried without a post mortem. Now I am no pathologist but if the wounds were such that the cause of death was on a balance of probabilities, as claimed, surely we did not have to have a post mortem.

Within sight, but still some way off, was the kraal. We were confronted with a deep gully which presumably experienced running water during the rainy season. Try as we did, we could not forge this obstacle.

We walked into the kraal. I knew from half a mile away she was still alive – the wailing of the woman folk had not started. We were still in with a chance. On arrival, I examined the woman. I did not have to have a degree in medicine to know she was in a very serious condition.

The deformity of both legs was incredible but none of her fractures had lacerated the skin. The arm was clearly fractured in more than one place, again no lacerations.

From my medical examination (so well qualified was I!) and my observations, it was apparent the old man had failed to provide, what some might consider crucial information I noted the young girl had to be **nine months pregnant**!! Most probably more if that was possible.

Now I had two people to keep alive. The nearest hospital was Kariba. I presumed if the mother died en route, the child may or may not have followed suit. The woman was exhausted and could hardly speak. She was frothing at the mouth. Obviously there could have been a possibility some internal organs in the chest or stomach had been damaged. The rib cage, front and back, was in good 'nick' so the elephant's foot or knee had not landed in that area!

I decided to try and get a chopper from Kariba, there was one there periodically, well more often than not. In my mind it was their only chance. Mother and child were not going to survive another few hours on the road and then the usual bumpy boat ride, which took an hour or so, back to Kariba.

I had a radio, whether I had to relay via Bumi or not I cannot recall. As always in unusual circumstances someone on the other end of your communications system seems to ask a lot of unnecessary questions. I always envisaged someone who had not been considered fit enough for operational duties sitting have a warm cup of coffee, smoking a cigarette while admiring a young ladies posterior, filled with self-importance deeming it appropriate to ask/demand superfluous information.

Usually followed by, "*Stand by! I shall find out where the chopper is and whether it is available.*"

I arranged for a mobile hammock to be constructed out of two long poles, and two blankets sewn together with string and twine and tied onto the poles with wire. A gang started to prepare a rough landing zone near the Land Rover. With the aid of the headman, a large group of woman stood on the banks of Kariba, so they would be easily visible from the air.

During the whole of my 'Hondo' service I never carried maps. I rarely got it right as to which gomo (hill) I was on and whether the river I was on was the same as the river on the map. So six figure grid references given by me where most unreliable.

It was my humble opinion the mother would probably die, she looked pretty ropey to me, but I thought it possible the child might make it.

The chopper eventually landed, we placed the woman in the back, did the thumbs up thing and they disappeared into the 'far blue yonder'.

A few weeks later I was visiting the police post at Bumi Hills when an opportunity presented itself for a 'piss up' in Kariba. A boat would take us there and guaranteed a ride back in a day or two. No one knew where we were, nor did they actually ever inquire. They most probably did not care. So Fani and I grabbed the offer with both hands. My friend DSO Ken Stewart (i/c SB) was of course part of the plan. He provided a Land Rover for official duties only!! Yeah!!

As we approached the port at Kariba I suggested to Fani we enquire about the woman and child. He agreed. We drove to Kariba Hospital. I introduced myself to a nurse as a CID DSO conducting enquiries into a case of an elephant stomping on a woman, some weeks previous.

"Oh yes, she is a star patient. Would you like to speak to her?"

"Yes please," I replied.

She took me to a ward. I stopped her at the entrance. "Which one is she?" I asked.

She pointed out a woman who was suckling a child, she had two legs and one arm in plaster of Paris. I told the nurse I would take it from there.

Before she left and with a big proud smile on her face the nurse said, "You know we are so lucky to have the Army we have – they travelled *through the bush, arranged for her casevac and saved both their lives. Such wonderful people the Army."* Then excused herself as she was very busy.

I placed a new cigarette in my mouth (we were allowed to smoke in hospitals in those days), offered one to Fani who produced the matches and we turned and walked out of the hospital.

*"It was us, the Mapolisa, not the Army. They were not there. Why did you not tell the nurse it was the BSAP?"*

I replied, *"Fani, look at the time, the bar is open, and the beers will be getting warm."* He shook his head.

Fani drove us to the Jam Jar (the police bar at Kariba), I asked him to wait, I went in bought two beers, one Castle, one Lion. The Africans had a preference for Castle. We stood chatting at the Land Rover for a while. Fani was not permitted entry to the European bar. That was a rule we as a nation got so terrible wrong and could have resolved with ease.

On finishing I told him not to 'prang' the truck as he left. I imagine he was confused by my failure to claim credit for saving the two lives. From my perspective it was our job, we did it and hopefully they survived the war.

\*     \*     \*     \*     \*

*I chose to walk alone,*
*Rather than follow a crowd*
*When I realised*
*The crowd was not travelling in the right direction.*

## PROMOTION IN THE FIELD
## & THE SMELL OF CORDITE AGAIN

*The image above shows the author's dog tag, his "given army rank" with a Russian can opener – by far the most efficient can opener available.*

W e were aware army units were weary of 'intelligence' supplied by 'Acorn reps'. Too often they resulted, firstly, in a hurry-up-and-wait situation, there after going through all their 'briefing' and 'deployment' by vehicle, helicopter or in some instances being parachuted in. Too many times the 'int' (information) failed to produce any 'contact' and was classified as a 'lemon'. Frustrating and depressing for them, it meant a return to routine patrolling.

Fani and I were on one of our 'bush stints' and for reasons unknown a Territorial Army unit/brigade or whatever, was holed up at the Karoi Show Grounds.

I had not supplied any information encouraging them to venture into my world. Fani and I had, over the many months operating in the Mukwichi TTL, managed to gain the confidence of a few locals in different kraals.

This TTL is the first habitation one gets to after crossing the Zambezi Escarpment.

We had had a few terrorist incidents. One involved some European fishermen who had been attacked. A man was wounded, late in the evening and being fearful of driving back to Mangula, they had remained at the scene all night. They had killed one terrorist in the incident.

The wounded man was placed on the ground and surrounded with stones by his friend, who then lay on top of him throughout the night to keep him warm. I believe his actions saved his friend's life.

There was another incident where terrorists attacked some miners. The miners shot one terrorist with a shotgun loaded with buckshot. I was in the operating theatre as medical staff attempted to revive him. As a decoy I had the terrorist, still technically alive but clinically dead, transported from theatre to the back of the CID truck, with the surgeon requesting that I transfer him to Salisbury. The terrorist was still attached to bottles of plasma/blood, oxygen tanks and all sorts of paraphernalia.

I had devised the plan, knowing many of the medical staff at the hospital were sympathetic to the gook cause. I hoped our ploy would get word back to his 'gang' who might be panicked into hasty activity, allowing the SF to get the upper hand. I disposed of the body when we got to Karol, using only SF operatives. We never realised any benefits from my devious act – at least we tried.

So all in all, there was a bit going on. Information received was that a number of groups had passed by, heading south. One day, as luck would have it, the army was in the north of the Mukwichi, when I received information of the presence of two groups of terrorists in the same area.

We located the Army Commander and I gave him as much information as we had.

There were no helicopters available to us but I was able to indicate which kraals they had visited the night before, which allowed them an opportunity to follow tracks. I cannot recall whether we had common communication links between police and the Army but let's hope so.

We left the Army doing their thing and drove around other kraals to see if we could get any further 'int' to assist the army's efforts. Somehow we got caught up in the army's affairs on that day. It was unusual for me to interfere in other people's business.

We heard the contact start – we were less than a mile away. Why or how I was contacted to provide assistance is beyond me. I always did and always will go to the aid of a fellow traveller in need, as long as he is on the same side. Fani and I ended up on the battlefield tending to a wounded soldier – always a tricky predicament when your full attention is diverted from what is essentially a dangerous situation.

I asked Fani to keep an eye open for any opposition as I went to the fallen man's aid – he had a Corporal in attendance who was not a medic and was needed on the battlefront. He told me he would get back to my position when he could. He asked me to casevac the wounded man to hospital. The situation was not conducive to lengthy discussions about the suitability or otherwise of Acorn vehicles in casevacs. I assured him I would make some plan. The corporal disappeared, towards all the noise.

I am certainly no medic and strangely we never carried any medical equipment with us in the Land Rovers. The grass was about two maybe three feet in height – typical TTL terrain – few trees and large barren patches. My injured patient seemed for all intents and purposes to be uninjured, there was no blood, and he was not distressed. He did not appear uncomfortable.

He was lying face up. He said he had been shot in the stomach area. I needed to get some appreciation of how bad he was. I could not, or did not dare to place him in the back of the Land Rover. My fear was exacerbating possible back injuries if I picked him up to seat him in the Land Rover. As I could not place him in the back, as land mines were prevalent in the area, I decided to remove some of his clothing and find the entry wound. Entry wounds are very small and often do not bleed much.

However unless the bullet had struck a bone and consequently ricocheted internally, one would expect an exit wound, and these can be very ugly.

On lifting his shirt gently I observed his water bottle attached to his belt had been hit twice by bullets. Slowly I moved his shirt off the abdomen area. I found no entry wound. He was a man endowed with a lot of body hair. I scanned his stomach area minutely.

He started to complain of pain and tingling. I then pulled his camouflage pants down to his knees. His underpants followed suit. He had no blood in that region. His genitals were intact, with no sign of injury.

It must be understood in an attempt to ensure I was not hit by stray bullets or possibly an intended bullet from a terrorist I was keeping a low profile. This meant I was positioned on my chest, face down and trying to ensure my derriere was as close to terra firm as it could be.

My patient had the largest growth of pubic hair I had seen on any human in my life.

That may sound like a big call but having been at boarding school (communal bathing), in Depot (communal showers), in constructions camps in the Australian desert and the jungles of New Guinea, I had seen a few male bodies in my time.

The two bullet entry points in his waist high water bottle, suggested, in theory anyway, the bullet that struck this man, would be laterally on the same line. That left an examination of his pubic region. If we weren't in the bush and trying not to be hit by stray bullets, we might have shaved him.

Funny thing, the word 'if' comes up in conversation so often – like, if my aunty were my uncle would she have balls?

So, there we were under a shady tree in the Mukwichi TTL my patient, now sans trousers, sans underwear, his legs spread as wide as possible, flat on his back with me lying, chest on the ground, in between his legs, my nose very close above his pubic hair with both hands sifting through the mass of human hair growth. At that precise time the Corporal came leopard crawling back through the grass. As I turned my head to see him, I could feel the pubic hairs brush my face.

The look on the Corporals face was incredulous. It dawned on me the scene he had come across would have suggestions of a simulated sex act with reverberations of the days of Caligula.

He enquired how we were doing. I replied, *"We are still trying to get to the bottom of this."* He left.

I eventually located a tiny, closed aperture. It was slightly larger than a pinhead with a small amount of dried blood that had leaked through the hair onto his skin. Progress was being made. My presumption was, it must have struck a bone, ricocheting through his guts and other organs.

The fact that he was neither faint, nor feeling languid, and the lack of pain was a vexing issue.

I suggested he roll onto his stomach so I could examine his back to confirm the presence or otherwise of an exit wound.

On engaging this position a visual scan of his back revealed the absence of anything unusual. He told me his bottom was stinging.

I think his actual words were, *"my arse is f\*\*king sore."*

In response I tried to lift his hips up and still stay low on the ground myself. I found this physically impossible.

Informing him of my intentions I raised myself up onto my knees, then I pulled the cheeks of his buttocks as wide apart as possible. I thought I saw some blood deep down inside one of the cheeks and had to place my face closer to confirm my findings. I had found the exit wound, small, with limited blood. I was as satisfied as a layman can be, internal injuries would be minimal. I straightened up and said, *"That's you done and dusted."*

You would not credit it, at that precise moment both the Corporal and the Sgt returned to the scene. Again it must have resembled the sexual conflagrations of the days of Nero and

Caligula – maybe that was just my mind. I told the two Army chaps of my findings and that I was now willing to place him in a seated position in our truck and transport him to the Karol Hospital. Which we did!

I am pleased to advise after competent medical x-rays it was established the bullet had travelled through his body, without interfering with any bones or organs and he was treated and discharged within a short period of time.

The Army had accomplished a good number of kills during that deployment, a lot of which came from 'Int' that had been provided by Fani and I, known simply as the 'Acorn reps'. Due to the amount of souveniring by Army units I had an agreement with them that was found suitable to both sides.

I allowed them to souvenir as much as they wished, as long as I could examine and deduct all the 'intelligence' available first. It was a plan that worked well and both sides stuck rigidly to the agreement. On completion of that Army unit's deployment, Fani came into my office at SB Karoi and informed me an Army Sgt wanted to see me. I invited him in.

The Sgt informed me they were 'pulling out' in the morning. He indicated there were two issues he would like to clarify.

He wanted to know my surname and rank. He also requested the company of Sgt Fani and me for a few beers at their camp that evening. I asked why the information he sought was so important – no one else had asked for it.

He said his lads had been really impressed with the limited number of 'Lemons' we had delivered and were thrilled at the amount of success they had achieved.

I gave him my surname and said my rank was an irrelevant issue to the production of intelligence, as it came from a number of sources, including police and locals. I might add in that period I managed to spend a lot of the SB float. It was $1,000 a head for each terrorist killed and $5,000 for a commissar's kill. I was the regular and private banker to the Mukwichi TTL.

Fani and I attended the Army farewell. The Army Sergeant stood up and declared that as I was reluctant to give my rank and as I wore none, they were going to provide me with an appropriate rank. I was required to step forward, where upon it was announced to those attending I was now a Lance Corporal and was awarded a single 'stripe' accordingly. It was an honourable gesture for which I was proud.

I asked my wife to sew it on one of my shirts and wore it with pride the rest of my service. It now sits in pride of place in my bar.

I jokingly mentioned to the Corporal, who had assisted me with the patient, that what he saw was not what it may have appeared to be.

He replied: *"Shit, I wondered there for a minute!!"*

And the war intensified amok.

\*　　　\*　　　\*　　　\*　　　\*

*When one door closes, another opens;*
*But we often look so long and so regretfully,*
*Upon the closed door that we do not see*
*The one which has opened for us.*

*Alexander Graham Bell*

## HOW NOT TO GET PROMOTED

I have been hesitant to relate these events, as I am a little hazy on some details – I always remain true to the raconteur's principle of it must be 'based on facts'.

One good reason for the 'hazy' memory is that I was often tasked with 'odd job' work that I undertook in the main only with one African policeman. I preferred to work alone, so to speak. Sometimes I was tasked with work from 'outside' agencies, with my Member in Charge not being truthfully appraised of my work. These were usually short in duration, and frankly most were never documented.

I received a phone call in Sinoia from D/I Opperman in Salisbury. He advised intelligence of some sort had been received that a group of six terrorists had or were to be deployed into Rhodesia across the Zambezi and were heading for Salisbury. Their instructions were not to make contact with any locals at all, including terrorist 'contacts'; they would be clad in mufti and they would also be carrying an 'abnormal' number of fragmentation grenades.

Their brief was to enter Salisbury undetected and then split up singularly, armed only with one grenade each, and at a given time and day, be positioned outside a European "crèche". As the children were playing, they were to toss the grenade amongst them. This was to be repeated. I cannot recall the time lapse.

With a critical shortage of 'troops' he had arranged with the Uniform Branch OC Lomagundi (C/Supt Hogg) at least one 'stick' would be immediately available, if and when I managed to pinpoint this group's exact position. My understanding being, they would be on permanent 'stand by'.

Now those are the facts 'loosely' connected with our deployment. Whatever it was, I was tasked with locating these gooks before they got to Salisbury. If successful, I was to contact the OC direct, he being fully briefed would deploy, 'whoever'. They would engage the terrorists, hopefully eliminating all. I would clean up and thus would end the 'third psalm'.

There were obviously certain difficulties with this deployment:

One, the actual date of the crossing was undetermined.

Two, if they did what they were told and did not make 'contact' with anyone – that would negate intelligence from our own sources.

Three, their intended route from an unknown point of entry to Salisbury was also undeclared.

For those who are not familiar with the area it covered five separate TTL's. If they followed the 'normal route', they would then enter either the Hartley, or Darwindale areas where I could be of little assistance. I told Opperman the chances of finding them were negligible. He concurred, but asked if I could just 'swan around' and see if I could pick anything up.

To ensure not having to move our own base D/Sgt Fani and I took up residence in the south of the Umfuli TTL, in a DC's rest camp. I might add, this was on our month 'off' operational duties.

For a week we must have visited every shebeen, clinic and any religious outfits preaching the gospel according to whomever. Our enquiries revealed the ever-popular answers:

*"Seen a few weeks ago."*

*"Fred saw them, but he has gone to Harare."*

*"My father's in the police."*

*"We are waiting for the rains; or the rains have damaged all the crops."*

*"I did not know about terrorists, when did the war start?"*

I did not bother shaving, not that I tried to look like the 'elite' troops of the Selous Scouts with their trademark beards. It was simply that I would never bump into anyone who would enforce regimental discipline.

In the second week we received, what we did not recognise at the time, a lucky break. A clinic in the Nyaodza TTL was broken into. We actually picked this info up in our travels. We paid a visit and found an unusual story. The premises had been broken into and only 'drugs' for use for people suffering from diarrhoea had been stolen. No money, no other assets.

Fani and I between us had most probably 35 years' experience in house breaking and theft crimes, but this modus operandi was a new one. Who would have the knowledge? I cannot recall the answer to the obvious question. Was the tablet box marked with the condition for which the tablets were designed? Fani and I went about our business, confused by our findings, but we had much bigger fish to fry.

A few days later a second lucky break – this time some bells started to ring. Another clinic had been broken into, this time in the Umfuli TTL, south of the first incident, same MO and now we took a hunch – it was our prey. Consolidating our area of enquiries, we worked with new vigour.

Still no information came forth. If it was our quarry, they were abiding by their instructions well.

We had been playing the Dr Livingstone game for two and half weeks when a third break, this time, within our area of interest.

A farmhouse was attacked one night. The European farmer had shot a terrorist as he was attempting to climb through his bedroom window. He killed one, and then fired at a few fleeing shadows.

I attended and while not having the Selous Scouts 'touch' for tracking we observed and followed a blood trail for some distance, back towards the Umfuli TTL. I always applied my investigations knowledge and principles to my work. I was after all just a policeman caught up in this situation. I had no anti-terrorist training per se. My intention was always to investigate and locate the perpetrators of a crime.

I had to adapt. Under normal circumstances I would effect the 'arrest', compile the docket and submit the docket via the normal channels to the Director of Public Prosecutions.

Now in the 'new circumstances', Fani and I effecting the arrest of six armed men, apparently trained in Russia/China or wherever, in our minds was sheer lunacy and suicidal. So the adaptation we introduced was that we called for those better trained and more capable. While they set about their work, we usually had a 'smoke or two' and when they were finished we 'cleaned up'.

If you recall I had been assured 'back up' was on 'stand by'. I called to speak to Hogg – he was out of town. I was told Supt Allen was the next most senior. I spoke to him and yes, you guessed right, he had absolutely no idea what I was talking about. Nor it appeared did anyone else.

I had no medical qualifications but the amount of blood I had seen told me the wounded gook was not going to venture too far. He may have died, in which case the other four would have moved on but I judged it a critical time to establish the exact state of play.

I explained to Allen as best as I could. The bird of time was on the wing, we were in a time critical situation. At least 30 minutes went past. No word: there were no choppers available. It was a three quarters of an hour's drive to my location. The amount of daylight was also critical. Allen phoned back and said he had done the best he could. He could not provide anyone. I just had to do the best I could. I was aghast – three weeks and now this situation. I was without any ideas.

Four or five hours later, I was still at the DC's camp – the phone rang. It was Allen. He had commandeered a passing TF Unit. They were on their way to my location. I was to do what was necessary.

A Major presented himself at the head of a long convoy of vehicles. I briefed him. Then I led his men to the blood trail, where I had left off. They went about their business. Less than thirty minutes later I heard the echoes of a 'contact'. I approached the scene. Soldiers confirmed five killed. I cleaned up taking possession of the bodies and armaments, leaving just spilt and drying claret. On examination of 'the evidence' I found the tablet boxes.

I was absolutely furious with Allen for his apparent dithering. I drove into Sinoia, walked into his office. I then made my next critical mistake.

From here lies two differing stories that were to have an influence on my career, not that it mattered. I knew, as did most the party was over. It was mid-1978. Twenty months later all was lost.

The first story is that related by myself to CID Officer Chief Supt Hobley.

I walked into Allen's office and said, *"If the heat is too much in the kitchen I suggest you let someone else in who can handle it."*

The second story was read by C/Supt Hobley; from a report submitted by Supt Allen.

*'DSO Stanyon walked unannounced into my office he was brandishing an AK. He was filthy, unshaven, he smelt, he had blood covering his clothing. He had a menacing attitude and told me to get out of the war and let someone more competent take control.'*

A bit like a 'divorce' – there is his story, her story and the truth somewhere in the middle.

What transpired next is also a first! After confronting Allen, with the five bodies still in the back of the Land Rover, Fani and I returned to the DC's rest camp to finish 'our clean up' requirements. I was seated on the veranda when a police car arrived and out stepped the junior Lomagundi Officer Supt Cassidy. He had been a Section Officer at Nuanetsi with me in 1968. We got on very well indeed.

On entering the house, Cassidy said, *"You have caused a major problem in Sinoia. There are a number of really pissed off people there, including Allen. You are going to be charged under the Police Act, most likely for insubordination. You will need a good defence team. I am offering to be your defence counsel."*

I offered him a cup of tea and we chatted, mainly about the old days. He was studying or had passed his LLB degree.

I thanked him and agreed when the gauntlet was thrown down I would let him know. He left saying I had not changed much over the years!

At that time I had written my promotion exams for Inspector. I passed and was awaiting the interview with the Board. I had come 'top Recruit in my induction training squad', followed that up, albeit a little later with the promotion to SO exam, coming top in the country.

I cannot recall who told me however less than 5% of the total people whoever served in the Regiment managed to make it to the 'top spot' in all three promotion exams. I thought it would be an achievement I could tell my grandchildren if I achieved 'top spot' for Inspector. I passed the board – no mention was made of the incident.

Sometime later I was in the CID Salisbury offices, Railway Avenue, and bumped into C/Supt Hobley.

*"Mr Stanyon, congratulations on your promotion."*

*"Thank you Sir."*

*"If you would only learn to keep your views to yourself and exercise a greater degree of diplomacy you would have done far better in the order of merit."*

*"Yes Sir."*

I remain outside the top 5% of those who served. I left the Police Force after 16 years' service, having never been charged. I was honoured to have made up the numbers in an exclusive Regiment and gained friends for a lifetime.

I may not have played exactly to the rules, but I gave my 100% every moment of my time.

\*      \*      \*      \*      \*

*I've taken my fun where I have found it,*
*An' now I must pay for my fun,*
*For the more you 'ave known o' the others*
*The less you will settle to one;*
*An' the end of it's sittin' an, thinkin',*
*An' dreamin, Hell-fires to see*
*So be warned by my lot (which I known you will not),*
*An, learn about women from me!*

**Kipling**

*The ultimate measure of a man,*
*Is not where he stands in*
*Moments of comfort and convenience,*
*But where he stands at times of challenge and controversy.*

**Martin Luther King**

## JUST ANOTHER
## DAY IN THE OFFICE

With the passage of time now a curse on my memory, certainly for detail, the dates escape me. As for some of us who have experienced the ageing process I wish I had maintained a diary. Reference thereto would have facilitated not only the detail, but replenished the chemicals of the memory bank.

My grandkids would have a rueful smile if we settled in for the night, lights down low, grandfather's breath smelling of the nectar of the Gods, his breathing shallow, affected by excesses of tobacco over too long a period.

Granddads can get away with a lot in the eyes of children but I should think mine would claim such stories were not real, they were told just for fun to put them to sleep. I could imagine on retreating quietly from the darkened room thinking I had lulled them to sleep, I would hear one reassure the other: *"Pops is just a fibber."* The sins of the aged.

Once again Mr McGuinness at Bindura had 'requested' our presence, well I like to think that way, possibly 'required' would be more accurate. So Fani and I were picked up by plane at Karoi and flown to Bindura. We experienced the same pleasurable hospitality.

*"I have a chap here, we are certain he knows the whereabouts of two issues important to us. Firstly a common entry point along the Angwa River and secondly what he describes as an extraordinary large arms cache. He feels confident, as we do, he shall be able to point out the area of these two locations from the air."*

Now gooks and arms caches, McGuinness and the Valley immediately brought back painful memories of haemorrhoids and loud noises. The essence of the statement was 'from the air'. That was the important difference. I thought at least it would be a lot safer up there, no chances of land mines, no Army to shoot at me and with a touch of lady luck, no return of the 'piles'. We were onto a winner!!!

I just hoped the Patriotic Front had not taken to the skies to carry out pre-incursion surveys or recces.

*"It will only take a few hours, then drop him back here and the pilot will take you home."*

It was interesting how people other than my wife, thought I permanently lived in Karoi.

I observed the gook was not armed, thank goodness, but worryingly he was not handcuffed or leg ironed.

*"None of that is necessary, he is 100% committed to us."*

We set off; it was a pleasantly warm day, with the sun beating down. (Those with the experience will know in those light planes, even with the windows open, it gets uncomfortably hot.) At 6, 4" room in the shotgun seat was at a premium, thankfully, with all my smoking I was 'slender'.

Sitting reasonably comfortably in the back was Fani, seated directly behind the 'driver', and behind me was our new chap who had apparently just signed allegiance to the illegal regime governing the last country to declare Unilateral Independence from Britain.

I had not enquired of anyone the protocols of seating arrangements in the plane. Clearly the jockey was behind the 'joy stick' and while it felt a little uncomfortable, the new member of the SF was placed, at my insistence behind me. Theory, he would have to crawl across Fani to get to the most important person, in whose hands we had placed our lives.

Just as a backup I drew my pistol from its holster under my shirt and clasping it in my hand, waved it openly, for our friend to see, returning it to my lap. While not a physicist, it was meant to be a warning, any unnecessary tap dancing and I was ready with the means to stop it.

So on we flew, over the top of Sipolilo, over the escarpment and along the Angwa River. Wars do have their pleasures. Here we were engaged in an aerial sightseeing tour of some of Africa's most interesting geological sites. If we had gone a lot lower, a game-viewing trip would have been included at no extra charge!!

As has been demonstrated in previous tales, I work with what I am given – in all facets of my job. When given the opportunity I am selective as to whom I 'break bread with'. So, what kind of plane? Don't know, but the wings were above our heads, those with wings fitted below seat level, make for spotting from the air difficult and cumbersome. How high we were flying was the pilot's problem, out of my control, so I wasted no time thinking about it. How fast and far, no idea. It always concerned me flying with only a single engine. I would have thought, a second, or a spare, would have been useful, bit like the spare wheel in cars.

To my immense surprise our newfound 'comrade in arms', chatting to us in very good English, was pointing out a few geographical features with which he was familiar. This was most encouraging. I was a hopeless map-reader, and silently was going to let the pilot plot the 'six figure grid reference' when we hit pay dirt.

There was no question as to who was going to transverse the ground and arrange recovery, but that would be another day. This was a comfortable gig and as long as 'Fred' behaved himself, I estimated the beers would be just the right temperature on my return.

I nonchalantly noticed the pilot scanning his dials with more intensity than usual. It's a pilot thing – they are always checking this, that and the next thing. I heard an unusual noise, a bit like a 'splutter'. I gazed across to my right and there was some urgency in the pilot's actions, his hands were moving from one instrument to the other quickly, then returning to a handle which he was pumping. His actions became more frantic. Things like that did not disturb veterans like myself!

Attempting to be as calm as a cucumber, and disguising any panic in my voice, I calmly enquired, *"Everything alright?"*

His reply was chilling and confusing, *"Engine freezing!"*

The splutters increased in frequency and volume.

*"Just how does an engine freeze in neigh on 100 degrees heat?"* I asked, feeling my bowels starting to move involuntarily.

I was having a look at what I could see of the engine, I was expecting to see ice or snow – Christ we must be high!

Then another disturbing event, with the pilot still franticly attacking every instrument he had, there was a silence. I mean a deafening silence, followed by wind noises, the high-pitch wind noises one hears as air escapes from a small hole, like letting air out of a balloon. That was immediately followed to my absolute horror, my observation, that the blades of the propeller were stationary. It was vertical. I could clearly see the top half.

Another glance at the pilot confirmed we were now, not in a good place. His hands were moving at the speed of light. I can assure readers your mind goes to places you have never thought of. Looking down at the earth, it looked like a photo taken from a spacecraft. We were a long, long way up.

Still attempting to be the calm passenger, I asked, *"Do these things glide well?"* Given the situation we found ourselves in, it struck me as a reasonable point of interest.

"No," he said. *"We were dropping at a rate of..........."* (Knots, MPH or whatever!!!)

Whatever he said, made me realise, this is how the war ends for DSO Stanyon. My bowels were now signalling immanent activity. I could feel the sweat running down my face, the palms of my hands were sweating. "F**k! What a way to go."

It was then I thought of the two passengers in the back seat. I turned with the intention of reassuring them, this was just a technical problem, easily fixed. To my astonishment I saw two white men seated in the back. I did a double take, and noticed while they had black hair they were as white as a ghost. They were speechless and looked terrified. I do recall thinking to myself if they are white, I must be transparent!!

The ground was starting to take on a much clearer definition, this made our speed of descent much more alarming. Did I think of loved ones, or long lost lovers? No. Did I ask God to forgive me for all my trespasses and sins? No. To be frank, unlike a 'contact', there is no adrenalin pumping. As the ground started to swell up, I had a fatalistic attitude. Thanks for the memories.

I knew it was all over. Then the splutter came back, the engine coughed a few times and burst back into life. The pilot levelled the aircraft out and resumed his patrol requirements.

*"Engines can tend to freeze in this heat,"* he informed his passengers.

You reckon!??? I am certain I needed a change of underwear. I also needed a smoke and a beer.

From that point on our comrade could not identify anything. A few more trips up and down the Angwa, half an hour maybe an hour, while he slowly returned to his natural colour, he was going to be of no further use. We headed back to Bindura.

That evening I sat quietly in the bar of the Twin Rivers Motel. I was thankful to be there. I was chain smoking and quaffing beers like the brewery had announced its closure. Rufus Snyman, whose wife held the license, asked how my day had been. He always had a smile on his face – one of the districts real characters. I really did not feel like describing the 'horror story' all over again.

I replied, *"Just another day in the office Rufus, your shout."*

\*     \*     \*     \*     \*

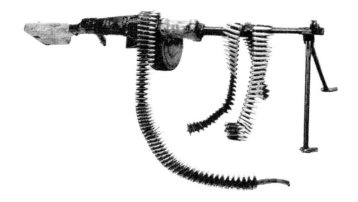

## IT'S JUST PLAIN
## COMMON SENSE

T here is no cordite, no shooting and no loud noises in this tale. No opposition and no heroics. Frankly it is a small and almost insignificant example of what most probably 99% of those involved in our conflict did on a daily basis over the eight years of our war and every war in history.

It does however have connotations of 'risk management', something very much in vogue in the commercial and industrial arenas when I arrived in Australia in the early 1980's. In my thankfully successful 25-year career in the commercial world, I remained on a steep "J" curve the entire time. I was fortunate in that my company, wanting to be seen as being in the vanguard of business had a qualified Risk Manager on the payroll. I was sent to the University of New South Wales to do an appropriate live-in course in the doctrine.

So what is the connection between the commercial world and police work in general, wherever it may be practised? There are of course, many. I refer specifically to the management of risk, something done almost daily in police work.

In my experience, it was not given a 'label', it was not a separate subject taught in Depot. In fact I never recall anyone giving me a lecture on its merits or otherwise. I think the average policeman might simply have referred to is as 'common sense'. It was the ability to consciously or sub-consciously review a given situation, with all available information, then devise the most appropriate plan of action which ensured a desired outcome, resulting in minimal injury to those involved and reduction of any possible collateral damage. That almost sounds like it came out of some textbook, I reiterate, no such instruction was available to the police force.

In the commercial world, the first and most important aspect to be considered in managing risk was 'finance'; a substantial difference in mentality. The assessment of any contemplated decision in a commercial sense, was 'what would be the commercial/financial impact on the business be'?

Now death was obviously the worst scenario in both worlds. The moral and personal loss was the same. All the aspects of dealing with such a horrendous outcome were identical and awful.

However in the analysis and determinations prior to the commencement of the event, in the commercial sense, there was always 'the financial consequences to the business' that never occurred in police work in my experience. The cost of the operation, losses incurred through damage to property, cost of expended assets, the cost of labour, impact on insurance, these were issues in the police that were of no concern.

It was evening, I sat quietly consuming my beer at the Twin Rivers Motel, in Karoi, the day's work had drawn to a close, no night op's planned, it was time to relax and enjoy when a phone call was received from the Karoi Charge Office – my attendance was required there.

Who, anywhere, would want to talk to me on the phone at this hour? The African policeman said it was a DSO Stewart. (Member in Charge SB Kariba) Not only well known to me, but a close friend and accomplice in past shenanigans and security operations.

I drove down to the charge office and spoke to him.

*"Thanks for coming to the phone, Shamwari."*

*"I hope you realise you have disturbed my beer drinking so there had better be a bloody good reason."*

*"Yes. I have just been involved in a light plane crash! The pilot is with the PRAW, and we have crash landed in the Urungwe or Rengwe TTL."* (We can't remember which- this was 40 years ago. Both TTL's were pretty well infested with opposition from time to time.)

Stewart advised me there were just the two of them and neither were in the slightest way injured – another good job done by the mostly unheralded PRAW – he had spoken to the Member in Charge Karoi, a chap by the name of Wilson, a Chief Insp; he had also spoken to the Commander of an army unit that had been in residence. Both, whilst sympathetic to their plight, had rightly concluded as there were no injuries, they were in a township where sustenance was readily available, their security predicament was not dire and they could sleep there the night and they would be retrieved first thing the following morning.

These decisions I presume had correctly been calculated considering the 'jeopardy' both commanders would have unnecessarily exposed their men to by a night rescue.

The plane crashing would have been visible from afar, as I presumed they had used landing lights to locate a safe 'ditching spot'. Also the noise would have been heard from a distance by any opposition in the area.

There was ample time for the opposition to arrange a welcoming party, because it was a safe bet an SF reaction party would be sent out. It would not have been difficult to arrange an ambush on the road between Karoi and the scene. The gooks knew the SF deployed with two or more vehicles. One has to remember that deployment of army required at least two vehicles and I think at least twelve men. I am not sure about PATU, I think there was always a 'stick' on standby at Karoi. Given the situation and circumstances I thought the decisions were appropriate and correct.

Having established exactly where he was, my take on the situation was I presented a far less risk to make a night recovery. My thinking being if we took two vehicles travelling together, it would increase the risk tenfold. While Land Rovers with their tell-tale, trademark light configuration, were not plentiful in civilian hands, they were not unusual. If I drove alone, the opposition would have to wait, until I was actually very close to confirm I was SF. Vehicle lights at night tend to cause temporary blindness. Only one significant issue to be considered was left; would the terrorists have time to lay a land mine? That is, if they had one readily available.

Seeing we would be operating just after sundown and there had been no reports of land mine detonations on the road I was to travel, gave me some assurance the day's traffic was sufficient evidence that the road, at sunset anyway, was clear of mines. With only two people to pick up, there was sufficient room in the front of my land mine protected vehicle for our return. I told Ken I was on my way.

On approaching the township I stopped the car, jumped out and disappeared amongst the building. I left the lights on, so if we had unwanted company, they would find it difficult to witness our re-entry to the vehicle, unless they were behind the vehicle's position.

I am pleased to enlighten readers we all returned safely to the Twin Rivers. Rufus, the owner, was able to provide accommodation. The bar was empty, because it had been closed, in compliance with the law, at 10.00 p.m.

We drank, again in compliance with the law (that was a change!!!), as a guest of the owner. At a ceremony attended by only three others and myself, I was awarded Rhodesia's highest award, a "free beer from friends."

This has been a narrative not of war heroics, as I said, everyone did something similar whenever possible, but the mentality and thought process of all normal policemen/women in doing their job.

In a war situation, the stakes are raised just a little higher.

\*　　　\*　　　\*　　　\*　　　\*

*The voice of conscience is so delicate
that it is easy to stifle it;
But it is also so clear that it is
Impossible to mistake.*

*Anne de Stael*

*Russian TM 46 Anti-Tank Mine:*
*8.6 kg's with 5.7 Kg of TNT*
*The Rhodesians most feared weapon.*

# WHAT GOES UP
# MUST COME DOWN
*Sir Isaac Newton*

In 1976, as previously mentioned, I spent a lot of time in the quaint Internal Affairs Department rest camp named Siyakobvu, in the Omay Tribal Trust Land. A sort of hamlet, built for the white aristocracy like PK van der Byl,(Rhodesian Politian) to engage in his favourite pastime of big game hunting; nestled along the banks of a small running brook, covered in the canopies of large leafy evergreen trees, where once they cooked on open fires whilst sipping pink gins and listening to the creatures of Africa settling for a nights repose, occasionally with the faint echoes of a far off lion marking his territory: all-in-all a most romantic retreat from the humdrum of daily life.

Being a person who has read poetry most of his life and been fascinated by those with brilliant minds, whether used for good or evil, I lay one bright starlit night, pondering my life and future. I had what turned out to be a prophetic thought. To fall asleep I used to try and recite poetry or quotations that I enjoyed. It was a form of mental escape from the vexations in my life.

I tried the famous Newton one that starts, *'I do not know what I may appear to the world; but to myself, I seem to have been only like a boy playing on the seashore…'* and then I got stuck. I tried another favourite, *'And to every action there is always an equal …'*, gone – *shit, I'm pissed*, and then one came to mind which I quoted verbatim; *'What goes up must come down'* - that will do me for the night and I drifted off into blissful slumber.

The following morning I moved out with Fani to go about the business of prosecuting the war. I recall we headed for the banks of Kariba; there really were not many other places to go. I was in the mood to 'win hearts and minds' – I was armed with boxes of fishhooks, bags of salt and mealie meal.

We drove and walked from kraal to kraal, explaining how we were the only alternative to the Makandangas. How life for them would improve tenfold, if they supported us and reported any 'strangers in the area'.

*"Oh my friend please take a box of quality fish hooks, and what about a bag of salt to dry the fish with, and you know what, because we think you will do the right thing, here's a bag of mealie meal, so you can change your diet once in a while."*

Much clapping of cupped hands, big toothless grins as a pair of snarled hands took the bounty. Then it was on to the next village.

*"Seen any strangers in the area?"*

*"No, not ever seen one, we live too far away from Kariba, no one comes here."*

*"What about those that come across the lake in boats with guns that have bananas hanging off the bottom?"*

*"What, who, what are you talking about, no one comes across the lake. Look see how far it is, you can't see the other land!!"*

*"Yes, well if they do come, we are just down the road* (about 35 miles) *at Siyakobvu, would you please come and tell us as soon as you can."*

*"Of course we will, I shall send my eldest son, he is strong and can run all the way."*

*"Excellent! May I help improve your life, with a box of fish hooks, some salt to dry your fish with, and a bag of mealie meal, milled and ready to eat."*

*"Thank you, you are most kind"*

Again the clapping of hands and a solemn promise any strangers would be reported immediately it was then on to the next kraal.

I told my partner and good friend, *"You know Fani we are doing a really good job, we shall have this whole Batonka tribe down at 'Camelot' just as soon as the next gook drops by."*

*"Ishe, you know they can't come, the Makandangas will threaten to shoot them if they leave the kraal, they will lie to them and say that they will wait on the path for them and kill them. They won't report."*

*"Yes. I know that only too well Fani, but some highly trained, educated and qualified witch doctor, whom us white men call a physiatrist, has worked out that they will come."*

*"Ah Ishe, has this man been here in the Hondo?"*

*"No, Sarge no but he has read a lot of books, based on past Hondos, all relevant to our current problem."*

*"When was that?"*

*"Oh most probably going as far back as Genghis Khan, Alexandria the Great, Anthony and Cleopatra and Caesar, then General Georgios Grivas, Mao Tse-tung and last of all the War of the Running Dogs."*

*"Ishe, I don't know these people — but you know, we not going to get any reports."*

As always with his happy character, he gave a good belly laugh,

*"They are not going to report."*

*"What say you Sarg, it's about beer time, let's go home, we have half the Batonkas converted."*

Now to be blatantly honest, whether we spent the night at Bumi and then went to the base camp or straight there I cannot recall, as in reality it is an irrelevance, the ending is the same.

We returned to camp and on entry immediately noticed the carnage. The camp had suffered a terrorist attack in our absence. P/O's were hurriedly going about their business of cleaning up. Now the exact details are sketchy. It was confirmed in our absence terrorists had attacked the base. There had been no injuries but a lot of the assets were damaged.

I do recall the resident cook had given up on the war and had taken to the hills. I also recall establishing that no one on base could cook more than a fried egg – including yours truly.

After my return home, I asked both our cook and my wife if they would call me into the kitchen, for cooking lessons, until such time I was self-sufficient in the art.

I recall having an 'O' group with interested parties and compiling a list of food and equipment which needed replacing. This included fridges, freezers and any amount of food, bedding and many 'sundry' items. We would never have ordered any more than our basic needs! Now would we?

I give the Karoi Police credit they got it together and advised a five-ton Bedford was on its way. At the expected time you could hear the Bedford lumbering towards us from miles away. I was standing in the middle of the camp, looking up at the front gate, as the driver slowly manoeuvred his way down the road towards the front gates of the camp.

Then right before my eyes, the truck detonated a land mine. Now as sad as it is, with the lapse of time, I do not recall which wheel was involved. I do recall the driver was not hurt, nor was anyone else.

Once all the dust had settled and I had picked myself up off the ground the first thing I saw was a volleyball net hanging in the trees. There were steaks and roast, mincemeat and vegetables all over the scene – some very badly bent and battered fridges and freezers. Closer examination found, well-mixed eggs ready for scrambling! The driver was OK which tends to make me think it must have been a rear wheel detonation. Most mine incidents I attended with Bedford front wheel detonations, resulted in horrific injuries.

We started cleaning up. I found the original supply list, which we had used to make the order from.

I called Karoi, and simply said, *"Same again please!!!"* Then my mind flicked back to Isaac Newton: *"What goes up must come down."*

Now I wonder how persuasive all those fishhooks and salt had been in encouraging the locals to 'come across to our side'. We could of course convince ourselves our exercise of 'winning hearts and minds' had in fact worked.

We could also ponder whether, 'one day, pigs might fly' too!  .

\*　　\*　　\*　　\*　　\*

*Half to forget the wandering and the pain,*
*Half to remember days that have gone by,*
*And dream and dream that I am home again!*

**James Elroy Flecker**

# WHILE THE FAT LADY WAS SINGING

*The Ride of the Valkyries & Come Sweet Death*

On the 1ˢᵗ May 1978 I was promoted and in compliance with dictum that had served the BSAP well since the occupation I was transferred. I was sent to CID Bulawayo. There were few Detective Inspectors engaged directly in combating terrorism – not in the field anyway. Det. Inspectors were in the main, either senior Investigators of serious crime, or Members in Charge of Sections and stations. They were taking the next important step in their careers learning the art of command and control, administration and direct man and finance management. The fact they had more hands-on experience, in the pressing needs of war, than the majority of those leading them, was apparently not a consideration.

On arrival in CID Bulawayo I was posted as the Member in Charge, Sabotage section. In 1963 as a Cadet in CID Bulawayo, I remember the members of 'sabotage' to have been shadowy, secretive figures, in offices hidden in the north wing of Bulawayo Central, dealing, in those days with African Nationalism, in the main ZAPU.

When I got there in 1978, I felt as though I had arrived in a time machine which had either stalled or been travelling in reverse.

When I met the current incumbent at the helm of Sabotage section, I asked if we were ready for the 'take over/hand over' process.

His view was that's your office, I am on transfer to Special Branch. It turned out he was less than enthusiastic when it came to matters relating to administration.

I completed all the administration requirements as best I could – the place was in a shambles really, from that point of view. The main task of the section was to investigate 'terrorist related crimes'. I was required to attend the JOC Bulawayo meeting whenever it was convened. On my first evening, I went to the venue, which was the local army barracks, where outside I met my SB counterpart, D/Insp Birch, a former squad mate and personal friend – the only D/Insp to be awarded a medal for continuous excellent work.

The meetings were often cancelled and when we did sit down there inevitably was very little to talk about. I came to understand other JOC's closer to the action in Matabeleland functioned efficiently. In CID Bulawayo I experienced an atmosphere of disinterest, the whole place lacked vigour and excitement, people robotically going about their business. There was terrorist activity along the border with Botswana, in Plumtree, Nkai, Wankie and other places. However, they were, all serviced by SB and CID staff on the ground. We did have one or two incidents of terrorist activity in the city, all of which I personally attended, mainly through boredom and most probably to the dissatisfaction of section staff.

After all the activity I had been involved in, it was to me a tremendous let down. From a political standpoint, my home and birthright was slowly eroding away, general opinion rightly claimed we had reached the end. We were now suffering the death throes, awaiting a political settlement, with the English delegation who had no experience in the matter at all.

I reported to a Chief Supt. who showed me scant interest after I had highlighted the lack of inspections and other administrative non-compliances of the section, for which he was responsible. This particular gentleman was a veteran of the early terrorist incursions and never tired telling me how they 'wrapped up each incursion within weeks'. He never quite grasped the fact, in the new war, single group incursions were numbering 100 at a time and multiples of these were occurring weekly. Nor it appeared could he fully grasp, in his day he had the whole Rhodesian army, Air Force and whatever police manpower required, all concentrated in one small area.

Now the battlefield was for all intents and purposes the whole country, certainly all the rural areas of the country.

By 1978 and certainly 1979 we were losing good men, men with a lot of 'war experience'. They were moving to other countries to kick start new careers. I didn't blame them. Those of us who had kept our fingers on the pulse, knew 'the fat lady was warming up to sing'. The dulcet operatic tones, practising for Bach's 'Come Sweet Death' and Wagner's 'Ride of the Valkyrie' could be heard echoing across the still, night skies of the country. Her voice was more prominent in some areas than others, always unseen but never silent.

In my opinion leadership in the CID was 'cardboard'. That is, it existed but lacked substance and I found there was little respect for those in command.

One morning very early in my stay, I was cleaning out the exhibit room. It housed exhibits of a terrorist nature only, weapons and mines, uniforms and other bits and pieces, which frankly, were unlikely to ever see the light of day in any courts in Rhodesia. I was auditing the books to ensure compliance with requirements. Ensuring each exhibit had a corresponding entry in the exhibit book was labelled correctly and the room was neat and tidy. It is a requirement, an officer carry out at least an annual inspection of the exhibits under his command and signs and date stamps the exhibit book, recording the date of his inspection. There were no such annotations. One example comes to mind, I found, an unlabelled AK 47, with fully loaded magazine attached, with one round in the chamber and the safety switch off. I was unaccustomed to such sloppy administration.

I heard a voice behind me it was the PCIO (the Officer Commanding of Matabeleland CID) Assistant Commissioner Eddy Webb. I reported to his deputy.

He said, *"Mr Stanyon may I see you please."* With that he turned and walked towards his office – our two offices were divided by the office of his secretary. I followed him into his office. A serious man, pipe smoker and rumour had it, a fine billiards player. He dramatically inhaled from his pipe.

*"Mr Stanyon I have perused some of your documentation, addressed to C/Supt Evans. I note with some displeasure every document has been incorrectly signed. You sign off as the Member in Charge and not Officer in Charge.*

*Also I have noted your absence from,* I though he said 'prayers' or 'parade' *on Friday evenings at the officers Mess.* You should be advised, all 'my' officers are required to attend Friday 'parade/prayers', the only acceptable excuse is your absence from town on duty."

For those unfamiliar with the quandary – Members in Charge were non-commissioned personnel.

Rumours had been circulating for weeks/months. Apparently a young twenty something Army Lieutenant has demanded a Police Inspector, aged thirty odd, salute him. The army officer correctly observing he was commissioned and the Inspector was not. The Police Inspector, obviously an idiot of some note, had refused and reported the matter to his OC, who escalated the matter to PGHQ.

It was incredulous we were in the middle or more accurately towards the end of a war, soon to suffer the loss of our country and birthright and we were arguing about who should salute who.

Over the period of the war I had experienced run-ins with Commissioned officers from both the police and army. Men sort these things out, immediately and alone. One can only imagine the number of meetings and consultations, references to legal precedents, lawyers and local contributions that were engaged in.

From the old school police officers, I envisaged the conversation something like,

*"Will they out-number us in the Mess old boy? Don't want any riff-raff in the Mess now do we?"*

*"There will be a lot more money coming in to the Mess! But they will need grooming – coming in one at a time we can cope with, but if we agree to this, there will be a hundred in the Mess on the first night, we won't be able to get a drink! Just imagine!"*

The result of the situation was simply a general circular issued by Police General Head Quarters, which dictated from a certain date all Inspectors and Chief Inspectors would be Commissioned Officers.

Just as an aside, I always found it "interesting" after promotion to Inspector, no further examinations were held. Promotion thereafter was considered, by perusal of suitability reports by one or more of the applicants OC's, a review of his Record of Service and then after an interview by three officers, who did or did not recommend promotion.

If failed the whole process started the following year. From what I gathered thereafter, promotion was on merit and by order of seniority. I did hear, senior officers could block junior officers' progress, if they decided such promotion was not suitable.

Another rumour had it that promotions in general were being accelerated, Patrol Officer to Section Officer as well as Section Officer to Inspector. This was to ensure as many people as possible would benefit from more lucrative pensions, once the inevitable occurred. A second rumour that was substantiated showed PGHQ was of the opinion certain current Commissioned Officers, with their 'wealth of experience' were simply irreplaceable from junior ranks. As a consequence, those chosen by PGHQ would be retired and then immediately re-appointed with the same rank and position they held when so retired. This effectively meant those chosen almost doubled their pay, with a presumed extended period of service.

Mr Webb was one such officer. Such 'nepotism' only fuelled the fires of discontent. To my knowledge Webb had never been involved in any war effort since 1972. Before that time, the experience he may have had, would have been worthless. What's more he was blocking the progress of all promotions down to the rank of Detective Inspector. In the nominal role, for Webb, it records the following wording under the heading discharge 'I.T.O. Pol Re-Appt. Rags."(In terms of Police Re-appointment Regulations) I note he went on to serve the terrorist regime until 1982.

Back to the meeting; I asked Mr Webb if he minded me explaining my position in regards to the fact I did not consider myself Commissioned and why. He agreed.

This was my explanation. I explained Standing Orders had not been amended accordingly, on a number of issues;

(a) SO's required a person to serve at least 24 months as an Inspector, before being eligible to apply for Commission

(b) He had to make application in writing in the approved format.

(c) The Inspector would have to go before a board of Commissioned Officers for them to consider his suitability for such Commission.

(d) If the Inspector was successful in passing the board, he would be placed on a list in order of Merit.

(e) Inspectors so pending promotion would have to wait for a vacancy to occur in their appropriate Departments to be promoted to the rank of Superintendent.

(f) Further to that my understanding was each Commissioned Officer would be issued with a sword (or cutlass/sabre) with their name and regimental number etched there on.

What's more in the CID and SB, Standing Orders required Commissioned Officers, drop the word 'Detective' before their newly appointed Commissioned Rank.

Therefore, as:

(a) None of those amendments had been made in SO's. I pointed out there was a precedent in place that commanded irrespective of any other form of notification, nothing would change until SO, had been amended by order of PGHQ and such amendments published.

(b) The fact being I had not served 12 months in rank, let alone 24 months, the whole exercise was superfluous.

The PCIO pondered this for a while – there was a long drawn out silence. He replied. *"That will be all Mr Stanyon, thank you."*

*"Yes Sir."*

I was never asked, requested or ordered to change my sign off as Member in Charge again nor was I ever questioned about my non-attendance at the Officers Mess.

Some months later, through sheer boredom I requested a transfer back to Salisbury. In good BSAP fashion they agreed and sent me to Fraud Squad CID Bulawayo. There, as the senior D/Insp, I was again the Member in Charge – I had two D/Insp's on staff, a DSO and a DWPO. Once again, there was nothing to do. All wasted manpower while the country slipped further into the abyss.

I had a Supt, to whom I reported, God knows what he did, because I gave him nothing, because I got nothing. One D/Insp and I took to playing chess to pass the time of day. The Supt. found us a few times, rebuking us on each occasion. Later calling me into his office, he asked for an explanation. I told him, he knew as well as I very few cases were coming across to CID Frauds.

It was not the sort of crime one could patrol the cities' streets for looking for criminals so engaged. I just can't recall his reply, but the matter was never spoken about again, the chess games continued.

In August 1979 – eight months before we lost the country, I was transferred back to Salisbury.

I lost my career, my country and my birthright to a bunch of savages, who had, it is rumoured rigged the election with the compliance of British intelligence operatives.

History now clearly highlights, what we as a nation had been advising the British of the inability of such people to run a country with efficient governance. Those people have totally destroyed a culture, its people, a thriving economy and the breadbasket that fed the country and three neighbouring countries – all of this simply because some British Prime Minister 'felt the wind of change'.

For those who may have the slightest interest in the two operas quoted

### Bach's "Come Sweet Death"
Relates in part the following sentiments:-

*Come lead me to Peace,*
*Because I am weary of the World,*
*O come, I wait for you,*
*Come soon and lead me,*
*Close my eyes,*
*Come blessed rest.*

### Wagner's "Ride the Valkyrie"
Is based on:--

*Norse mythology,*
*A Valkyrie is a female figure*
*Who decides which soldiers die in battle?*
*And which shall live and be sent to Valhalla.*

\*　　　\*　　　\*　　　\*　　　\*

*They are able who think they are able.*

Virgil

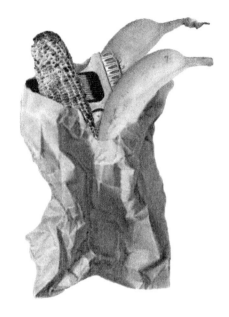

## SOME FOOD FOR
## WHEN YOU GET HUNGRY

This is a story that exemplifies the relationship between the African and European in Rhodesia. There existed what some might call, a blind understanding between the two races. With the exception of the extremists on both sides, there was always an overall harmonious cohabitation.

This is the story of three average members of the Regiment of the BSAP – devoid of political indoctrination. As individuals they merely made up the numbers, their names will have long faded into the obscurity of oblivion, not recorded in any history books. Frankly in the wider world they would be an inconsequence.

They were merely policemen carrying out their duties to the best of their ability, on a daily basis. It was fate that caused them to be serving in an era when the country endured internal war. It would not have been their choice, however given the ever-widening threat and suffering of the people whom they served, it was their duty to ensure law and order at any cost.

What is about to be related happened multiple times, daily, involving any number of different people in differing circumstances. It is what the BSAP was famous for - it was called Esprit de Corps.

It mattered not, the colour of your skin, nor your creed, the level of your education, neither your caste nor status in society. It was not confined to the Police Force, it happened in all aspects of life in what some called 'Gods Little Green Acre'.

It was the very fabric of Rhodesian society, the foundations on which we lived our lives; it was our duty and an expectation to assist a fellow traveller. We were world renowned for our consideration to others.

In either April or May of 1980, Rhodesia had fallen foul of the dishonourable and treacherous politics of the British Government. The terrorists had gained government control.

D/Sgt Nemberi and D/Cst Timot had been passengers in what I can describe as 'an illegal taxi', which provided services to the local populous. This service was renowned for poorly qualified drivers and mechanically unsound vehicles. The taxi was involved in a serious accident, resulting in the hospitalisation, at the Harare African Hospital, in Salisbury, of both serving policemen.

Once stabilised, they were housed in a general ward. They soon realised, the ward was filled with wounded ZANU and ZAPU terrorists, who had been brought in from Mozambique hospitals. Compounding this unsatisfactory situation was the hostile attitude of the African nurses towards the two men. After a day or more, word had spread amongst the confined terrorist patients, that there were 'enemy within their presence'.

With the encouragement of the terrorists, the nurses began threatening the two policemen with death – injected or overdosed drugs were threatened. The nurses, much to the overzealous sneering and laughter of the terrorists, started to ridicule the men. What was most disturbing and caused sleepless nights, was a number of the terrorists had their weapons leant up against the walls next to the beds. From time to time these weapons were brandished, in simulated acts of shooting, aimed at the men.

Rightly they feared for their lives. They sought assistance from the one person they believed would assist, an overworked and indifferent European doctor. When laying their complaint to him, there was a nurse present. The Doctor showed no empathy for their plight. They requested, to see someone of higher authority, this was denied them. Such was the nature of both their injuries that discharging themselves and walking out of the hospital was an impossibility.

They discussed what options were available to them. Members of the BSAP (both were SB representatives) were considered. Being stationed in Karoi for years, they had few personal contacts in Salisbury City. The few senior African staff they managed to talk to apologised and were sympathetic but unable to assist.

Nemberi suggested they contact DI Stanyon – that was no good he was now stationed in Bulawayo and would not be able to help. No. Nemberi had heard along the grape vine he was recently transferred to Salisbury.

Stanyon was sitting out his notice period, as Member in Charge Sixth Floor Fraud Squad, having requested immediate discharge. As this had been refused, he had refused to do any further work.

Stanyon's phone rang. It was Nemberi. He had tracked him down. There was obvious anxiety in his voice. He related his predicament and asked for help. He believed his life was in danger. I drew the opinion Nemberi, a fine man and totally dedicated officer to the cause, was acting in a melodramatic manner.

Armed with the bed numbers and location of the ward, I drove down to Harare Hospital. I did not seek permission to enter I merely located the ward and walked in.

I was astounded by the sight of at least six AK's leaning up against the wall all of which had magazines fitted. One could not differentiate between terrorists and 'others' as they were all in hospital garb. I walked very slowly, my mind in turmoil. I had been warned by D/Sgt Nemberi of the AK's but had disbelieved him.

My presence was despised. That was obvious from the looks of utter contempt and loathing from patients. The nurses also looked at me with derision and disdain, clearly avoiding me and leaving me to my own ends. Plan A immediately came to mind, I would have the doctor order their immediate discharge, have them conveyed to the Frauds Peugeot, and I would drive them to Kaori myself, taking whatever equipment and medications were necessary. Both agreed with me.

I found the doctor, who flatly refused to accommodate my intentions. I demanded to speak to his immediate superior, which was permitted. Another European doctor who informed me the war was over, there was no threat to the lives of Nemberi and Timot. On top of which there were no vehicles (as in ambulances) available, and they were unlikely to fare well if I transferred them by car.

His best advice was to tell them to get used to the new order. The days of special treatment for the lucky few in Government service were over.

I told Nemberi I would be returning, I needed to approach this from a different angle. There were some 'nannies' selling foodstuffs like mealie cobs, bananas, ground nuts and bits and pieces, outside the hospital. On seeing this I walked back into reception and asked if I could be supplied with a paper bag. A large brown paper bag was soon located and given to me. I walked back out to the 'vendors' and chose some 'food stuff' – I walked down to the car.

I placed my Tokarev (an Eastern Bloc manufactured automatic side arm) into the bag and covered it with foodstuff. I briskly walked back into the ward and to Nemberi's bed. I spoke loudly, so anyone could hear me saying I had brought them some food – he thanked me. I told him to examine the food, to see if he needed some more when I returned. His examination of the contents brought a sparkle to his eye, he thanked me and I left.

Now here comes the twist – some time prior to this incident, rumour had spread amongst CID/SB, two European men had 'jumped ship' and were now working for Mugabe directly – not the organisation but the man himself. I knew them both. I had been on ops with them both. I had been totally dismayed at the news. I had no proof, but my sources were impeccable. For reasons I am unable to explain, I chose to contact the senior man. He knew me well. Rather than enter a discussion of what had allegedly occurred, I merely said, *"I wonder if you could help me please."*

I might add there was, if we can call it such, 'favour owing' not that the past was ever mentioned. The current situation was discussed and he asked for half an hour where after he would get back to me.

In due course the phone rang, *"It's all be fixed, they will be transferred this afternoon"*

He gave me a time, which I do not recall. I thanked him and wished him well.

I returned to the hospital an hour before the allotted time. Both men were as I had left them. My re-entry caused an atmosphere that could have been cut with a knife, the looks of hatred went right through me, I felt a chill. I was unarmed, vulnerable and I guess scared. What if one just lifted his rifle and wasted me!!

In due course and not a single minute too early, there was a lot of activity with the two men, who were wheeled out of the ward. I noticed Nemberi clutching a brown paper bag on his lap.

Outside was an ambulance – both men were loaded. Just before the doors were closed I stepped into the ambulance and shook both their hands and thanked them for their service.

Nemberi proffered the paper bag. I declined suggesting he might get hungry on the way.

*"Tantenda Kwazo, Ishe."*

I got out and the doors were closed, I watched as the ambulance slowly moved out of the grounds. I had not seen either of them in over 13 months and I never saw either of them again. It was my total honour to have served with them – they were fine men.

On returning to my vehicle I was approached by the two European doctors. The senior fellow asked,

*"Who the hell do you know?"*

I replied,

*"The good tooth fairy, Squire, from the old Order."*

\*　　\*　　\*　　\*　　\*

*What is originality?*
*It is being one's self, and*
*Reporting accurately what we see.*

*Ralph Waldo Emerson*

# FAREWELL TO THE BSAP
# & RHODESIA

T he 18th April 1980 was, to my mind my last day of service in the Regiment of the BSAP. My late father served for 14 years, four of which were in the Second World War, in the Middle East. I served for 16 years and my late brother served over three years. We were all immensely proud to serve King, Country and People. Although the Rex /Regina bit did get a bit lost after 1965.

My father died with few assets but with the love of his family around him, he was too old to start again in 1980. Unfortunately my young brother suffered a tumour to the brain and his life was cut short too early. He died in 2015.

While the last day to my mind does not reflect the actual last day of my service, it was the last day I worked for the police. I was on the CID 'graveyard' shift (11pm-7am) on the night of 17th and morning of the 18th April 1980. I was serving with former DCI Paddy Anderson, the then Senior Security Officer for the Reserve Bank of Rhodesia.

We were as usual required to attend to any serious crimes, we actually only attended scenes in the townships of Salisbury South.

There were a few murders where we arranged to recover the bodies; the collection of any evidence was nigh on impossible with never an eye witness. These were random killings, presumably politically motivated, or scores of old, settled, under the guise of politically motivated incidents.

As we sat at the Southerton Police Station, there was an eerie silence. We were both in deep thought. I cannot speak for Paddy. The stark reality suddenly hit me. This was the last day of Rhodesia. I was not concerned with all the political shenanigans revolving around Zimbabwe/Rhodesia and Muzorewa – this was the last day – of my home, my country, and my birthright.

I suggested to Paddy I could not sleep, as one would expect after a night shift – heaven knows what was to befall my country. I suggested we play a game of golf at the Royal Salisbury Golf Club, on the last day of 'Gods Little Green Acre', or the 'Jewel of Africa', as described by the Prime Minister of Tanzania.

We hired clubs and caddies and slowly hacked our way around eighteen holes. We had a beer and bid each other adieu. I drove back to my office at the Fraud Squad located on the sixth floor of a building not far from Railway Avenue. I typed out my Form 46 (Application for Discharge) and walked into my OC's office (A/Commissioner Burrell)

I handed him the form and made this request, *"I seek immediate discharge with no notice period."*

Burrell replied with no threat, nor intimidation, but merely observation, *"If you do not work your notice, you shall be deemed a deserter and a warrant for your arrest will be issued. You will lose your pension emoluments and suffer whatever punishment deserters are given."*

I presented my argument, claiming I had signed on to serve the legitimate Governments of Rhodesia at the time and any future appropriately elected Governments. The terrorists, had rigged the elections, there was ample evidence of that. I had not signed on to serve savages who had committed the most heinous crimes imaginable. I refused to owe any allegiance to whoever won the election. The consequence of serving these people would be to provide legitimacy to their existence – which they did not deserve. Within time they would unlawfully annihilate all members of their opposition. There would most probably be war crimes set up, which would be nothing more than kangaroo courts.

Burrell, who had lost a son to the terrorists, purely acknowledged I was entitled to my opinion, and advised the easiest course of action was to serve my notice. I did as little as possible over the next three months.

I received information on the grape vine a coup was being arranged by the Army. I was requested to wait for a period of time after I took my discharge and if successful I would continue with my career. I had built up a small arms cache, which I took with me to a farm of a friend and awaited the coup. It never transpired.

Prince Charles did his duty in attending the lowering of one flag (ironically the Union Jack) and the raising of the other. On the 30th August 1980 with nothing left to fight for, having been sold down the drain by the very people who had set us up in the first place, I boarded a flight with my family bound for Jo'burg and places beyond.

The airlines were still practising the ground to air missile diversionary tactic. As we lifted in a steep J curve into the morning sky, tears rolled down my cheeks. I watched as my birthright disappeared beneath the clouds. I remember a sense of guilt coming over me – had I really done enough? Should I have transferred into a full time anti-terrorist role, would it have made any difference?

For those of us who attended the University of Hard Knocks know, one of the cardinal rules of success in life is '***Failure is not falling down, it is refusing to get back up***'.

Irrespective of what we were in days gone by, it is the here and now which really counts and there is no greater force for continued success in life than persistence and determination: they alone are omnipotent.

       \*         \*         \*         \*         \*

*Oh for a lodge in some vast wilderness,*
*Some boundless contiguity of shade,*
*Where rumour of oppression and deceit,*
*Of unsuccessful or successful war,*
*Might never reach me more.*
*William Cowper*

# TRANSITION TO
# THE COMMERCIAL WORLD

### *Comparisons with the police*
### *And using the Forces training and standards*

Not unlike many of us, I maintained contact with many former members. There was this spiritual essence in the Regiment, which was difficult to comprehend; it was invisible, untouchable and rarely if ever discussed in depth. I believe the last 37 years is sufficient evidence to define its formidable power.

It was simply 'Esprit de Corps'. What exactly is that? What my research exposed was that the Regiment probably defined it best, if you will excuse the seldom-revealed parochialism. It is defined as 'a feeling of pride and mutual loyalty, devotion and enthusiasm shared by the members of a group'.

Due to the work I was engaged in after my police career, I travelled the world extensively, meeting members of law enforcement and private security operatives in a multitude of countries. I am not going to venture into the conjectural discussion of the comparative qualities of the organisations, but without fear of contradiction, I never again felt the spirit that was the Esprit de Corps of the BSAP.

The BSAP had a means, which again, I have failed to positively identify, to inculcate into its members a sense of professionalism of task or duty if you will, without any structured tuition.

One last incomprehensible value the BSAP had was its selection and training processes. Certainly the recruitment officer in Rhodesia was a serving member, usually a junior Superintendent, having come through the ranks – there would have been no human resources training, no physiology training, and yet so few 'misfits' were ever attested.

I attended Depot training and re-training three times – that's not smart on my part. There was a lot of emphasis on fitness, looking smart, knocking the sharp edges off, learning to type, poor old

Annie Lovell (in my time), a fair amount of law and police training (investigations and legal precedents) – but no overt and apparent focus on all the other requirements so important to the standards of the Force.

One did not have to be a serving member for long before a devotion to duty was displayed and a determination to ensure a respect for the law was abided by. That 'close enough' was never good enough and wherever possible, 'it' had to be done right the first time. We seem to have raised the level of the bar, on such common trivialities as punctuality, respect, humility, dignity, restraint, courtesy and service.

I acknowledge the BSAP, seldom if ever produced world leaders, Nobel laureates, Captains of Industry, tycoons or world financiers.

During my travels I met many former members and found it interesting how they had successfully managed or failed the transference from the structured life of the police to the devious, deceitful and often compromising world of commerce.

I thought some might be interested in my journey from former BSAP CID 'doppie picker extraordinaire', to the new commercial world where 'the mighty dollar' provided the main focus and controlled every aspect of ones work.

With the age-old adage of 'winners are grinners and losers can do what they like' ringing in my ears and a total adversity to serve terrorists, I did what I liked, I waited for the 'coup' that never eventuated. In hindsight thankfully, there would have been a lot of unnecessary blood spilt and a lot of broken-hearted people, I packed my bags and left Africa.

My family had been resident of the Continent of Africa for 120 years, immigrating to Natal in the early 1800's, to Kenya (where remnants remain) and then to Rhodesia. I am surely one of the white tribe of Africa.

There was a saying in Africa, from Cairo to Salisbury and now of course to the Cape itself, 'if you leave Africa after the Jews, you have left too late'.

I headed for Australia – some called it 'the lucky country'. I had twelve cardboard boxes, one containing an elephant's foot. With me were my two infants and my wife. Cash, in hand, bank or under the mattress, was enough to get by with, as long as work was obtained immediately.

As you read the following abridged narratives, one should bear in mind I was a fourth year secondary school educated Rhodesian boy, all I had to fall back on was my police training, standards, ethics and principles. No Rhodes Scholar in this camp.

My first job, obtained through a newfound contact, was as a warehouse 'gopher' for a large hardware chain. I had a supervisor above me who had a Warehouse Manager to whom he reported. A dead end job, but it was money coming in.

About a month into my new career I was invited to a Saturday BBQ (Braai). I thankfully attended, bringing a piece of steak and non-alcoholic beverages.

After an incident during the war one Saturday afternoon when I was just about as 'blind as a welder's dog', I was called out to attend to a security incident. I took a wrong turning and things turned ugly – I have never consumed alcohol until after sundown since.

I arrived at the house. One car, with its boot open, appeared to be the focus of attention. There was a very large crowd in attendance, only a handful from work. Closer inspection showed a 'boot sale' (an Aussie custom) was in progress. In charge of the sale was my supervisor. Assisting him in cash collection and product distribution were my work mates.

The product was obviously 'stock' from the warehouse!! Within half an hour, all deals were done – cash divvied up and very happy customers departed. The braai was a resounding success.

I asked my supervisor what it was all about. *"You didn't nick anything this week, so we just invited you to see what happens. Each week we all nick stuff, and then sell it at the weekend – kind like a bonus!!"* I resigned on the Monday morning, wiser indeed.

I became a pallet rack erector, working in rural Queensland mines and around the factories of Brisbane. Twelve months had passed and I had submitted 96 unsuccessful written job applications. I was starting to wonder where the hell the 'lucky country' was. Whether or not a Police Inspector was of any significance in Rhodesia was one thing, in Australia it meant 'jack sh-1-t'.

I became nauseated with explaining I had not served in either the British or the South African Police, and that Rhodesia, was not part of Indonesia. Former police officers, irrespective of where they served, were referred to as 'bloody coppers' and were not the first choice of most Human Resources Managers for companies.

I managed to snare a job as an Insurance Assessor – I had no idea what they did and was lucky to get hired by a one-man-band outfit, with good connections in the insurance world. It was a step in the right direction, I was supplied with a company car and I managed to double my salary.

I would probably bore you with what happened in that industry – suffice to say, part of my job was to assess insurance claims, covered by insurers (who had hired me) then obtain three written 'quotations' to resolve the matter and to satisfy myself the client had been placed back into the same position he was before the suffered loss.

Certainly among the artisans that were on our books, there was fierce competition to get 'the work'. They had great difficulty with my decision-making, in that I did not accept *'there is a quid in it for you'*, when an envelope placed on my desk was followed by absolute horror and I threatened *'to tape the conversation'* and hand same to the police, for prosecution. The practice stopped immediately.

After some ten months my wife showed me a large advert in the State newspaper, looking for a State Security Manager for a Cash in Transit Company. I assured my wife I had learnt it was necessary for large companies to show transparency during employment and to advertise, when in actual fact, the position had already been filled. In this case, I suggested the position would already be filled by a former officer from the local Federal or State police.

I ignored the advert. The following Saturday it re-appeared, with some unusual wording – 'those who had applied need not re-apply'.

Not thinking I had much chance, I concocted my curriculum vitae and posted it. I was invited to the offices. I was interviewed by an Englishman, a former member of Scotland Yard's Flying Squad and a week later I received a phone call, I had been placed on the short list of 'three'. I again presented myself and was interviewed by the person to whom I would report, the Australian National Manager, should I be successful.

As luck would have it – the National Manager of Australia had hired a Rhodesian some months before – thought he was an excellent worker and thus I had made the short list. It turned out, this chap had been a Prefect at the school that had attempted to educate me, in Umtali. After which he attended Gwebi Agricultural College.

He had been hired as the supervisor in charge of the 'Coin Depot' in Sydney. If we came from, where was that place? Oh Rhodesia! That's right, and we went to the same school and we knew each other that augured well for the Manager. There were no questions regarding my suitability for the Cash in Transit industry. I have no idea what happened to the other two candidates: ill health, car crash, second thoughts, who knows? A week later, I was hired.

On my first day at work, the 'London bobby', told me he would have to build me an office and wanted to know what I knew about the 'C.I.T' industry. I replied honestly – nothing at all, I had no idea what the company did.

He suggested, *"For the first week I want you to go where and when you like, and maintain notes of your observations – I shall see you next week."*

My salary had increased by eight thousand dollars per annum; my company car was brand new and much flashier than the last one. Oh and I could have my work suits and clothing dry cleaned by the company employed to do the "Armoured Car Crew Uniforms", a significant savings.

Maybe I had found the lucky country!!

In the first week I arranged to travel in an armoured car to see what happened therein. About a mile out of the depot, the truck turned around and went back. I asked what had happened.

*"We have been called out on strike."*

*"What happened?"*

*"You are management and not allowed in armoured cars."*

Everyone had two days off – the Transport Workers Union and the manager came to an agreement. On the third day I joined another crew who came back in at lunchtime. I had struck up a conversation with the crew in the back (a former Queensland policeman) and I joined him in the crew room for lunch. Once again all the trucks returned to base, they were on strike because I was in the 'crew room' and I was management. Two more days, no pay for the workers, lots of meetings and it was agreed then, in future no management were allowed in trucks on operations or at any time in the crew room. I was being educated at an alarming rate.

A week passed and I presented my written findings on my observations. There were 12 pages of it, purely on matters I considered to be poor security, possible exposures to theft and in my humble opinion inefficient work practises, not necessarily of a security nature. These covered inadequate screening of applicants within the industry, total lack of firearms training (all crews and supervisors were armed), the highest risk being litigation, lack of quality induction training for crews, cash room counters and supervisors, inadequacy of physical security on the armoured cars against very simple and nonviolent attacks, including radio transmission immobilisation. The biggest threat I saw was the opportunity for the crew to act in concert with criminals, and lose the contents of the truck – averaging $4 million per truck.

Over the next twelve months I was directed by the national manager to carry out similar surveys on the other sixteen businesses nationwide and all airport operations. Just over 12 months later my boss was fired, a young up and coming Director took the reins. He appointed me the National Security Training and Risk Manager. My predecessor was fired.

My first job was to reduce the countrywide 'internal losses', which affected 'the bottom line'. Internal losses were unaccounted for missing money, usually taken (read stolen) by staff in small amounts for lunches; if debts at home were getting a little out of control; to assist car re-payments; extra cash for the weekend; etc. etc. As long as the amount was less than the cost of trying to locate the loss, management accepted it as part and parcel of 'the business'. Until then nobody had bothered to add up all the branches 'internal losses'.

How much was the figure? The new boss advised he had had the head office accounts tabulate these losses countrywide. The loss to the bottom line averaged $1,880,000 per annum. This was part of the net profits of the company.

I hired a computer programmer and for a cost of $8,000 we 'nutted out' a system allowing me to track names, dates and patterns of losses. (Some of you might notice some similarities from the police) I introduced a 'paper form' to be submitted on every loss of

$1 or more – much to the annoyance of most of the 2,500 odd employees. The net result in the first year was a decrease of over one million dollars and then down to a steady level of about $300,000.00 per annum. The new man was thrilled, his career, remuneration and reputation was judged on the level of 'net profit' alone.

I was responsible for a $1.2 million per annum expenditure budget. In the beginning I had many business suitors inviting me for lunch and 'other' favours, all of which were reported to my superiors and politely refused, bottles of 'grog' left at reception for me at Christmas were returned.

The consternation this caused was remarkable. I was interviewed about 'my attitude' by the world CEO and some directors. I stuck to my guns – it is I advised them, simply called 'corruption', in which I have no dealings.

BSAP training, logic and determination to get the job done at any cost came to the fore after the Australian Government introduced legislation in an attempt to combat the rising crime rate involving the importation and distribution of illegal drugs, the base of the legislation was that the proceeds of crime, in any form, could be confiscated by the Crown, if so proven. Banks and armoured car companies were frequent targets of armed robbers.

Two armed robbers went on a three-year spree robbing banks and the two armoured car companies. They were arrested after robbing one of the ATM machines for which we were responsible. It is almost tradition in Australia for robbers to first remove all weapons from security guards before the commencement of the crime. When police searched their residences, the idiots had kept the handguns as souvenirs of their exploits. This provided direct evidence linking them to a number of crimes and shortly thereafter admissions were obtained for other crimes.

I asked the police to instigate the new 'proceeds from crime' legislation. They refused as in their opinion the legislation only related to crimes involving illegal drugs. The police approached the DPP, at my request, who confirmed the police take on the new legislation. I read the legislation in detail and could not agree.

I used $60,000 to hire a decent lawyer. The matter was heard before a judge who ruled in my favour and we (well I) set an

Australian legal precedent, which is now followed wherever possible by all State and Federal Police forces, stating that 'the proceeds of **any** crime' was in fact covered by the legislation.

They had stolen $ 4.6 million over three or four years. The net result was the recovery, by myself of racehorses, ocean going yachts, three mansions, bank account contents, and other assets, worth about $2.9 million. The new Director was thrilled although the recoveries were split proportionately between victims. After all, he saw the potential in this bloke – where did he come from?

It was interesting, all I had done was correctly interpret the written law and refuse to accept my interpretation was not accurate.

I say this because I believe one should always give credit where credit is rightfully due. In this case credit is given to the systems, standards and ethics of the BSAP, which in the main churned out good quality operatives time and time again.

Many of the ever changing company directors and national managers experienced difficulty working with me because I was quote: 'unable to see the grey areas and had an inability to act like the tide, which comes in and goes out' – in other words my world was inflexible, I saw only black and white. The rules were the rules, if you want to change them, change them but do not violate them – very much a BSAP trait. Thankfully underwriters at Lloyds of London liked what they found in me and supported my continued employment.

Why have I told this story? It is simply this – everything I did from day one for the next 17 years was based solely on my training from the BSAP. Many of the documents I introduced were based on those we all knew and used daily in the BSAP.

I ended up hiring six security managers. (One of the most successful was an ex-BSAP District Branch Inspector) I provided the induction training for the company based on what I had learnt from the BSAP – all appropriate staff underwent an annual re-training to reaffirm standards and procedures. I wrote a procedures manual for crews and other employees based on the 'old Black Instruction book'.

The first National Training Manager I hired was an ex-BSAP District Branch Inspector who brought a quality of training, inclusive of leadership training for all managers and supervisors that was so successful it was copied in parts by other divisions of the company (about 20,000 people in all). The International Cash/Values in Transit Manager asked me to find him a Security Manager 'just like you' – I arranged for the employment of a former D/Insp. from the BSAP and my understanding is he enjoyed a successful career until the company was sold and I have not heard of his fate since.

Lloyds of London, who were the only organisation large enough to underwrite CIT operations worldwide, were complimentary in their praise for the company's risk management.

The image below represented a 'days' banking by one branch out of sixteen branches owned by the company I worked for. I was a signatory to the company's bank cheques. It was one of the larger financial cheques I signed. A large amount in an ordinary man's life let alone in the life of a poorly paid policeman and world travelling bum.

*One days banking*

The risk management of the company that I managed was simply drawn from the training and standards I had undertaken on behalf of the BSAP plus a live-in university course of about two months. I made sure I mentioned this 'fact' at every opportunity I had.

The past is exactly that, it is of no consequence at all now. I retired 14 years ago – an international conglomerate purchased CIT Division – the BSAP and Rhodesia no longer exists.

BSAP numbers are dwindling rapidly. On the morning of the 22nd September 1964 I had been the most junior European policeman in the BSAP. Now 71 years of age, there are not too many alive who were senior to me, then.

My post police career in Australia was, thankfully extremely successful allowing me to retire as a self-funded retiree at the age of 57, having arrived in Australia at age 34. I was a senior national manager within an Australian company, with International interests that enjoyed a position as one of the top 25 companies in the country. There is no doubt at all the BSAP training, ethics, standards, professionalism, self-sufficiency, initiative and an ability to work against the odds constantly, was the foundation which allowed whatever level of success I achieved.

I live a quiet, comfortable life in retirement now, with my small canine friend.

I believe I remain in the Regiment's debt.

For all that has happened in my life. I do have regrets, though I acknowledge I have been fortunate in life, for which I am thankful.

\*     \*     \*     \*     \*

*Believe you can, and you can.*
*Belief is one of the most powerful of all*
*Problem dissolvers. When you believe that a*
*Difficulty can be overcome, you are more*
*Then halfway to victory over it already.*

*Norman Vincent Peale*

# THE BEER MUG
# NAMED 'GOOK'

There is a beer mug named '**Gook**' which commands a place of significance in my watering hole at home. Purchased circa 1972/73. Printed on the mug the Rhodesian advice to terrorists. They say if you hold the mug behind your head and a mirror in front, the reflection will reveal the advice. It is in a state of uncleanliness, for one reason alone, I have never washed it since it was last used in December 1979.

All the artefacts in the bar have a history attached to their existence. Some merely of exotic places I have visited, purchased purely for the 'bragging rights', at a time when that seemed important to me - others providing contemplative and reflective thoughts of wild parties and unforgettable characters. Most of course the instigation of questionable yarns of times long gone.

In my dotage a few months ago, in a land far from where it all began, I was seated in my bar alone, indulging in a quiet drop of the nectar of the Gods. My eyes fixed on 'Gook'. With little else to do, I pondered, "if only 'Gook' could hear and talk, what would it say of its 45 years of existence".

I allowed my imagination to drift into the surreptitious world of deception and fabrication, where only old people and young children dare venture.

This is what 'Gook' told me:

When my new owner purchased me and quaffed from my lips for the first time there was a group of them, drinking from mugs decorated like myself, at the watering hole.

They were brim-fired and filled with adrenalin, confident of their invincibility, intrepid, and claimed to travel where angels feared to tread. I heard talk of a few dissidents who planned to upset the 'status quo'. Oh how they laughed and sniggered, some part choking at the jokes about these fools.

It was unanimously agreed the terrorists were in for a rude awakening. *"History,"* one claimed *"repeats itself"*. Another interjected: *"we have always successfully eliminated all previous insurgents. This will be no different."* With an air of self-confidence, one added, *"Just a few weeks, a month at most, and we would return to Utopia, the very Garden of Eden, that was our land."*

'Gook' mused; I have played many parts during uncontrolled drunken sessions, and performances of the Regimental song and other rude ballads, I have been filled and emptied while those around me bragged of the countries unquestionable belief of bringing a few dissidents to heel. Repetitions of **"never in my life time"** and "**not in a thousand years**" reverberated across the walls, in which I was confined.

There have been more sombre periods when it had taken longer to drink a quota of my sustenance. I bore witness to more serious discussions of how they alone were holding back the tide of world communism. They knew the Western world were thankful and would remain in their debt. World sanctions were a farce – "stuff" was coming in – through Beira and South Africa - nothing to be concerned about. The Powers that Be gave the incursion a name, they always did. This one they called, 'Hurricane'- like 'Pagoda' in 1966 through to 'Lobster' in 1971 and the 26 in between. One said, *"Same old same old."*

I guessed this meant, the end result would be the same.

After each session, I would be washed and placed back on the shelf. I watched as people staggered to bed. One by one the nightlights were doused. As the night drifted into silence, save the sounds of those that made the night their playground, frogs and owls, night jars and crickets.

While alone on the shelf I hear faint whispers, in the distance - unheard by my master? Or did he choose not to heed the warnings of distant drums.

Tomorrow I shall be filled again. Tomorrow I shall hear of the triviality of the recent 'incursions'. The dismissal, as farfetched, that dissidents were gaining ground. I hear too of internal bickering, *"Why did we not know sooner?" "Who was responsible?" Why did we not react?* I hear of dissension within the ranks.

In April 1974 I recall a group sitting quietly, each apparently lost in their own thoughts. Attempted encouragement to enjoy falling on deaf ears.

One muttered, *"This is a serious problem."*

*"Blind Freddy,"* said another *"could see we were now in a difficult predicament, possibly we were now facing the beginning of the end."*

There had been a coup in Portugal – it would have far-reaching and disastrous ramifications on the 'Garden of Eden'.

People came and went from the bar over the months. Fighting now a way of life. It was discernible all remained determined to fight. True to their cause. I noticed 30-day periods of absence from the bar. Stories unfolded of horror, and barbarism, heroics and humanitarian deeds. The frivolities had diminished. There was a determination and commitment to stay and fight, unyielding until some reasonable and acceptable resolution could be achieved.

In 1976 I sensed a mood change, 1000 people a month were reported emigrating. One patron claimed desk pilots were becoming numerous. Rumours were rife, senior army personnel believed they had 'moles' within the ranks of the Security Forces. One apparently knowledgeable consumer spoke of pressure being applied by South Africa, the last ally the country had.

1976/77 fighting and its consequences remained the norm. I saw no evidence of a lack of determination, nor lack of patriotism, nor an inability to fight, or lack of will power. I heard hushed whispers about those who had paid the supreme sacrifice and others suffering physical and psychological incapacitation. Unlike the Ops before, no longer talk of outright victory, or of mopping up. People spoke of other operations named 'Thrasher' (Feb '76); 'Repulse' (May '76), 'Tangent' (August '76); the consequences they spoke of, lack of manpower, equipment shortage. Increasing numbers of dissidents.

But never, never, they repeated, never would they surrender. The patrons professed they were prepared to pay the supreme sacrifice.

Some talked of the "chicken run."

*"Good riddance,"* said another.

Guests accepted the situation, conversation never revolved around new careers, or emigration. I detected a discernment of hope that 'someone in politics could produce a 'rabbit from a hat'. Soon conversation changed to the unnecessary waste of life. Common ground maintained, it was essential, to remain true to the principals of democracy, and universal suffrage, of decency and honesty and credible governance.

Those that named operations added two more, 'Grapple' in August 1977 and 'Splinter' in June 1978. By the end of 1978 the entire country was at war.

Talk now centred on accelerated emigration. The enthusiasm of many to continue to fight was waning. With Smith having agreed to majority rule within two years, it was now no longer a war to be won, but a peace to be formulated. The Government came out with a new national strategy, 'Winning the Hearts and Minds'.

1979, I bore witness to discussions of the loss of many key and experienced operatives leaving for greener pastures. The situation was no longer under the control of 'the fighters'.

From mid-1979 a new conversation dominated the watering hole - The Lancaster House Constitutional Conference. It started on 10th Sept 1979. Concluding in Dec 1979.

I never saw the same faces again. There was no more laughter or banter. The odd man dropped by. I was never used again.

Now 38 years later, I sit on another shelf 11,500 kilometres from home, still unwashed. From time to time I have witnessed people visit, only when I hear their names do I recognise them. Like my master they are all old men now grey haired, faces creased by the weather and the severity of lives lived, their gaits lack the spring they once had in their step, backs bending, shoulders rounding.

One thing has returned though, it is the laughter. They tell stories of 'the war' that they find amusing. They recall the characters of old, some of them have passed on, some down on their luck, and others mastered the change in life. Still the same people gather to drink and break bread at the same table.

I am looking down at the man that bought me 45 years ago. He stares up at me, alone but for a small dog. I wonder what he thinks. He would remember the waters that have passed under the bridge.

He moves slower now, with a limp, his hands arthritic, his eyes lightly sunken, the glint long gone. The eyes reveal the pain of loss, tolerated, but not forgotten nor forgiven. Maybe one day he will quaff from my rim again.

What will the world know of those who gave their all? Where history has already proven the folly and erroneous, culpable decisions, made by politicians by placing power into the hands of dictators and savages? The British lords and aristocracy, thought it simple to rid the world of a handful of belligerent whites. They lacked the capacity to foresee it would deliver millions to starvation, destitution and adversely affect the populous of five other countries.

And what of our future? He will pass before me. And I, I may be sold to a stranger as part of some militaria collection. What will he know of what I have seen and heard, renditions of Kum-a-Kye and other drunken songs, of raucous behaviour, wild bar games, laughter, and youthful boasts, of loves made and lost, of dreams shattered, promises broken and hopes devastated? What concept, if any will he have of the Garden of Eden? Will he really care?

Or maybe I shall just be discarded onto some foreign garbage dump, and covered with the next load of rubbish. An inevitable and similar fate awaits both my master and I: *sans* wine, *sans* singer, *sans* Song and *sans* end.

History shows the Rhodesian advice to Terrorists, printed on my surface is exactly what happened to the Rhodesians themselves!!!

\*     \*     \*     \*     \*

*If my hands were filled with truths,*
*I should be careful not to open them.*

*Le Bovier De Fontenelle*

# Ashes of Tradition

We who call ourselves wise are otherwise;
Mudzimu, now gradually dying,
We crushed her prestige to sand....
And who shall rebuild on the ash of tradition?
Who can kill time without harming eternity?
Knowledge has come, but wisdom lags behind.

"
                                        Mudzimu" by Gibson Mandishona

# Of All Wild Things

The hot blood sings
Like summer in the veins.
Up the Sanyati Gorge
The barbell mass to spawn
Churning the water white.

Deep in the mopani scrub
The Sable bull
Taps the shoulder
Of his resting mate
Persuading her to stand for his delight.

                                        "Season" Phillipa Berlyn

# African Soul

### One

Within my Soul, within my Mind,
There lies a place I cannot find.
Home of my heart. Land of my Birth.
Smoke coloured Stone
And flame coloured Earth
Electric Skies / Shivering Heat
Blood red clay beneath my feet.
At night when finally alone,
I close my eyes and I am home.
I kneel and touch the Blood warm
sand
And feel the Pulse beneath my hand.

### Two

Of the ancient life too old to name,
In an ancient land too wild to be tame.
How can I show you what I feel?
How can I make this essence real?
I search for words in dumb frustration,
To try and form some explanation,
But how can a heart and soul be caught
In one dimensional written thought?
All love and longing are a fire
And Man consumed by his desire.

### Three

Then this love is no simple flame
That mortal thought can hold or tame
As deep within the Earths own core
The love of Home burns evermore.
But what is home? I hear them say,
This never was yours anyway
You have no birthright to this place
Descendent from another Race,
An immigrant? A Pioneer?
You are no longer welcome here.

### Four

Whoever said that love made sense?
I love is an imperfect tense.
To love in vain has been man's fate
From History to present date.
I have no grounds for dispensation,
I know I have no home or Nation.
For just one moment in the night
I am complete, my Soul takes flight.
For just one moment. Then it's gone
And I am once again undone.
Never complete, Never whole.
White skin and African Soul.

Authot Uknown
London Daily Dispatch

*The authors residential "Bar" in Australia.*

## WELCOME
## TO
## THE LAST WATERING HOLE

*Prodigal sons and Poetry lovers, Dreamers and Romantics,*
*Veterans of conflicts, who fought honourably for good causes,*
*Those left alone, with little more than chosen memories;*
*Artists and Readers, Aging scholars and the Friendless folk,*
*Unselfish Charitable souls and they who chose the road less travelled;*
*You are welcome, to sit awhile, quaff your fill and tell us your tale.*

*Those who toil, now with bent and twisted bodies,*
*People who offered their all for their fellow man,*
*Optimists filled with Compassion, Integrity and Humour,*
*Fearless characters who dared to challenge the status quo.*
*Those who were dealt poor hands and still played without protest,*
*Come sit a while, rest, do not repent the past, and tell us your tale.*

*The waters of our time, like the watering holes, are drying now,*
*Tarry not, the bird of time is on the wing.*
*Regrets we have, let them be the lessons of our lives,*
*We have played life's game, we did what we thought well.*
*Whomever your deity, draw comfort there from.*
*Join us, there will be no judgement here, tell us your tale.*
*Before we too into the dust descend,*
*Sans Wine, Sans Singer, Sans Song, and Sans End .*
**Doug Stanyon**

# IN CLOSING

There remain many stories, I have not told, especially of the years spent in the war – it is frightening what man will do against man in times of conflict, to what depths of depravity the human race can lower itself.

I hope the reader has experienced some enjoyment, from these stories and possibly a little insight into another way of life.

I wish upon you and yours, good Health & Happiness.

Thank you for your time.

*Some wisdom to close with*
*from*

<u>*The Masai Tribe of Kenya.*</u>

*"The Lords of East Africa"*

*"You think your thoughts you have to live with them."*

# GLOSSARY OF TERMS

| | |
|---|---|
| ACORN REP. | Radio call sign for CID or Special Branch operative. |
| AK 47 | Soviet Automatic Rifle – Kalashnikov 7.62 x 39 mm |
| AP | African Police |
| Babalas / babelaas | Hangover; to be drunk. (Zulu word babalazi) |
| Body Box | Aluminium Box for carriage of dead bodies. |
| Braai | B.B.Q's |
| BSAP | BRITISH SOUTH AFRICA POLICE |
| BSAP Motto - | For King, for Law, for Country |
| Chirundu Bridge | Boarder between Zambia and Rhodesia |
| Claret | Blood (Slang) |
| CMED | Central Mechanical Equipment Department |
| DC | District Commissioner (African Affairs Dept) |
| DCI | Detective Chief Inspector (European) |
| Depot | BSAP European Training College |
| Depot Hairstyle | Short Back and Sides |
| Det. | Detective (African and European) |
| Dik Dik | Minute African Antelope – Royal game |
| DISPOL | Police Officer in Charge of a District |
| Doppies | Expended rifle cartridges – collected for Forensic Exam |
| Doro | African Beer – brewed in many ways. |
| DSO | Detective Section Officer (European) |
| First Call | District Branch person on first call-out |
| First Reserve | As above |
| GMO | Government Medical Officer |
| Gooks | Rhodesian Security Force slang for Terrorist. |
| Gungene | The Bush |
| Gwaza | The harder one worked the larger the wage |
| Hendon school | London Police standard of Motor Vehicle Driving |
| Hondo | War (Shona word) |
| Hooley | Drunken Party - slang |
| Internal Affairs | Dept., dealing with African affairs. |
| Ishe | "Sir" or "Chief" (Shona word) |
| J.O.C | Joint Operations Command |
| Kaross | Traditional Blanket made from animal skins. |
| Kit | Personal possessions – clothes/uniforms |
| Kopje | Small geographical hill – usually with rocks visible |
| Kum-a-Kye | BSAP Regimental Song. |
| Kwazo | Very Much |
| Kwete | Shona for "No" |
| Majonny(ies) | Police/Policemen (Shona slang) |

| | |
|---|---|
| Makandanga | Shona slang for terrorist |
| Mapolisa. | The Police. |
| Means | Communication means – radios, phones |
| Member in Charge | Person in charge of a Police station/section |
| Mess | Police Single Quarters |
| Mini Moke or Moke | Small Austin vehicle trialled by the BSAP |
| Moola | Money |
| Moswa | Business/Matter/System (Shona word) |
| Nannies | African women |
| Nganga. | African Witch Doctor |
| OC | Officer Commanding |
| Old Dart | England |
| Patriotic Front | Amalgamation of ZANU and ZAPU |
| PCIO | Provincial Criminal Investigating Officer |
| PEA | Portuguese East Africa/Mozambique |
| Piccaninns | Young children |
| PRAW | Police Reserve Air Wing |
| PROPOL | Senior Uniform Branch Officer |
| Route Instructions | Instructional Document provided to Police |
| RSA | Republic of South Africa |
| SANAC | South African National African Congress |
| SDD | Sudden Death Docket of Investigation |
| SF | Security Forces |
| Shabeen | Illegal bar and/or brothel |
| Shamwari | Friend (Shona word) |
| Shangaan | Small African Tribe |
| Sibam | Firearm (Shona slang) |
| SitRep | Situation Report |
| Skuzapos | Security Force personnel acting as terrorists |
| SO | Standing Orders of the Regiment; Section Officer |
| Squads – Depot | A number of Recruits under taking training |
| Stables | Early morning parade used to clean transport |
| Tambo | Rope |
| TARB | Traffic Accident Report Book |
| Tatenda | Thank you |
| Tokarev | 7.62 mm Russian Automatic Pistol |
| Troops | Junior European District Policemen |
| TTL | Tribal Trust Lands – African occupied area |
| Two Bar P.O. | Patrol Officer with three or more years' service |
| Veldskoens | Plain leather shoes of a Khaki hew. |
| ZANU | Zimbabwe African National Union |
| ZAPU | Zimbabwe African Peoples Union |
| ZEF -7 | Radio call sign for stations - 7 was Victoria Province |

# BSAP MEMBERS IDENTIFIED.

Staff Crown Sergeant John Roger PEARCE 4756
Recruit Constable Andrew Daniel Varkevisser 7177
Inspector Alfred John Worden 5334.
Senior Patrol Officer was Harvey Burr 6753
Staff Inspector William 'Bill' Coetzee 4752.
PO Isaak Johannes Vorster 7145
Senior Sergeant Taringvandisho 11886.
Senior PO Daniel Petrus van Schalkwyk 6225,
Officer Richard Howard Williams 7336
PO Graham Beit Hardy 7282,
PO Thomas Andrew Crawford 7154
PO John Steven Botha 7479
Insp. Bernard Edward Cavey 4038,
Section Officer, Eric Saul 5562/5898,
PO Reginald David Graham 7157
PO Ian Leslie Harries 6588/8954
Former Det.Sgt. Herbert John Stanyon 3835
Former Constable Michael John Jupp 6608,
Section Officer Keith Jarrett 4438
PO Nigel Stanyon 10203
6090, DSO Neville Henry 'Paddy' Gardiner
Inspector 5332 Geoffrey Edward Hedges
SO Charles Cassidy 6548
PO Christopher John Philip Russell 7184.
PO 7146 Anthony Patrick St Clair
Supt Bremner 4303
D/Insp Edward James Frank Painting 6097
D/Sgt Nyenya 15885
DSO Peter Begg 5875
D/Const Ndhlovu 19811.
DSOJames Gordon Greenwood 7900
A/Comm Jack Denley 4261
Snr Asst Comm Peter Allum 3939
Section Officer Thomas Bruce Matthews 9010
Assistant Commissioner Edwin Alfred Webb 4416

Printed in Great Britain
by Amazon

58691690R00224